Reading with Clarice Lispector

Theory and History of Literature
Edited by Wlad Godzich and Jochen Schulte-Sasse

Volume 73. Hélène Cixous *Reading with Clarice Lispector*
Volume 72. N.S. Trubetzkoy *Writings on Literature*
Volume 71. Neil Larsen *Modernism and Hegemony*
Volume 70. Paul Zumthor *Oral Poetry: An Introduction*
Volume 69. Giorgio Agamben *Stanzas: Speech and Phantasm in Western Culture*
Volume 68. Hans Robert Jauss *Question and Answer: Forms of Dialogic Understanding*
Volume 67. Umberto Eco *On the Concept of the Sign*
Volume 66. Paul de Man *Critical Writings, 1953-1978*
Volume 65. Paul de Man *Aesthetic Ideology*
Volume 64. Didier Coste *Narrative as Communication*
Volume 63. Renato Barilli *Rhetoric*
Volume 62. Daniel Cottom *Text and Culture*
Volume 61. Theodor W. Adorno *Kierkegaard: Construction of the Aesthetic*
Volume 60. Kristin Ross *The Emergence of Social Space: Rimbaud and the Paris Commune*
Volume 59. Lindsay Waters and Wlad Godzich *Reading De Man Reading*
Volume 58. F.W.J. Schelling *The Philosophy of Art*
Volume 57. Louis Marin *Portrait of the King*
Volume 56. Peter Sloterdijk *Thinker on Stage: Nietzsche's Materialism*
Volume 55. Paul Smith *Discerning the Subject*
Volume 54. Réda Bensmaïa *The Barthes Effect*
Volume 53. Edmond Cros *Theory and Practice of Sociocriticism*
Volume 52. Philippe Lejeune *On Autobiography*
Volume 51. Thierry de Duve *Pictorial Nominalism: Marcel Duchamp, Painting and Modernity*
Volume 50. Luiz Costa Lima *Control of the Imaginary*
Volume 49. Fredric Jameson *The Ideologies of Theory: Essays 1971–1986, Volume 2*
Volume 48. Fredric Jameson *The Ideologies of Theory: Essays 1971–1986, Volume 1*
Volume 47. Eugene Vance *From Topic to Tale: Logic and Narrativity in the Middle Ages*
Volume 46. Jean-François Lyotard *The Differend*
Volume 45. Manfred Frank *What Is Neostructuralism?*
Volume 44. Daniel Cottom *Social Figures: George Eliot, Social History, and Literary Representation*

For other books in the series, see p. 170.

Reading with
Clarice Lispector

Hélène Cixous

Edited, translated, and introduced
by Verena Andermatt Conley

Theory and History of Literature, Volume 73

University of Minnesota Press, Minneapolis

Copyright © 1990 by the Regents of the University of Minnesota

Published by the University of Minnesota Press
2037 University Avenue Southeast, Minneapolis, MN 55414.
Printed in the United States of America.

Library of Congress Cataloging-in-Publication Data

Cixous, Hélène, 1937–
    Reading with Clarice Lispector / Hélène Cixous ; edited and translated by Verena Andermatt Conley.
        p.   cm. — (Theory and history of literature ; v. 73)
    Includes index.
    ISBN 0-8166-1828-3. —ISBN 0-8166-1829-1 (pbk.)
    1. Lispector, Clarice Criticism and interpretation.
    I. Lispector, Clarice.   II. Conley, Verena Andermatt
    III. Title.   IV. Series.
PQ9697.L585Z58   1990
869.3–dc20   89-20512
                                                                    CIP

Contents

Acknowledgments   vi

Introduction *Verena Andermatt Conley*   vii

1. "Sunday, before falling asleep": A Primal Scene   3
2. *Agua viva*: How to Follow a Trinket of Water   11
3. *The Apple in the Dark*: The Temptation of Understanding   60
4. "The Egg and the Chicken": Love Is Not Having   98
5. "Felicidade clandestina": The Promise of Having What One Will Have   123
6. *The Hour of the Star:* How Does One Desire Wealth or Poverty?   143

Index   167

Acknowledgments

I would like to express my gratitude to Iowa State University and James Dow for making the initial stages of this project possible through a summer grant and to Miami University for providing me with a research leave leading to its completion.

My special thanks to Marguerite Sandré for her patient recordings and general help, to writer Mary Howard for her readings of my translations, and to Claudia Guimaraes for helping me with the Portuguese passages.

I would like to thank David, Francine, and my parents for their patience and above all Tom Conley for his continued assistance as well as for his unflinching Irish sense of humor.

My greatest indebtedness is to Hélène Cixous, whose readings are the basis of this project.

V.A.C.

Introduction
Verena Andermatt Conley

The pages that follow have been excerpted from Hélène Cixous's ongoing meditations between 1980 and 1985 on problems of reading, writing, difference, and
related themes, including exchange and the gift, love and passion, poverty and
riches. The texts gathered are all readings of Clarice Lispector or, rather, readings
by Cixous with Lispector in the context of seminars given at the Université de
Paris VIII—Vincennes at Saint Denis and at the Collège International de Philo-
sophie. This in part dictates the format of the texts and an ordering reflective of
Cixous's preoccupations rather than one that would follow Lispector's chronol-
ogy as a writer. Cixous discovers Lispector at a time when she studies questions
of sexual difference in connection with what have been called libidinal economies, that is, with ways the body is engaged in exchanging with and finding its
limits in, a social world.

Paradoxically, Cixous begins her reading of Lispector with one of the Brazilian writer's later texts, *Agua viva (The Stream of Life)*. Cixous claims to
have been overwhelmed by her encounter with *Agua viva*. In it she finds the finest practice of *écriture féminine*. Outside of the seminars, it appears as a somewhat controversial term and has often been misunderstood among literary and
social critics. In the relation that Cixous holds with Lispector, *écriture féminine* is
a working term referring less to a writing practiced mainly by women than, in
a broader logical category, to textual ways of spending. It suggests a writing,
based on an encounter with another—be it a body, a piece of writing, a social
dilemma, a moment of passion—that leads to an undoing of the hierarchies
and oppositions that determine the limits of most conscious life. By virtue of its

poetry that comes from the rapport of the body to the social world, *écriture féminine* disrupts social practices in the ways it both discerns and literally rewrites them.

For Cixous, in *Agua viva* Lispector insists on the effacement of the subject, which results in opening on a limitless perspective and undoing the frame of common or representable human experience. Lispector practices what Cixous has been looking for. It is the kind of affinity she feels, the kind of shock she receives at a first reading of *Agua viva*, that prompts her to take a long detour through much of Lispector's work, some of which is more thematically oriented and marked in its style by existentialism. Lispector's contact with the world is immediate: her language portrays the struggle that human beings engage in with their social milieus and with themselves. Yet the writing does not work through philosophical or dialectical terms that make up the heritage of Simone de Beauvoir or Jean-Paul Sartre. The will to encapsulate that world by writing it is now turned into a far more immediate relation of language and sensation. Cixous accounts for this difference by forging the concept of *écriture féminine*, fraught with the existential and historical position of the female in the world that marginalizes the human subject, but that effectively redeems it through the ways it offers anyone, male or female, a *living* relation with language and experience.

Lispector's voice transforms Cixous. It comes to her by way of Brazil, in bilingual editions or in French translation. In fact, the work raises questions about the status of readings done from texts in translation, not unlike the problem of American readers of Cixous who face a poetic writing inspired at once by Hegelian philosophy and James Joyce. Phonic and graphic effects, so important for the ideological status of the text, are sometimes changed or even lost in translation. Cixous works through the difference of French and Portuguese, and in turn encounters what her own readers face when they follow her novels (at least from *Angst* to *Limonade*). Now Lispector's idiosyncratic use of punctuation is often modified by translators, thus affecting the meaning of the text. A comparison of French and English translations of Lispector for this volume also reveals numerous conceptual discrepancies, often inflecting interpretation and thus further complicating the translator's task. Wherever possible, I opted for the French translation of Lispector for the sake of holding to Cixous's reading as it is articulated in the seminars. All modifications of published English translations have been indicated.

On another level, Cixous's dialogue with Lispector is interspliced with other voices, especially that of Heidegger's essays on poetry — something already evident in one of the first texts by Cixous on Lispector "L'approche de Clarice Lispector," in *Poétique* 10 (October 1979). In no way are Cixous's readings of Lispector the work on a single author, of the type "the author and her work." Rather, they are a theoretical practice of Cixous as a writer who — in her own words—wants to go always farther in her readings (*toujours plus loin*), in keeping, perhaps, with a highly accessible relation to space and with a psychoanalytic notion of ongoing freeing, conceived as (re)birth or as a subject's perpetual rediscovery of himself or herself.

The chapters in this volume have been transcribed from audiotapes. The oral aspect of the readings has been purposely kept in order to retain the flavor of a style using simple sentences and a certain degree of repetition. A truly didactic type of diction is at work, and its syntax, the obverse of Cixous's other writings, evinces a litanic style, in which a pedagogical discourse is mixed with that of a poet. One of its most recurrent expressions is *il y a*, or "there is." It implies a theoretical position that refers to Heidegger's *es gibt*, "there is (to give)," an utterance that is charged with theological and philosophical undertones. It inaugurates an originary moment by calling to attention the positioning of an individual in the world. The words suggest that as a collectivity we have the great grace and privilege of being born into the world through an act of language, simply put, that comes with and is enclosed within all . . . *there is*. Cixous uses the phrase adroitly and rhythmically, but in a style that cannot sustain the same force in written expression. A necessary rephrasing has sometimes made the implicit idea of the gift, which virtually goes without saying in the repetition of *il y a*, disappear in English. Adequate equivalents for the expression *mettre en question* (to call into question) or *il est question de* (it is a question of), have been difficult to find. Cixous tries to avoid all statements that tend to closure or to authorize the speaker's mastery over what he or she is stating. Thus put, her observations call questions into question, and undo the speech of a "master's voice." Further, she repeats formulas so as to turn them into elements of oral poetry. For the sake of obtaining variety in the written translation, some of the expressions of questioning have been replaced by declarative sentences.

A specifically French expression, *une problématique* (a "problematic"), conceived and used as a substantive in the social sciences to designate an issue taken up in order to study—but not resolve—its irreconcilable and multiple paradoxes, has been avoided. As such it would be a gallicism and has thus been rendered as "dilemma" or as an adjective modifying a noun. Inevitably, some of the word play of the seminars cannot be translated. It is indicated, where possible, parenthetically in French terms. Cixous refers to Lispector as "Clarice," in an obviously poetic and political gesture insisting on an intimacy beyond language that avoids labeling the author as a dead fact. She follows Mallarmé's remarks to the effect that the act of naming deprives the referent of the poetic qualities that reside in it prior to its designation or placement in a social body or in a scheme of history. It should also be noted that Cixous adds adjectives to nouns in order to animate them. She never closes a circuit of descriptions with conjunctions, such that the ostensive negligence in composition (for example, "words lyrical, powerful, excessive . . . '' instead of ''lyrical, powerful, and excessive words'') is not so at all.

The readings of—or with—Lispector were originally interspliced with other texts. Cixous's literary 'history' consists of what she calls contemporary, rather than synchronic or diachronic texts. In other words, she chooses different texts that share certain affinities and that fit into a program with her own readings; she studies their various ways of dealing with similar issues through a prism that, by way of multiple comparisons, breaks writing into ''colors'' or ''tones'' of composition. Although the cultural referents are not obliterated, her readings clearly do not dwell primarily on literary history and may risk not appealing to those studying a work as it reflects specifically a given culture. Instead, Cixous chooses to discuss questions of the highest possible logical category, that is, of life and art or life and death. She intersplices her readings of Lispector with other texts, be it those mentioned by the Brazilian writer herself, such as James Joyce, Franz Kafka, or others, Heinrich von Kleist, Maurice Blanchot, and Jean Genet. Some of these texts have been kept here, others have been set aside for inclusion in a second volume, with readings of the aforementioned authors, as well as by Paul Celan and Marina Tsvetayeva in the context of writing and history. Often, Cixous doubles or laminates her readings of a Lispector text with other Lispector texts in order to probe similarities and differences as well as to break up the continuity of a single reading. For example, although there is no specific study of *A paixão segundo G.H. (The Passion according to G.H.)*, allusions to it are numerous throughout Cixous's readings. Similarly, comparisons with one of Lispector's early texts, *Perto do coração selvagem* (Close to the savage heart) abound. And ''Domingo antes de dormir'' (''Sunday, before falling asleep''), a short but crucial text, is one where, for Cixous, the position of Clarice Lispector's writing in relation to the father is evident. It inaugurates the following readings; allusions arch back to it time and again. More specifically, a study of *The Apple in the Dark* is spliced with readings of ''E para lá que eu vou'' (That's where I'm going) and ''Tanta mansidão'' (Such mansuetude). Such a reading process breaks up a continuum in favor of what might be called a braiding of voices, or multiple resonances of textual echoes. Cixous's gesture proposes to ''*mettre en regard*,'' to put texts side by side, somewhat like Jean Genet's later writings through the use of double columns in ''Ce qui est resté d'un Rembrandt déchiré en petits carrés réguliers et foutu aux chiottes'' (What remained of a Rembrandt torn into small, very regular little squares and rammed down the shithole) in volume 4 of *Oeuvres complètes*, a technique that since has been adopted by many—for example, Jacques Derrida in his *Glas* (1974).

Not all of Cixous's readings of Lispector have been included, since our project is limited in length. The texts retained are for the most part those available in English translation with the exception of ''E para lá que eu vou,'' ''Tanta mansidão," "Escrevendo" (While writing) and "Felicidade clandestina" (Secret happiness).

The readings of Lispector are part of Cixous's ongoing quest for affirmation of life over death and power in all its forms, including those of academic institutions and practices. The texts are read from within the general problem of the philosophy of the subject, through which Cixous joins her own contemporaries Michel Foucault, Jacques Derrida, and Julia Kristeva, to mention just a few, in her questioning of the so-called rational, "Cartesian" subject and of what she perceives to be the increasing power of the social and applied sciences that seek to establish control over the human being. At the crossroads of Hegel, Freud, Marx, Nietzsche, and Heidegger, no less than the many writers and poets, Cixous develops a reading of what, in France, has been a common concern since 1968. Like others in her decision to move from Hegel's "master text" of the philosophical institution to a reading of Heidegger, or from an academic to a poetic model of philosophy, Cixous insists on deliverance through language, in the sense of freeing, of giving birth and of being born, which, for her, goes through as much as possible of an effacement of the constituted subject. She wants to let alterity speak as alterity. Her gesture implies acceptance, tolerance, and noncomprehension of the other. Her insistence on joy and pleasure in reading Lispector is close to a French reading of the Heideggerian "subject" that is there, exposed to and traversed by, the other. Cixous does not simply advocate a divided subject, nor does she imply a return to some Anglo-Saxon *volontarisme* that would fight power with new repressions through univocal conceptualization. Cixous insists on an emptying of self or of what she calls, somewhat summarily, the unified, narcissistic subject. Hers is not a subject that is being subverted but one that is exposed to the other or, better, that is always being born. Critics (among others, Michel Beaujour) have labeled her work as something of a "neotenic style," that is, a half-born, willfully premature writing that allows the genesis of its articulation to be part of its at once aesthetic, social, and corporeal beauty. This is where her voice dramatically rejoins that of Clarice Lispector. Mixing different styles, the resulting tones in Cixous are more of affirmation than of negation and vindication. Her writing strives toward what Clarice Lispector both asserts and performs especially in her short text "Tanta mansidão," that is to say, toward a writing of the "rainy aspect of rain," in such a way that the rain is not grateful not to be a stone. Cixous, with Lispector, strives toward a mode of reading, writing, and speaking nonexclusive differences so that the other is other without being thought of in merely negative or positional terms such as that of the nonself. Of course, by definition, language forces us to go through negativity, since the words replace things, but, following her work, the question that we can ask is exactly of how to go about inflecting that negativity.

Cixous thinks that she finds already present in Lispector what she herself has been looking for, that is, ways of giving, of spending, and of inscribing pleasure. This would come close to what she, Cixous—in the wake of the French philosopher Georges Bataille rephrasing Freud—had called a feminine economy, a libidinal organization based on spending, rather than on retention and which, for cultural reasons, would be more on the side of women. Here it can be assumed that the force of *écriture féminine* works especially in the play between thematic and linguistic registers. For this reason, *spending* in Lispector is not just organized topically but is also worked through language, especially in later texts like *Agua viva*. Clarice Lispector is known for her writerly innovations and experimentations, and Cixous is much aware of this. This kind of writing, with no exchange or market value, with no "useful purpose," can be called *écriture féminine*, be it that of a woman, like Clarice Lispector, or of a man, like Jean Genet. The concept may be difficult to understand for readers whose habits are strongly influenced by useful productivity or cultural pragmatics. It is there that poetry, with its overdeterminations, replaces the univocity of a concept that reappropriates, creates new exclusions, hierarchies, repressions. In the context of the French debate of the subject that focuses on difference and alterity—hence on means of articulation and linking rather than on fullness and on a continuum— Cixous is most attuned to Lispector's ways of inscribing textual interruptions, into meditations about the "self," that is, of marking limits, of linking self and other at all levels.

Reading between poetry and philosophy, always close to analysis, Cixous insists on the notion of a path to be traced, rather than that of the *beautiful road*, or the method to be applied. The figure of the road is a truism in the patrimony of French philosophy and literature. Descartes had conceived his method as a path to be followed, just as most French writers seek their knowledge by way of a quest along the roads of life. Hers, however, are literary inroads, or trails leading nowhere or rather, elsewhere. They effectively complicate Heidegger's figure of the *Holzwege* that, in translation, are precisely "roads going nowhere." As Cixous reminds us, a feminine reading (hear: one of spending, more often practiced by women in our present historical and cultural setting) must have both its part of logic and improvisation. Hence some of the novelty of her readings of Lispector, some elements of surprise and risk, contrary to a reading based on retention and appropriation and needed to follow the right road, one that is set on being simply conceptually correct. Cixous favors listening to the text to derive certain values or rules, lessons (of life). In accord with Lispector, reading and writing become an apprenticeship, but not one that leads to mastery.

This does not mean that Cixous says anything. Her readings are guided by the text she reads. One cannot make the latter say anything, but rather one has to let it speak. That is why she finds it preferable to proceed affirmatively whenever possible, reading what she enjoys, rather than negatively by writing *against*. She avoids mastery and incorporation as much as possible by working on several texts at once and leaving them "open," by going back and forth, by breaking up the order of the text, by proceeding by leaps and bounds, touching down here and there at nodal points, not in linear fashion, but by making connections. At certain points Cixous works minutely on lengthy passages, perhaps in the continuation of the French tradition of *morceaux choisis*, or of textual analysis, but also as a way of working at the level of sentences and of enunciation rather than simply through conceptual reduction. Thus she avoids closed structure and stages an approach. Her sentences reduce the *I* to the more impersonal French *on*, difficult to render in English but kept here wherever possible to efface the presence of the subject. The use of the conditional and turns such as "I would say," of adverbs such as "perhaps," or "almost," avoids a heavy statement or appropriation of truth, closure, and finality. Such formulations are used to suggest the possibility of a multiplicity of readings, the necessity of brushing against the text rather than of rolling over it like a tank.

The question of sexual difference, although—possibly for historical reasons—never addressed from any feminist point of view by Lispector, is omnipresent in her texts. Cixous's own reading of Lispector shifts over the five-year span from a more overtly political and feminist reading to one that takes up human relations analyzed in terms of giving and receiving, with each pole of the exchange studied in its tones and shadings. But contrary to earlier work, the reader no longer encounters an a priori privileging of woman. Studying the "nakedness of relations"—never clinically but always with a bit of idealization—Cixous is most attentive to Lispector's capacity of writing incisively about male-female relationships, as in *The Apple in the Dark* where relationships portrayed are just one example among many but cannot be generalized as a model.

Assuming a position different from that of most of her contemporaries, Cixous searches for a desire not based on lack but for a love that lets the other live, that does not incorporate, but lets the other be other. This mood is reflected perhaps in her article "Reaching the Point of Wheat, Portrait of the Artist as a Mature Woman," recently published in *New Literary History*. The title—an adaptation of one of Lispector's poetic metaphors may serve as a clue to Cixous's present focus on a maternal love that cares for and gives birth to the other. Something of a more Heideggerian resonance of *Fürsorge*, of caring, is evident, supplanting what had been taken up in the 1960s, when Lacan preached his lessons about the deadliness of desire. As mother, midwife, and analyst, Cixous insists on the disinterested gesture of helping the other actively to have his or her birth, to join body and mind. These issues percolate through Lispector's stories, such as *Legião estrangeira* (*The Foreign Legion*), included in a second volume, or here in "O ovo e galinha" ("The Egg and the Chicken").

In an effort to rearticulate presence, absence, life, and death, Cixous had suggested elsewhere, working against a millenary tradition, a possible reading of the world that would insist on the pleasure of eating the apple. The act opens to a new possibility of orality, of access to language. This she thinks she finds in Lispector. She writes less against symbolic castration than in another economy altogether where desire knows "how to have what it has," as she is able to inflect it in her reading of "Felicidade clandestina." This implies an art of taking and of letting go, of continuity and discontinuity, yet of sliding over the moment of interruption. It allows a certain pleasure in having without appropriating. It can be added that the wisdom of knowing "how to have what one has" is of vast implication in the world of political and feminist criticisms. The concept deflates aggression that is often welcomed in the name of pragmatics. It returns to a clairvoyant sense of the language of exchange and of nonappropriation in its most immediately somatic and perhaps even ecological sense.

Against accusations of being utopian—an accusation perhaps better founded during her days of more militant feminism in the late seventies—Cixous's ongoing analysis takes an ascetic turn not devoid of religious overtones in keeping with the recent climate in France, due, in her case, less to interest in a resurgence of Catholicism than through readings of Heidegger. There again, an adventurous, even daring reading of Heidegger intersects with Lispector's interest in humility and grace. The common quest is one of progressive impoverishment, of a wealth that rejects false values. She had already ended "Sorties" in *La jeune née* (*The Newly Born Woman*), through a reading of Shakespeare's *Antony and Cleopatra*: "And far from kingdoms, from caesars, from brawls, from the cravings of penis and sword, from the unnameable 'goods' of this world, far from show and self-love, in harmony with each other, in accord, they live still" (130). This absence of false gold haunted her not only through her readings of Shakespeare but also in the ubiquitous allusions to Rimbaud in her text. It becomes increasingly insistent in a double reading of Jean Genet's texts asserting the equivalence of all human beings, as in "L'atelier d'Alberto Giacometti" and "Le secret de Rembrandt," as well as in Clarice Lispectors' texts, *A hora da estrela* (*The Hour of the Star*). Meditating on wealth and poverty, Cixous shows how Lispector's writing of the infinitely small can be brought into view. Like Genet's writing, it is outside exchange value, or matters in the domain of the useful. For those more concerned with utilitarian pragmatism, based on the equation *riches = money + happiness*, such a text will remain unreadable. For those who might take issue with the luxury of such a gesture in the face of real poverty, it might be recalled that real destitution is the inspiration for much of Genet's writing.

Again, not without Heidegger's poetic overtones taken out of their historical context, Cixous insists on the archaic, the primitive, on something uncultured to be saved from culture, or from whatever is equivalent to the law or the symbolic. She inserts herself in a tradition that, with the German romantics and Nietzsche, adapted recently by some French writers and thinkers, believes in the creative forces contained in the archaic and in the necessity of their unleashing. This tradition from Schiller and Schlegel to Nietzsche and others shapes Cixous's thinking, both in its insistence on untying bound forces and in its belief in the importance of art for social change. It insists on the broader human scope of the reason of unreason over reason, on the mythic and the poetic over science and technology. Such an appeal to something archaic, she finds in Clarice Lispector, who writes from a civilization in which technology, less immediately omnipresent, is not yet part of the imaginary realms that everyone shares. Refusing technology, less in terms of financial exploitation than as the older paradigm of dehumanization, Cixous joins Clarice Lispector's imaginary worlds where the question is not yet addressed. If *technè* is present through writing, Cixous nevertheless insists on a fiction in which technologies are absent. Like Heidegger, she stops at the hand. As she writes and teaches by hand, she also stresses the use of the hand in Lispector as what humanizes the human.

At the same time, the German romantics—always high on Cixous's list of influential writers, as is obvious from her constant references to Kleist—inspire her with a notion of the absolute. The absolute concerns singular people who are out of the ordinary with its moral law. In a certain sense, the thinking of the absolute leads to an ascending thinking, to a group that—like Stendhal's Happy Few—is made up of those who have "dared to leave the common behind." The question is often, as in *The Apple in the Dark*, how to be understood by the common vision, and how to shuttle back and forth from people and places known by all. There is, in Cixous's reading of Lispector's absolute, an ever so slight slippage that glides toward a separation of the ordinary from the extraordinary, there where Lispector insists on the extraordinary in the ordinary.

Like many of her French contemporaries, Cixous distinguishes between an artistic "avant-garde" and the masses, between the extraordinary and the banal, between the poetic and everyday language. She expresses a slight contempt for the latter, and with it comes an implicit reconstruction of power. The attitude is one that may indeed give pause. On the contrary, Lispector's existential writings privilege a calm, often mock-heroic disposition in a brutally common condition of everyday life that—disaffected from its phallic system of value and evincing a great deal of humor, even joy—seems to underline the extraordinary in the very wealth of the ordinary. There is a strange tension between Cixous's ongoing thinking of the "new" that—relinquishing earlier traces of a writing more patterned on linguistic generation—privileges in Lispector epiphanies and moments of initiation closer to modernist or specifically Joycean aesthetics. Cixous situates herself resolutely outside a "postmodern" aesthetics of indifference that refuses any redemption in favor of its economic return or self-valorization in its acts of negotiation.

Next to theoretical attempts at "banalizing" our experience of love, Cixous, reading Lispector, keeps a noble, somewhat mythic and by definition always idealizing approach. By choice, Cixous, through Lispector, insists that the other be loved, not in any maudlin, sentimental way, but by respecting difference. Those looking at the world as an eternal power struggle will see in this no more than lofty idealization. In accord with Lispector, who insists on transformation from her existential point of view, Cixous stresses consciousness as well as the unconscious, desire as well as strength and need for self-improvement. One is not born knowing how to live; one learns how to live. A book is not just an intellectual exercise of aesthetic enjoyment but a lesson and nourishment.

Both Lispector and Cixous question knowledge as appropriation and go back to "The Book of Life" as a learning experience. They insist on a total experience of body and mind as well as on a distinction between intellectual knowledge and bodily knowledge. This comes as no surprise from Lispector, whose writings seek to grasp the sensory world through their existential commitment to language and real experience. But at this stage, and in contrast to philosophers who dismiss the empirical world, Cixous can be seen as clearly demarcating herself from those for whom the other is but a verbal construct.

Her insistence on, and at times almost hypostasis of, the poetic is helped by Freud's century-old assertion that poets are ahead of scientists and common mortals alike, and more apt to capture the subtleties of human rapports. A poet like Clarice Lispector universally questions the moral law and the law of language — different from political laws — and without which, in Cixous's view, there can be no social change. By choice, Cixous, with Lispector, insists on rewriting relationships in terms of giving and receiving rather than in assuming the ideologue's more leftist ways of battling institutions to replace them with other institutions. Both Lispector's fiction and Cixous's reading practices have been accused of staying too much within a traditional woman's sphere of everyday life rather than of speaking in sweeping terms from a more symbolic sphere, attempting to change the universe. It can be said that it is precisely the articulation of life and death in the most banal, the most unremarkable detail that is of interest to both writers, but perhaps those intent on making sweeping generalizations will be deaf to this.

Neither Cixous nor Lispector may be easy to read for those in North America who tend to read the work of Michel Foucault upside down, that is to say, by insisting on reverting power relations where Foucault—perhaps somewhat flatly—had declared the end of man. It may be difficult for American readers, whose mental habits seem to be set on thinking in terms of power, to conceive of a relation to the world based on pacifism, nonviolence, nonpower such as the one Cixous projects through a reading with Clarice Lispector.

In a mixture of improvisation and logic, of poetry and philosophy, Cixous raises questions from Lispector's texts and, in accord with contemporary tactics, follows rather than answers them. Her unfoldings and complications may seem to make, if Shakespearean language can be invoked, much ado about nothing. Or it can be seen that Cixous maximizes what could be called Lispector's minimalism.

A page of "Sunday, before falling asleep" turns into ten pages, and two pages of "E para lá que eu vou" grows into a twenty-page reading. Yet a textual system never takes over. Cixous speaks lightly, with overabundance but in generous rather than repressive terms. Hers is a hand that caresses—despite its repetition—rather than a fist that pounces on the text. Clearly, Cixous brings her own inflections to her reading of Lispector's texts, and those looking for Brazilian authenticity (folklore) will be disappointed. Also, at times, Cixous's increasingly ethereal readings seem a bit at odds with Clarice Lispector's often almost irreverently material ways, especially in texts like "E para lá que eu vou" and "Felicidade clandestina."

But the very possibility of a transcultural reading is nonetheless opened. One of the major questions common to both writers is that of the proximity of writing to life, of programs that rewrite and reread the relation between art and life in such a way that art—here writing and books—does not merely function as sublimation. Cixous's and Lispector's effort consists in revalorizing life and the living as opposed to burrowing into books and bookish knowledge. The irony of course concerns the choice of medium itself. For her reading practice, Cixous prefers a light and airy discourse from which erudite apparatus is all but absent. She is interested neither in legitimizing knowledge nor in subverting laws that imprison, define, but in writing elsewhere. Hers is a writer's reading often more intent on the "writing itself," on its techniques. Her own reading-writing, influenced by Lispector's, acquires the simplicity of a fairy tale or of a children's story. Cixous reads Lispector with other contemporary texts that bypass established bibliographies. She positions herself and then lets her discourse be modified over the years by Lispector's texts she is reading. (At the same time, her position of course inflects the texts read themselves.) Such a reading can, at the limit, lead to a certain impoverishment, since Cixous is looking for the same points—ways of articulating life and death—and finds them. The same concepts recur in her reading, and the absence of bibliography silences other voices speaking on Lispector. Yet the simplicity and transparence are deceptive and the analyses remain refined. Cixous reminds the reader that it is not necessary to cloak, necktie, and often strangle or smother a text. Overelaborate constructions often hide—or shy away from—simple truths. Close to clinical analysis, where detours and complications are signs of neuroses, she prefers a language simple and direct of those who have access to their desire or to those who let themselves be traversed by otherness.

Yet, Cixous also complicates her text through her many repetitions and insistences, and her readings at times have, to repeat, a didactic, litanic quality due in part to the pedagogical nature of the seminar. Her text, questioning power, is not devoid of power when she asserts the superiority of her own reading. Although she has no preconceived notion, no method to be applied, she lends the text her ear in certain ways that presuppose liberation through textuality, that is, through poetry and art viewed as an agency of social change. The seminars, so aware of reading from a contemporary point of view inflected by a certain historical position, prevent a critique on those grounds. Although Cixous does not say so, hers is, of course, largely a French position that accounts for other work in philosophy and psychoanalysis, dominant since Lévi-Strauss's and Bataille's revival of Marcel Mauss's famous essay on exchange, "The Gift" ("Essai sur le don") first published in 1925.

Cixous, with Lispector, insists on the effacement of the subject. Sanctity and saintliness are recurring terms (as in "Felicidade clandestina," where the tall thin girl alias Clarice Lispector agrees to be the other's spool in a complicated sadistic game of *fort-da*, without entering into her economy). Clarice, insists Cixous, writes in the nakedness of human relations with every shading possible while—consciously—checking herself on a way toward a better way of spending. Thus the subject as nonsubject is reintroduced with existential overtones, not as full nor as divided subject but as one that—like the analyst—is constantly in the process of *having* birth and helping others *have* their birth. Paradoxically this implies a certain passivity in someone who accepts and tolerates rather than represses: the ultimate power move or the ultimate disempowerment that allows the other to be other. This is also the reading gesture that Cixous performs vis-à-vis Lispector. She lets her speak, follows her, and, in following her, makes her come alive for us. Does Lispector lose some of her "Brazilianness" by being read in a tenth-floor Parisian apartment or in the historical classroom in the Château de Vincennes? That's up to the reader to decide, a reader free to take the leap and enter the text, or to turn away.

Reading with Clarice Lispector

Chapter 1
"Sunday, before falling asleep":
A Primal Scene

When we read a text, we are either read by the text or we are in the text. Either we tame a text, we ride on it, we roll over it, or we are swallowed up by it, as by a whale. There are thousands of possible relations to a text, and if we are in a nondefensive, nonresisting relationship, we are carried off by the text. This is mainly the way it goes. But then, in order to read, we need to get out of the text. We have to shuttle back and forth incessantly. We have to try all possible relations with a text. At some point, we have to disengage ourselves from the text as a living ensemble, in order to study its construction, its techniques, and its texture.

To arrive at a possibility of reading "Sunday, before falling asleep,"[1] I think of a children's game, a game of weaving with colored paper that is both homogeneous and heterogeneous. One has to find the color threads of the text, the semantic threads, and see how "to see," "to drink," "to get up," are linked. There are verbal chains and nominal chains that can be worked on with a grammar of meaning. One can work on the text from many different approaches, at many different levels. One can climb up and down a tree or sit on a bench in order to read it. Each time, one has a different level, another view of the scene. The text signifies massively; it is an egg. There is some of *King Lear* in it, but it has been effaced. There are many cultural referents too. There are fifty possible ways of entering this text, and it is up to the reader to find them. In terms of a quest, we can set out in many different directions. What counts is to find ourselves in the process. We have to work on a certain syntax, on a certain style that is as strange in Portuguese as it is in French. The tone of Clarice Lispector's text is that of the little girl in the big girl.

3

A capacity for improvisation should mark a reading process that could be qualified as feminine and that is one of improvisation as well as logic. The signals of our displacements are: paths, to go, not to go, Ovomaltine, to begin, Saturday, Sunday. We err between Saturday and Sunday in this story, which touches on genesis, or the first and the last day.

We do all this in order to follow, *not* to answer, the question, questions, which in French are feminine. Questions can be thought of as women. We *follow* the "feminine" questions, asking: what is "feminine" writing? "feminine" pleasure?

One of the efforts we make is to be transgrammatical, the way one could say transgressive. It is not that we despise grammar, but we do not have to obey it absolutely; and we have to work to some degree on degrammaticalization. From this point of view, it is good to work on foreign texts—Clarice Lispector's, James Joyce's and others'—because they displace our relation to grammar. In everything we do, we are questioning femininity. We work on texts as quests, that is, a questioning of femininity, on traces that are perceptible. Of course there is the trap "man" and the trap "woman." Those are denominations in language and on identity cards. They are only social indicatives, part of our role playing. In every individual there is a whole complex play of femininity, of masculinity.

I want to ask the question of the subject of enunciation and not that of the *énoncé*, of the statement. In Clarice's text—as in Joyce's—there are effects of naive writing. In *Portrait of the Artist*, Joyce begins with: "Once upon a time . . . " Clarice uses a narrative effect that refers to a similar process. It marks a primitive episode. I want to emphasize what is naive, primitive, in Clarice's little text. *Sunday, before falling asleep* would be the subject of the text. In a first story that the text tells, without interpretation from our historical position, we would have: one goes to see, or to be seen, to be looked at from different points of view. There is everything and everyone, except for the missing mother. It is a text of initiation. The center is *Ovomaltine*, Ovaltine or *top of the world*, even at the level of construction. Of importance is the way the text is written from the perspective of childhood. We could say that the narrative is "about five years old."

"Sunday, before falling asleep" tells the story of a family's Sunday outings. On Sundays, the family goes to the pier and the father stares out into the oily waters: "On Sundays, the entire family would go to the pier to watch the ships. They would lean over the buttresses and, if Father were still alive today, perhaps he would still be watching those oily waters which he used to examine so intently. His daughters became vaguely restless, they would summon him to come and look at something more interesting: look at the ships, Daddy! they would point out to him impatiently. As darkness fell, the illumined city turned into a great metropolis with high revolving stools in every café [translation modified]."

Following the complete trajectory of looks in this story, we first arrive at a system of objects from where we can go back to the subjects. We arrive at a primitive *mise en scène* where everyone is standing around, waiting, and in the middle, there is *Ovomaltine, top of the world*, in English in the text. The path of the subjects and of subjectivity begins with Sundays, then it unfolds to family, and, finally, we arrive at "she." From Sundays, we arrive at "Sunday was." One has to visualize this text, which is organized from and around the look. It takes place between father and daughter. The daughter's look is caught in the look of the father, which is directed toward the horizon, toward the water and the boats. There is also the intervention of the daughters, who teach the father something else. Father, have you seen? The daughters are saying: "Look at what I want you to see, and do not look at what I am afraid that you are looking at and that you see." It is a scene of a father with his daughters. The latter ask the father not to look at the sea, at the boats because they are afraid of losing him. Ambivalence is inscribed in the first sentences where we do not know if the father is alive. We jump from the living to the dead father. The daughters' love is invested in the father. The structure is very complex and it is probably no longer ours today. The writing is taken in a father-daughter rapport. The daughters, in the plural, are the older ones. The little one is going to be the heroine of the story, as in *King Lear*. She is going to be *the top of the world*. The older ones direct the look of the father toward the inside. The story consists of at least ten or fifteen short scenes. The oily water announces, at the same time as it pushes it away, Ovaltine. The two function as a couple. We have to work on the father in the daughter, on the daughter in the father. The story turns on the revolving stool. We have to work on the system of concentricity, which is going to give *the top of the world*. The text is at the same time a primal scene and a metaphor that can be found again, at different moments, throughout Clarice's work.

The force of this text makes us feel all the work done at the phonic and graphic level. There is a middle in this text, like a tree in the middle of paradise. It is *the top of the world*. The lexicon is as important through the choice of words, as through an alternating system of long, short. For example: "the daughters obscurely wondered" (*se inquietavam obscuramente*) is inscribed as long in the Portuguese text while in translation that dimension disappears.

I come back to the side of the primal scene. The text is immense while being very small, and the questions of time are especially complex. Fairy tales always start with "once upon a time . . . ," and the reader knows that it began long ago. Primal scenes, on the contrary, are scenes of rupture. They are situated after "Once upon a time," and talk about "since." Clarice's story is a story of "since." There is also some "was," because it could perhaps be said: "There was the father." It is a strange question of survival. From the beginning, we are very surprised by the sentence: " . . . if Father were still alive," which is violent and very clever on the part of Clarice Lispector. It plays doubly on childhood and on its opposite. The sentence can be read as something naive, like a childhood memory. But it is falsely naive. Everything is perfectly ruseful. The beginning of

James Joyce's *Portrait of the Artist* mimes the style of early childhood. In "Sunday, before falling asleep," there are mimetic outbursts, but generally there is a mixture of absolute knowledge and innocence. In the first sentence, "On Sundays, the entire family would go to the pier to watch the ships. They would lean over the buttresses and, if Father were still alive today, perhaps he would still be watching those oily waters which he used to examine so intently" (translation modified), there is a transition from the living to the dead father. It marks a kind of violence in a writing that, at the same time, stays perfectly calm. One goes out with the family, the father included, and in the next sentence the father is dead while the story is being told during the father's lifetime. To say "if he were still alive" means that he is dead and that he is still alive. Here, one never does without the father. Everything takes place in the ruse of the tenses.

The singular-plural system is incredibly rich. It adds a collective element. There are "Sundays" in the plural, in a series, and there is "Sunday." Father and daughter will detach themselves from a collective ensemble. The mother might only be the sea, the water toward which the father looks, absent.

The questions of value are important. They are related to questions of economy. There is "dear" and "not dear." It cannot be restricted to, but goes beyond, a financial equivalence. They are symbolic and narcissistic values. Sunday is the day of the Lord, the day of the Father. A first reading can miss the enormity of the story, which is completely within the father. The text draws an inclusion, an inscription, not an incorporation, in the father. Clarice says it. The general schema is brought back and reinscribed in the last sentence.

The text is caught between Sundays-as-a-series and Sunday. The protagonists are the little girl and the father. And there is Sunday. This allows Clarice to say in Portuguese: "On *Sundays*, the entire family went to the pier . . . ." But in the last sentence, we have: "*Sunday* was always that immense night . . ." When the family goes to the pier to watch the ships, it was not yet that night. There is a slippage that is gathered in the last sentence. We see that the originary night that engendered is masculine. The immense night is feminine. I could translate it as the father who is the mother. In mythologies, at the origin of ancient cosmogonies, the universal mother is associated with a night that gives day to the day. The mother engendered all the other fathers, the cargo ships, water, milk with foam. There is a multiple engendering because everything comes out of this Sunday. It is a case of masculine genesis. In this system, the egg is inscribed under the Ovaltine. It is the question of the chicken and the egg, or should we speak of the chicken and the *coc(que)*, the she-rooster and the shell?

At the level of the structure of filiation and genealogy, it is a story of father and daughter. It is related to writing. *Perto do coração selvagem* begins between father and daughter. It is the story of Clarice Lispector, a story of father and daughter, and whatever it may have meant to her.

From the beginning, there is the question of the look of the father. It can be interpreted on the side of the screen or on the side of offering. The oily water in front of his eyes is important. We leave with an idea of spying, and if we follow the look with another look, we have a key to the text, which deals with a level of evaluation that goes through the look. One evaluates with the look. It proceeds through narcissism. The look works in many different ways. One sees the father looking. The daughters were disquieted and brought back upon themselves, toward the inside, the look of the father. They try to control the look of the father. The child shouts: I want to control your look. I want you to look at what I find better to look at. It is the look of the father that is, as always, going to be carrying an evaluation, bestowing value.

The story leads to the access of the look of the father, to the ascension of the youngest, the favorite. We are led into town and "as darkness fell, the illumined city turned into a great metropolis with high revolving stools in every café." It is a fake sentence from childhood. The structure of the city is made of "high revolving stools in every café"; it is also the locus of the father. "The youngest daughter insisted upon sitting on one of those high stools." There is an irruption of a simple past. It was the famous Sunday of the primal scene. But what scene? It begins with: "The first time she wanted to sit on a high stool, the father found it amusing." The father likes her. It is a narcissistic moment. Right away, we have the evaluation of the father. It is biblical, it is good, and gay; it was joy and it is over: "Then the child would demand more attention and it was no longer quite so amusing." It looks like nothing, but all is lost. It reminds the reader of a scene in Kleist's *Über das Marionettentheater (On the Marionette Theater)*. The narrator tells about a young boy who loses grace. The boy lives in a kind of absolute happiness. He is full of grace, and one day the narrator mentions to him that he reminds him of a statue of an adolescent with a thorn in his foot. This gives him a kind of *coup de grâce*. He accedes violently and negatively to narcissism. From then on, he spends all his time trying to reproduce this famous work of art. Kleist cruelly writes how the adolescent becomes absolutely grotesque. The narrator surprises the boy, who tries to imitate the work of art and bursts out laughing. The sublime boy becomes an imbecile forever. Clarice's text is also about grace and loss of grace. The youngest daughter wants to sit on a stool. She has a spontaneous desire. The father finds it funny. Her desire is sanctioned by the father, who legitimates this spontaneous grace and, by legitimating it, renders it less spontaneous. He approves, recovers. The little girl begins again, this time in order to please the father. In other words, she prostitutes herself. She sells her desire to the father. She no longer does it because she wants to give pleasure to herself, she no longer eats her apple, but she does her little curtsies to please the father.

There is no commentary on the part of Clarice Lispector other than: " . . . it was no longer quite so amusing." This is the fall. It touches on what elsewhere

I called two types of knowledge. One would be confused with pleasure and would not be separated from the necessity of bodily pleasure. Another, a type of reproductive knowledge, is not part of, but is superimposed on, the body. It is a kind of "doing it on purpose." Instead of having a living scene, we are in the theater. In Clarice's text, they are linked together very quickly, under the guise of a simple childhood memory. "She chose something to drink which was not expensive, although the revolving stool increased the price of everything." One does not know who chose, the father or the daughter. The latter is now taken in the discourse of the father, in his values. The father says when they go home: "Without actually having done anything, we have spent so much money." We are in the paternal economy. The daughter took something that was not expensive. The father must have said something we do not know: the text is the epitome of discretion. But the daughter keeps the stool. She is nevertheless at the pinnacle, at least in appearance.

What gives, establishes value? We are going to see now all the systems of symbolic value. While the youngest daughter sits on the stool, "the rest of the family stood around, waiting." This is the test. One is not aware of it right away. "A child's timid and voracious reaching out for happiness." We are in a system of mirrors, and from the moment when the father looked and when the daughter saw herself being seen, one is in a scene of mirrors. The family looks on. There are systems of voyeurism, at the level of perversion. But elsewhere, delegation is in question. The little girl sees that she is now the keeper of familial pleasure, hence of all pleasure. She feels it because it is being signaled to her. The others surround her in order to find out what she feels, if she will have pleasure. It is also this way because the family is already too removed from pleasure. It cannot have pleasure. The family has to delegate its possibility of having pleasure to the little girl. They will take pleasure in her pleasure, eat and drink her joy. At the same time, she is able to keep a little of this timid and voracious curiosity.

One cannot not see that *Ovomaltine* is at the center since it is in italics in Portuguese. *Ovomaltine*, Ovaltine, is full of *o*'s. It is a foreign word, inscribed here. It establishes a multiple rapport between pleasure and strangeness. In the Bible, the apple is strange. It is desirable because one has not tasted it yet. From the very moment the girl desires, she tastes distance, difference, strangeness. One can say that pleasure is not of this world. It belongs to another world, another language. There is a magnificent sentence: "This was when she discovered *Ovomaltine de bar*, the Ovaltine they served in cafés." The sentence is from childhood, but at the same time it is the great event. Luxury is condensed in a tall glass: "Never before had she experienced such luxury in a tall glass, made all the taller because of the froth on top, the stool high and wobbly, as she sat on '*the top of the world*.' " All the signifiers of the first part of the sentence intersect with, and multiply, each other. The first sign of warning is the "high and wobbly stool." Something trembles. We know that one does not stay "on top of the world." Everyone was waiting. The Portuguese word *esperava* is stronger since it intersects with hoping. Here comes the drama: "The first few sips almost made her sick, but she forced herself to empty the glass." While they are waiting, she is struggling against nausea. She fights but goes all the way. The carrier of pleasure, she has the responsibility of an unhappy choice. She has to like what has to be liked, that is to say, the law. She is literally absorbing the juice of the law. At the same time, she resists. She is on the side of pleasure. Her resistance is marked by a mixture. She does not adhere completely to the law. But she is going to conform because of the others. One could think that she only reproduces a classical structure, but there are specific traits. For example, the sentence: "Was it dependent on her that they should believe or not in a better world?" That is Clarice Lispector's question. It is the origin of her morals. It is a question. She will never know. It is from a possibility of a belief in a better world that she is going to pretend, that she enters into something in which she does not believe. There is a scene of the mixture: "There was also the startling suspicion that Ovaltine is good: it is I who am no good." The exchange is classical. It is I against the world. It is at the lowest moment of her fall, at the sublime moment, when she blames herself, that she also sublimates: "She fibbed, insisting that her drink was delicious because the others were standing there watching her enjoy the luxury of happiness which cost money: was it dependent on her that they should believe or not in a better world?" She has to abandon her own demand, her own erotic requisition. She has to believe that her body lied. So, she is going to lie. The lie is always conscious. She does not lie; on the contrary, she gives back her false truth. But it is her body that she belies.

The positions are important. The youngest daughter is sitting on a high stool, at *the top of the world*. Everyone is standing around her. "She fibbed, insisting that her drink was delicious because the others were standing there watching her enjoy the luxury of happiness which cost money." She pays for the family. Her happiness costs her a lot. There is ambivalence at all levels.

"Was it dependent on her that they should believe or not in a better world?" is also the writer's ethics. She chooses to say that it is good while she feels like vomiting. She does choose not to say that there is no better world. It is at this point that one goes over into a better world that is marked by the shadows. One goes into the father's world that is supposed to be better. One is taken in a kind of return, a kind of turning back: "On the way home, her father quipped: without actually having done anything . . . " He says this while *she* has done, gone through, learned a lot. "Before falling asleep, in bed, in the dark," marks the last phase of retreat, of reflection. Now we are going to have the vision toward which the whole story leads. It is the vision of a better world: "Through the window, on the white wall: the huge, swaying shadows of the branches, as if they belonged to some enormous tree, which in reality did not exist on the patio." One has entered the world of shadows that does not exist. The little girl makes the apprenticeship of the shadow. Appearances are much greater, much more beautiful than reality, for example, this gigantic shadow of a tiny little tree of which it could be said that it is the father.

That is how one arrives at: "Sunday was always that immense night which engendered all the other Sundays and engendered cargo ships and engendered oily water and engendered a milky drink with froth and engendered the moon and the giant shadow of a little tree" (translation modified). One was in an episode of discovery where all had stayed quiet and mute. Then, Sunday suddenly becomes this "immense night," as if this silence took over. It becomes a symbolic night, not only a real night. As if Sunday had to remain this night, not the day that in the shadow engenders things with their appearance. And things with their appearance — that is the better world. It is the water and the oil floating on it. It is the milk and the froth, the Ovaltine and the name of the Ovaltine. The little tree and its gigantic shadow. The engendering of the moon. One goes back through a trajectory of elevation. There is a moment of jubilation. She had left in an ascending movement of pleasure to the top of the world. So one talks again of water, of milk, goes up to the moon, arrives at a "giant tree" and little by little arrives at the "little tree" and finishes on *pequeña*, on a "little" girl.

1980–81

Note

1. "Domingo, antes de dormir," in *A legião estrangeira* (Rio de Janeiro: Editôra do Autor, 1964). Translated by Giovanni Pontiero as "Sunday, before falling asleep," in *The Foreign Legion* (Manchester and New York: Carcanet Press, 1986), 140–41. All quotations are from this translation; all modifications have been indicated.

Chapter 2
Agua viva: How to Follow a Trinket of Water

Questions of Reading

Agua viva is a text that can produce resistance and anguish in the reader because it is governed by a different order.[1] One could say that from the point of view of a classical order, it is completely disorganized. But as poets know and keep repeating, the law holds only through its name and by its name.

Let us attempt an overview of *Agua viva*, alighting here and there in the text, at various points. Others could have been chosen, but I prefer the following, which are like answers to the problem of the law, the word, writing, and the (libidinal) structure of the writer. Elsewhere I have said that the system that puts a keeper before the law, the secret of which is life (the secret of which is that there is no secret), is symbolized perfectly in the scene where there is a sentence, like a legend in a vignette, a sign in front of the biblical apple that says: "Thou shalt not enter." That is the other side of the law. But if we do touch, we will discover that the apple has an inside and that it tastes good. We will run over to the side of pleasure that goes through the mouth. This is what Eve does in the scene with the apple. Writers have rewritten this scene in many different ways. In a story like Kafka's "Vor dem Gesetz" (Before the law), it is enunciated thus: "You will not go through." Because if by chance one does, one will discover that the law does not exist. To protect it, one has to do everything so that the law will be respected. In other words, one has to remain in front of the word, so that the word dictates the law. This is what books tell us everywhere, and what is being said everywhere in books. But the law is cunning because there are always men from the country who nevertheless feel like going in — just to see. Yet the word always remains stronger than anything. That is why men were believers and women were witches. Those whose interests led them to sublimation will be deaf to these remarks. There is something of the other that is not transmittable unless there is a political revolution such that the believers in the law will be capable of letting go somewhat of their position and accepting even without comprehending the possibility of something else.

This is the path I take in my reading of *Agua viva*. I could have taken it in any other text by Clarice Lispector. She says the same thing everywhere. The question of the law comes up everywhere.

Clarice speaks all languages, including those anterior to Sanskrit, including silences. It is good to live in languages on the condition that they not lay down the law. When we name in our ancient world, we attribute an identity to the thing or being in such a way that it takes its place in a general classification and falls under the *coup* of all the laws. Clarice names through love. She dictates the law of love, but she does not fall into chaotic indifferentiation. She distinguishes, sees differences, does not ignore the necessity to regulate. She is not into a law that represses differences, but into one that formalizes, that gives form. To name is one of the thousand gestures that one can make toward the other. It is like caressing, looking, silently calling. She says that God does not belong to any language. In the text, he nevertheless belongs to a language, to that of *Agua viva*. But while saying, ''God does not belong to any language,'' while naming him, Clarice does not imprison him. She gives him a name, but she does not take him by the name. She does not give him a name in order to take him. She gives him his name, a name that does not belong to any language, and that is not going to capture him, put him in a structure and come back to him.

Clarice works on language itself and on its relationship to the body, on the paradox that makes it so that things without body and reality are found and said more easily because they are nothing but words, for example, the law. She works on differences between humans and animals. She regrets not having been born an animal. In other words, she has to find the animal in herself. At stake for her is not the realm of science but that of life and death, of love. This agrees with what Freud had described as the formidable narcissism of animals, of the singular power of animals that goes with the fact that they have no intellect nor unconscious. They have another relation to life that can teach us a lot. This is what the law wants to avoid at all cost. It does not want us to feel regret, or desire, for a mode of life that would take as an example not God and the saints, but animals. This mode would not repress the animal part in us: ''An animal never substitutes one thing for another,'' says Clarice. It could be said that an animal does not speak, therefore it cannot substitute one thing for another. True, but it is good to remember that replacing is an act that is not simple and that is to be questioned. Substitution, the foundation of the symbolic order, also functions as repression.

Every moral law wants to go back through this simple sentence, which is not simply naive.

One of the major scenes of this text (42-44) begins with: "To write you I first cover myself with perfume." It is a scene that puts into body the gesture of writing and its verbal meaning. It begins with something very simple, which could be an effect of style, a coquettish movement. But it is the contrary. Clarice with this sentence declares war on writing conceived as death or corpse. By saying this, she situates the paradoxical enterprise that is going to be hers. It is not a trait of style. It brings about a long, absolutely astonishing and dazzling meditation on Sagittarian writing. By association, there appears an image that is introduced by metonymy: "I'm going to die, there is this tension like that of a bow ready to release its arrow." From this hybrid and strange body of the one who writes, living and not living, a scene of writing emerges: "I am going to write now as my hand moves." In this passage, the attempt is made to repair the dreadful cut between book and body. For Clarice, to write is a human act. She does not write in the space without body of the law, but with the hand. "I won't interfere with what it writes." She attempts to render corporeal a gesture that in general is so heavily symbolized that it allows for all the lying lies. I say lying lies because we will be led to read about falsehood and truth.

One of the recurring sentences that punctuates the space of Clarice, is: "I trust in my incomprehension, which has given me a life free of understanding, I've lost friends, I don't understand death" (42). With Clarice Lispector, there is no naïveté. She does not simply say: "I do not understand anything and I like it." She is in a "life free of understanding," that is to say, of the moral law. Clarice's search for another economy, another mode of existing, with other modes of relation does not become another moral law. If it does for us, that means we belong in too deep a way to the old world of moral law and that we come back incessantly to that model. Moral law has its interior coherence. That is precisely not Clarice's law. We could replace the term "law" with another term, but only if the functioning of the first term in the text is made very clear. We can call it rules, like biological rules, or laws, vital structures. That is why it is so important for any reader of Clarice to work on *Perto do coração selvagem*, which is an originary work. Clarice wrote it when she was very young, and for me she is the only example of someone who, from the beginning, did not enter into the moral law. What may appear as hyperelaborated in texts toward the end of her life is already there, in its uncultured state, but already mature, already thought through. In the first texts of her life, at the end of her adolescence, what she gives the reader to see is something entirely different. It is something that is not given as a model. If the various states of Clarice do violence to the reader, the reader is on the other side, on the side of the moral law. If it is lived in its immediacy, it is proof that one has in oneself a savage part that is the ultimate refinement of culture. Clarice's law, rather than the law that imposes, is an appeal, a calling.

A Question of "It"

In an interview, Clarice says, "I want the thing itself," and this "thing" is written everywhere in her texts. To write it is almost an impossibility. There is always something left of a self. But for Clarice, it is a question of "it." She also mentions that she does not rewrite or touch up words. This is both true and untrue. As she says, she lets her hand write and puts herself into an intense relationship of listening. She is tuned into her unconscious and becomes a scribe. She transmits. At that moment she is in a relation of respect, of sacralization with what she writes. She considers that she is not the one that writes but that the word is already a thing in itself. So when I say that it is not true that she does not rewrite, it is because the operation of rewriting precedes. At the moment when she puts herself into this state of writing she is already rewriting. Elsewhere in the interview she tells the story of the little pieces of paper. She tells her maid not to throw anything away. That too could be interpreted as her holding on so much to what she writes that she is on the side of avarice. Her remark is completed by another that she makes a little later when she says in relationship to *Agua viva* that for three years she had been afraid to publish it, because there is no story, as she says. Obviously there are fragments. The question of the fragment is essential and of interest on several levels: on the one hand, there is the question of the value of a fragment. What does it mean? What is the economy of the fragment? Clarice's fragments are not just any kind of fragment. They are not, for example, the fragments in the sense of Maurice Blanchot. It is on the contrary the kind of fragment on a piece of paper that the maid might throw away because it is nothing but a piece of paper. And that is related to the story of the hand and to the story of "I do not touch up words." What is happening in this formidable impulse is such that she probably will have gone as far, at a given moment, as to destroy the frame, the kind of writing practiced in an office, on paper, because for her, when writing comes, it comes. She notes on pieces of paper, in the present, at the very moment it presents itself. So rather than staying on the side of a fragment, we have to go over to the side of the remainders, of cutoffs, of small pieces of the whole. If she hesitated to publish *Agua viva* for three years, it is because the text raises the question of the law. Given her libidinal economy, Clarice does not like narrative and all it entails in literature. The genre with its laws does not correspond to her pleasure. At the same time, literature has produced narratives, has structured things. So perhaps, belatedly, she was worried about the idea of a non-narrative pushed to the extreme, that is to say, a text without the law of narrative, like *Agua viva*. She imposed the law on herself since she asked if it was bad. Does this mean that she believed in narrative? When there is narrative, there is a path. The reader can follow this path, look right and left. It facilitates a certain type of reading that comes back to the law, *lex*, to something that binds, links, reads. And if Clarice herself reread *Agua viva*, she would reread it the way she wrote it and as we read it, without a gathering point of view that allows to carry one and only one judgment. *Agua viva* is a text that disobeys all organizing laws, all constructions, and that goes very far.

Is the text readable? One may have to find other modes, other ways of approaching it: one can sing it. One is in another world. The text does not keep, hold back, and one cannot retain it. Does this mean it is only water? Absolutely not. It is living water, full water. It escapes the first rule of text. It is not linear, not formally constructed, whereas most other texts by Clarice Lispector are somehow constructed. As there is no story, one can start anywhere, in the middle, at the end. There is no exterior border. But there are a good many interior borders; there are some very precise ones that could be drawn. They have to do with the infinite line of separation between moments, epiphanies. There are no borders of montage, as in James Joyce, and the text is without ruse. It is always a question of beginnings. It is hard to imagine a text that would be more violently real, more faithfully natural, more contrary to classical narration. Classical narration is made of appearances, caught in codes. Here there are no codes. Yet Clarice is not mad; there are living codes with a beginning and an end. She says it: Now I begin; now I close; I leave and I come back. The text follows movements of the body and enunciation, but it also follows a theme. Rather than a narrative order, there is an organic order.

There are keys for reading. In *Coração selvagem*, Clarice Lispector says that she continues to open and close circles of life. In *Agua viva*, she performs this statement. In style, it is rendered through the ubiquitous gerunds and present participles. The question, constantly raised—because there is no life without somebody to live it—is: Who lives? Who lives there? Themes relate to life: there is the constant inscription of birth in innumerable ways. It is a process that recurs from circle to circle, often dealing with the birth of the subject itself, the birth of moments of subject. First, there are moments of gestation during all the very moments of gestation. The subject is yet to come, and in place of a subject, one has that which constitutes itself, a presubject. It is stated all the time that "I write" or "I live" before she or he, before the subject differentiates itself, becomes personal, determines itself. Clarice dwells inside those moments, in the space of the not yet and the already. There, in those moments, it is a question of pleasure. Although Clarice does not say it, one can raise the question of saying-having pleasure-prohibiting (*dire-jouir-interdire*). *Agua viva* is the inscription of a certain kind of pleasure, of a pleasure that does not keep itself for itself. Generally, one holds back one's pleasure: I am having pleasure, but I do not say it. This brings us back to the Lacanian predicament: woman has pleasure but she does not know that she has pleasure; she is incapable of saying it. Lacan keeps on saying that women have nothing to say about their pleasure. This is not true. Pleasure is all *Agua viva* is talking about. It is caught between two prohibitions that are not the same. There is one that *Agua viva* talks about all the time. It is that to say and to have pleasure are not simultaneous. To say something always betrays something. What is tragic is that the word separates. There is a difference in language between the subject who has pleasure and the one who says it. That is the very theme of *Agua viva* where Clarice writes incessantly: "I'm trying to capture the fourth dimension of the now-instant"; "I want to take possession of the thing's *is*"; "I want to possess the atoms of time"; "I want to capture the present"; "at the same time I live (the instant), I hurl myself into its passage to another instant" (3–4). That is all she says. I want to capture my essence. I want to capture, not I capture. Clarice knows it is a struggle. Beings, femininity resist capture. Women know that something between having pleasure and capturing that pleasure is lost in the act of love. Says Clarice: " 'Time' is something that one can't count." That is the point of departure. What will she do? She will struggle against the drive to capture to which she so strongly opens herself. Generally, culturally, women do not capture pleasure. They do not say it the way Lacan does. It is in their interest not to say it in a Lacanian scene where there are no sexual relations, because at that moment it is heard through a masculine ear, which captures, which is dressed to capture in a mode that would not be a feminine way of capturing it. One must think of another way of capturing it, without appropriation. This is what Clarice tries in *Agua viva*.

"I Want to Capture"

To read *Agua viva* involves a double task. On the one hand, one can follow themes. There are themes in *Agua viva*. There is no harm done by respecting a certain order while remembering that the text is completely organic. One has to follow all that is of the order of truth, genesis, fatality. There are thousands of little important themes. On the other hand, one can follow that which brings pleasure. The text is full of springs. If we take a theme, it does not have to be absolutely isolated. In other words, if we take a thread, we will see that it is a thread that is going to produce a web. On the first page, Clarice repeats four times "I want"; "I want to capture"; "I want to possess"; "I want to capture." This linguistic chain crosses the whole text. When Clarice says "I want," this "I want" is immediately doubled. It is an enormous inaugural drive to take. She takes in order not to keep. All she does is put into syntax. There is a perpetual phenomenon of overflowing in the text. *Agua viva* deserves that one dare to let oneself overflow but, at the same time, not be afraid to border it.

How to Follow a Trinket of Water

A few words on what presents itself as what one could call at the same time "the most and the least" in this text. What does this mean? The least is that which

does not announce itself. For example: "Now I am going to talk to you about
. . . flowers." It is a thread. It is inscribed over and over. It is also the earth of all
that grows or of all that swims in *Agua viva*. It is a question of style. We have to
laugh when we read a sentence like: "I write you, seated by the window." Examples like I write you, I am writing to you, I write, I write to you abound, yet
the text is put together with few words. There are many repetitions as in musical
scales. The text practices its scales without stopping. There are also variations. I
have the vertiginous impression of never knowing what page I am on. All these
relations of false anteriority, posteriority are something of a *déjà vu* that is not
déjà vu. There are repetitions — like the chair or the apples — which contribute to
disorient the reader. Disorientation is the orient of this text. It is not pure repetition of the identical. The same theme resurges and draws a little flower, simply
because there is never a radical cut. Because, in a vegetal mode, there is interminable ramification, with burial and resurgence. I am still in metaphors; I do
not fear them; I am obedient to what this text suggests. The text is metaphor itself, a metaphor that is not a metaphor but *agua viva*, living water, an ongoing,
gigantic metaphor, a facsimile of a book, which permanently works with a coun-
termetaphor "with." If, for example, one says that one is going to work on a
fragment, if one takes the text one is going to work on a priori, visibly, it becomes a very chopped up text. In *Agua viva* one could say that it is a coast. On
the level of signification one cannot find a whole. One could find one on the level
of form. Again, one must ask the question: what is form? It is what marks articulation. It is not the beginning or the end of an image, although that can happen.
Clarice's gesture, which listens to itself write, does not hide form. It says it in
permanence. The means of transport of this text are inscribed everywhere. The
text is its own echo, like a person or a vegetal form. Like a plant it buries itself
and surges up, or like a person it reflects upon itself. The text says what it says,
which makes reading very difficult. One has to read the very phenomena of writing and reading.

Elsewhere there is something of a first point, a first sentence: "It's with such
intense joy" (3). In Portuguese, the *e*, "is," only has one letter. At the limit, this
would be the unit of reading of the text, a sentence-word, one and only one word.
A word of one letter alone. The first sentence, which propels the text, is deceptive. One waits for a proposition to come: that this text is born, for example. The
sentence triggers a wait for something that is already there. It does violence to the
classical sentence and sets the tone for what is to come. There are only beginnings, hundreds of them. We take off, without end. It is impossible to divide the
text into fragments. There is no narrative, no story. None of the usual narrative
instruments are operative here, so one can only obey the text. One reads in one
movement, which does not mean anything. Rather, one should say, one reads in
a circle. One follows the text's breathing rhythm. All this completely explodes
the temporal reference marks. It is put in place from the beginning by the sys-

tematic recourse to the present tense. The present imposes itself. One cannot not write this text in the present.

Interruption-Continuity

Every reader is struck by the story of the flowers (45–48). In the passage on the victoria regia, there is this sentence: "é de se morrer delas," literally, "one could die" of the pleasure they give. The rule of the text consists of a release, of a setting in motion, of an insistence until, and I stay in metaphors, one arrives at the acme, at the incandescence of something that is orgiastic, but in a feminine mode, at something that goes over to the limit. Then, one can say no and everything starts up again. One needs to see the system of starting up again (*relance*). At times, the mechanism of pleasure can be read clearly. It may be the mechanism of breathing or it may be called music. It always corresponds to bodily rhythms, of a worldly, not a brute body that produces a reading of the world. The body makes love; it is taken in moments of exchange with the other, hence the rhythmic variations. Yet, on the level of logic or discourse, there is no plot, no evident causality, which makes reading difficult. If one takes the book as an ensemble, it openly declares that it does not interrupt itself. There are no chapters. The first thing, other than obviously writing itself, is: it is about. This is active. With the body it leads toward noninterruption. Let us return to the proof of noninterruption that is continuous, but which is inscribed in most obvious fashion at a certain moment. There is the sentence: "I think I'm going to have to ask permission to die. But I can't, it's too late" (48). Two paragraphs later, we read: "I'm tired. I tire easily because I'm an extremely busy person" (48). If one works on this passage, for example, on the sequence of sentences introducing the paragraphs: "I think I'm going to have to ask permission to die"; "I have to interrupt this because—didn't I tell you? didn't I tell you that one day something was going to happen to me?" and "I'm tired," it so happens that these three incipits of paragraphs inscribe interruption: "I think I'm going to have to ask permission to die . . . to stop," "I must interrupt . . . interruption"; "I am tired . . . I am going to rest," that is to say, I am tired . . . I am going to rest. Perhaps one goes toward an interruption, but exactly: my fatigue comes, my fatigue is going to be put to work, and I am going to work on the fatigue that overcomes me and makes me interrupt. If we look at the temporal shuttle, we have: "I think that I will have to ask permission to die": one advances. "I can't, I can't, it is too late": it is already past. Because the time of interruption is the third moment of this paragraph, which explains without giving an explanation. One is never in what would be of the order of linking, of heavy binding: Period. One has the impression that "I listened to *Firebird*" is juxtaposed, and if we followed the wordplay on "fire" in the Portuguese verb *afoguei*, "I became enflamed entirely.'' First there is something like a premonition or a preparation. It does not happen in the text; therefore we are told: ''I can't.'' Truly, one could read: I am no longer. It is too late, but it has already happened. Obviously, death cannot ''happen'' other than in this way. Clarice died between two sentences: ''It's too late'' and ''I listened to *Firebird* and I became enflamed entirely.'' Here are all the themes of *Agua viva* at once. We have: ''First I listened.'' There has been sublation of ''to be dying'' through music and not through any kind of music: ''I became the *Firebird*'': I became music again by going through fire, through the ear and of course through writing. All this happens on the theme that is not mentioned, because that would be vulgar, the theme of the Phoenix. The firebird in Brazilian is the sparrow of fire. At the level of the signifier, there is another very subtle play on passage through fire and water, because *afoguei* in Portuguese literally means, ''I drowned.''

Clarice is the champion of the sublime metaphor. Her mechanism goes so fast and so subtly that the reader is caught in it and carried off into the general motif of the text that amounts to nothing but transport. A statement as seemingly banal as: ''I'm tired. I tire easily because I'm an extremely busy person'' (48), could be read from the point of view of the technique of writing as ''to go on while following oneself.'' Clarice accompanies herself and follows herself. One could define her thus: she follows herself, she follows herself. ''I am tired.'' This leads to a paragraph on fatigue. She follows her own remarks, which she re-marks.

The middle paragraph of the three begins with ''I have to interrupt this because.'' There is a staging of interruption. She effectuates the ''didn't I tell you? didn't I tell you that one day something was going to happen to me?'' I want to emphasize the formulation ''didn't I tell you'' because it is one of the most frequent marks of the text. There are a certain number of questions, and the question is part of the general technique of the text. There are questions that are followed by answers, and there are questions without answers. If I distinguish between the two, it is because in the ensemble of the play questions and answers, the convention calls for real questions, not rhetorical questions. The questions here address themselves sometimes to you, sometimes to herself. A question like ''And what if dying tastes like food when you're really hungry?'' has no answer. Another—''What am I in this instant? I'm a typewriter'' (70)—has an answer. ''Or is the portal already the church, and when you're in front of it you've already arrived?'' (63). No answer. ''Will my song of the it never end?'' No answer. These questions inscribe the generality of a theme that could be called the ''I don't know.'' Sometimes the question mark is the answer. One could talk of the putting into question of this text, as one could talk about its staging. ''Didn't I tell you that one day something was going to happen to me?'' What is inscribed in the interruption is the arrival. One has to interrupt so that something can happen. ''Have I not said it'' also inscribes the movement of retrospective anticipation.

Here and there in the text there are pseudonarratives in the past, like that of the man with one foot or the story of Zerbino. They deserve our attention because they are uprooted in relation to the classical space of narrative and reinserted in a microscopic form in the vast elementary text of *Agua viva*. They are no longer simple narratives but are closer to plants or animals.

Clarice talks a lot about flowers. Let us go back a few paragraphs, to the sentence: "The chrysanthemum is profoundly happy" (48). It produces deep joy, comes from deep joy, distances itself, takes off. One is left not with death but with the life of the chrysanthemum: "It speaks through color and dishevelment." Afterward one has the other system of the plant that speaks, the disheveled part. This is rather banal. It has been overexploited by Georges Bataille in relation to the hair of flowers: there is growth, overabundance of the hair, excess, something uninterrupted. The flower is *descabadelamente*, which is there, on the page, like a disheveled chrysanthemum. The word contains so many letters that it is through its dishevelement that the chrysanthemum controls its own wildness. In other words, it is through its wildness that it controls its own wildness. That is the text itself, its model of spending; it is because it is disheveled that something of the dishevelment becomes domesticated. When Clarice says proper, she introduces a tension between wild and domesticated. Wild is detached and proper comes back to the same. It also functions as a textual metaphor, hence the violent surging, while one is in full dishevelment, of "I'm going to have to ask permission to die." This is moving because it deals in addition with the problem of dying. Again, there is the whole question of interruption, of the recharging of energy that is going to be spent, hence a whole circuit of energies. But there is also the relation to human dying and that brings across what can be called passion, because it implies a calling of the other. In Portuguese, permission is license. One should work on license because in Latin it is *licet*, which means "does that please you?" It is not simply permission, but "may I please die?" In other words, it still puts into question the system of pleasure: I need to die of pleasure, but perhaps you will not like it; my pleasure may perhaps bar your pleasure.

To continue on the "I continue": as already said, we cannot interrupt our reading of this text. The last three pages are indicative of this. We read: "What I write you is a *this*. It won't stop: it continues on. Look at me and love me. No: look at yourself and love yourself. That's what's right. What I write you continues and I am bewitched" (79). The text stops saying "I continue" just as to die is only the pulse of life, the passage of my pleasure to your pleasure. But if we read the last lines: "What I write you is a *this*." "This" is between quotation marks. "It won't stop": colon, I stop, "continues." This is exactly the *mise en scène* of the sliding between a stop and continuity. The text is strewn with colons. There are also dashes. What is the use of the colon? What is a colon? Generally, it opens onto an explanation, but it is always done with the help of an interruption. The colon is not the period; it is the period of the period, what cancels the period, a moment both mute and marked; it is the most delicate tattoo of the text. It is also in place of, instead of, everything that would be causal. For example, when we read: "It's simply that: secret." "Secret" is a sentence; it is the shortest sentence perhaps. But it is a sentence in one word. It is a sentence that is secret and that at the same time says its name. One could invert and say: "Secret: it's simply this." This is secret, the secret of the *this*, a word that makes infinite sense all by itself, a sentence that performs the secret itself. It is the greatest economy, waiting is once again deceived. Clarice makes massive use of "this" throughout the text. For example: "This isn't a story"; "I paint a *this*"; "I write with *this*, it's all I can do." "This" is often between quotation marks and in those instances becomes a substantive. There is an interminable substitution between demonstrative and substantive, between verb and substantive. There is a disturbance of grammatical categories in such a way that a continuity is being produced in the ensemble of sentences at the grammatical level and that continues to double the value of the present tense.

Let us come back to the question of reading, to the question of bordering. We are told, repeatedly, that the text continues whatever may happen. It is we who stop. One must say that life has an underlying style that does not depend on the human rhythm: "I'm unexpectedly fragmentary." Let us point out the paradox and comical effect of the juxtaposition of these words *inopinadamente fragmentária*. The length of the word undoes the meaning. To read it, one must be "unexpectedly fragmentary." One cannot do anything else but surrender oneself to the flow of the text, accept its stake of continuities. If we want to become aware of it with an instrument other than writing, that is to say, with speech, we may indeed feel out of breath or anguished. The text has its punctuation at the level of themes. Instead of a plot or a narration that would formalize something of an interruption, of cutting, of pure cutting, one has the simplest thing in the world, therefore barely visible: the paragraph.

"This Improvisation Is"

There is the story of the chair and two apples. Chairs and apples can never be added. This is exactly like the text itself that never amounts to a sum, to a whole. What can be found everywhere, like a series of callings or new beginnings, are little words. Toward the end of the text (77–79), there is a rhythmic precipitation, and Clarice writes: "Ah, this flash of instants never ends. Will my song of the *it* never end? I'm going to end it deliberately, with a voluntary act. But it continues on in constant improvisation, creating always and forever the present which is the future. This improvisation *is*. Do you want to see how it continues on?" "This improvisation *is*," is the law of the text. "My song of it never ends." I must stop it somewhere, so I stop it deliberately, but it stops in constant improvisation, period, onto the next line. "This improvisation *is*" signifies the presentation of the present. It is a sentence that leaves us hungry. It has a finality without end, be it affirmative in the mode of the Bible, or—as often in Clarice—in the mode of subversion of the classical sentence, the basic sentence, with subject, verb, and predicate. One would expect: "This improvisation is beautiful or tiring," but we have: "This improvisation *is*." We have a construction that is so condensed, interrupted, and still complete, with only the subject and the verb "to be" that is the predicate. It qualifies itself. It insists on the theme. It could be both at once. There are repetitions that give the feeling of *dé jà vu*. There is a massive recourse to the verb in this complex mode, which doubles the effects of the present. In addition, there is recourse to demonstratives, to a deictic usage that points and underlines.

Here is another example of Clarice's syntax: "Oh, living is so uncomfortable. Everything presses in: the body demands, the spirit never ceases, living is like being weary but being unable to sleep—living is upsetting. You can't walk around naked, either in body or in spirit. Didn't I tell you life presses in?" (78). There is a repetition of the verbal system of nouns as subject. The verb functions as noun. There is a double activity. These are pseudodefinitions. One has this strange expression: "life presses in" or "constricts." There is no subject. "Constrict" has a strong verbal value, as if to live did not depend on a self, on a subject. To live has become a noun. There is a passage to the nominal, as if the ordinary mass of words was attracted to the nouns, and as if there were an ascension from the banalized common name toward the proper name. In the absence, in the effacement of the personal subject of enunciation, everything in the utterance becomes subject. There is a great mass of subjects: to live is subject, apple is subject, so is tiger. Never have there been fewer personal subjects, and fewer subjects said to be impersonal but attracted to the personal through this kind of grammatical play. If we followed those grammatical systems, they would lead to the question of: who writes? who speaks? But at the most refined level since the question of the author is still here, although obviously reversed into that of without-author. Clarice can leave from elsewhere, as she says toward the end: "Now I am free." The text continues.

At one point (69–70), there is an element of plot: "The ring you gave me was made of glass and it broke and love ended. But sometimes in its place there comes the beautiful hatred of those who loved each other and who devoured each other. The chair in front is an object for me." One is caught in a long pseudo-narrative, which starts with an interruption, with the breaking of the glass ring. By the first breaking (it is the song of a child), the ring is the link; it links; there is linking and then comes the chair: "The chair in front is an object for me. Useless while I'm looking at it." The work on objects is very important. There one of the major messages of the text disengages itself. It is the displacement of the value from subject onto object: "The object-chair interests me. I love objects insofar as they do not love me. But if I don't understand what I write the fault isn't mine. I have to speak because to speak saves. But I have no word to say." "But it would be salvation." The series of conjunctions, "but," comes instead of the broken ring. "What would a person say to himself in the madness of candor? But . . ."

A little further on, Clarice writes: "Who could have invented the chair?" "Behind my thought is the truth that is the world's. The illogic of nature." Illogical is what lacks logos, what is silence. " 'God' is such an enormous silence that it terrifies me. Who could have invented the chair? You need courage to write what comes: one never knows what would come and frighten. The sacred monster has died. In its place was born a girl orphaned of her mother. I know full well that I must stop." One must look at the braiding of interruption and noninterruption, which, in addition, has at stake the creation of a world without subject, without author. It began earlier, at a moment when there was no more subjectivity because the latter had been interrupted. The ring was broken; there was no more love; then, given Clarice's writing, when one arrives at the one who has invented the chair, one is effectively projected toward the chair: "The record player is broken"; "the ring broke." "I look at the chair and this time, it is as if it had looked and seen"; instead of the scene of love, there is a scene of love with the chair that is not announced; it is inscribed as it produces itself: "This time it's as if it too had looked and seen. The future is mine — while I'm living. I see." Now one begins to take off in a new relation between subject and object, in a nonsubjective world. Here one finds all the themes of *The Passion according to G.H.*

Agua viva is not calculated in mathematical fashion. It is, as Clarice constantly reminds us, a text that follows itself, which lets itself be led, which takes risks with the acacias and is not afraid to let itself go. It is not an unconscious populated with Freudian scenes. True, it always takes place "behind something," as Clarice says. It is prelogical, prediscursive. It happens because there is, because "there takes place." This place is largely that which would be delimited by the range of the body: within reach of hand, ear, or the senses. It always goes through something concrete. There is a propagation that does not allow for the imaginary or phantasm. A reading that works on themes must work on big, large themes, for example, on everything that takes root, is source of the act of writing. These are acts, always. They all lead toward the final episodes, because there is a progression. It is not by chance that the final scenes are scenes of grace, because, as Clarice says, grace is without object, without subject. These scenes are the most naked. In this strange *corps-à-corps*, one does not know if it is one of love or of struggle; she stops at the end and the text continues. Something disengages itself and even if there is no story, there will have been a movement, a movement of liberation, of interminable propulsion, which effectuates itself, which insists, and which performs at the end.

When Clarice writes, "What I write you is a *this*" (79), to whom does she address herself? To the reader, to you to whom she spoke in permanence, to whom she did write this letter. The "this" orders, orders the reader, shows a direction. "It won't stop: it continues on"; it is no longer she but perhaps the text that continues. Then, there is this extraordinary sentence: "Look at me and love me. No: look at yourself and love yourself" (79). What does one hear? "Look at me and love me" is an imperative, an order given, an injunction spoken. One has in return: "No: look at yourself and love yourself." What that inscribes is something that the grammar would perhaps negate, but the order has been executed. In other words: you look at me and love me, no: interruption, substitution, while you look at me and love me. In fact, in the act of writing, the truth, let us say, of the first sentence is in the second: "Look at yourself and love yourself." That is to say, you think you read me, but what you do is look at yourself and love yourself. Once again, there is a relay of you. It is caught in the general problem of the *not I*—and there is no humbler way of saying *I*. But in the meantime, there has been all the work on effacing the subject *I*, as in *The Passion according to G.H.*, and given the fact that there are only objects, now *I* is an object among objects.

The Question of the Author

Again, I take the plane and go through colors, painting, and touch down at the question of mirrors (62–65). Clarice is interested in the mystery of mirrors: "The tiniest piece of mirror is always the whole mirror." The least page of *Agua viva* is always all of *Agua viva*. "Take away its frame or its contours and it spreads, as water pours." The frame is undone and it ends with: "No, I haven't described a mirror—I've been one. And the words are themselves, with no discursive tone." And this ends with: " 'X'—I bathe myself in that this. It's unpronounceable."

There is no more division between inside and outside. The most subtle movement can be seen only if one takes the plane, metaphorically speaking. It can be seen only from above. At that moment one perceives the threads that Clarice claims to have woven in the text. They are barely noticeable when one moves along a path. One is always in the forest, in rooms, on chairs, but one does not see the threads because on the ground, they are cut. The remains of a trace can only be seen from above.

Yet, at the same time, the text is not calculated in mathematical fashion. It is, as Clarice continues to say, a text that follows itself, that lets itself be led, that takes risks with acacias, that is to say, a text that is not afraid of letting itself go. It is not an unconscious populated with Freudian scenes. It is always happening "behind something," as Clarice says. It is prelogical and prediscursive.

It happens because there is a place, itself largely defined by the range of the body, of what would be within reach, within earshot, within the range of the senses. It always goes through something concrete, through a kind of propagation that does not allow the imaginary or the phantasm.

When I say that we can work on themes, I think of large themes, for example, of everything that turns, takes root, is the source of the act of writing. These are acts. They lead up to the final episodes because there nevertheless is a certain progression. It is not by chance that the last scenes are scenes of grace. As Clarice says, grace is without object, without subject; it is what has been completely stripped, bared. In this curious bodily encounter that we can never know to be either of love or struggle, at the end, she stops and the text continues. Something is disengaged, and even if there is no story, a movement will have taken place, even of liberation, which, at the end, performs.

When Clarice says: "What I write you is a *this*," *this* orders, gives direction. It is all taken within the problem of the effacement of the subject, as in *The Passion according to G.H.* Here Clarice says that there are only objects, and that she is an object among objects.

The reader goes through the fabulous experience of the question of the author, of the mirror, and of grace, which are like supreme moments of baring where the subject spreads into water and bathes in the very matter of the mirror. This experience of the mirror is a passage toward you. At the end of *Agua viva*, the reader must go on while Clarice stops:

"And behold, after an afternoon of 'Who am I?' and of waking up at one o'clock in the morning still in despair—behold, at three o'clock in the morning I awoke and found myself. I went to meet myself. Calm, happy, plenitude without fulminations. I am, simply, I myself. And you are you" (79).

From then on, separation, which was so badly effectuated at the beginning with the birth pain and the story of the girl who was orphaned of her mother, can take place. She can rest, and the world continues. This does not bring about death or absence in the world, since there is I and you and it is. "What I write you continues," because now it is what I write you that continues. One should even hear the what-I-write-you-continues in one word. It is what I write you that continues and brings *I* into continuity. But the *I* is no longer an author who masters.

Cut-Adherence

We can take up the passage on the flowers, especially the tulip. The wild tulip is beautiful. This is being developed in a text by Kant reworked in a very systematic reading by Jacques Derrida in *Parergon*. It is a curious text. Working on the definition of the beautiful, Kant distinguishes two types of beauty: a free beauty and a simply adhering beauty, a beauty suspended to, dependent on. What interests Kant, Derrida, and us, of course, is the free beauty. The independent beauty is the only one in Kant's judgment that gives way to the pure aesthetic judgment, that is, to the declaration: it is beautiful. These two types of beauty produce another supplementary level of analysis in Kant. There appears the free, ideal beauty, which only human beings are capable of perceiving. The choice of examples is comical. As examples of free and natural beauty, Kant cites colibris, birds of paradise, wild flowers. Then one notices that the poor horse is excluded from the world of beauty. This is easy to explain because Kant's theory of beauty is animated by a finality without end, and the horse has a finality. The horse is for people, and one cannot say that it is beautiful.

In terms of free beauty, or a finality without end, Kant works on the explanation of the condition of an aesthetic effect and its effects on the body. Kant stages the funny story of a mouth. For Kant, where beauty is at stake, nothing can be said. For him, the story of the tulip is without why. This is not true. One can say a lot of things about the tulip but without why. The "one has nothing to say," is dictated to Kant because he is in a philosophical dilemma. He cannot treat it otherwise, outside philosophical reason, for example, by thinking analytically. Everything can be rationalized on the horizon, and then there remains something without why, since Kant's why can only be rational. Here is what Derrida unfolds around these sentences:

> The wild tulip is, then, seen as exemplary of this finality without end, of this useless organization, without goal, gratuitous, out of use. But we must insist on this: the being cut off from the goal only becomes beautiful if everything in it is straining toward the end (*bout*). Only this absolute interruption, this cut which is pure because made with a single stroke, with a single *bout* (*bout* means blow: from *buter*, to bang or bump into something) produces the feeling of beauty. If this cut were not pure, if it could (at least virtually) be prolonged, completed, supplemented, there would be no beauty.[2]

This is simply a commentary on Kant's text. There is a cut, but without finality; there is tension and a pure cut. The pure cut, the *coup du tranchant*, is Clarice's practice. It is what, while reading, comes to us as a shock. It is something at the level of intensities, something absolutely determinable. "The tulip is beautiful only on the edge of this cut without adherence" (Derrida, 88). Kant cites the example of a tool with a missing handle. The tool is said to be ugly because it is cut off from its goal. It lacks something; therefore it still adheres. We begin to see that the cut is a bad, impure cut:

> But in order for the cut to appear—and it can still do so only by its edging—the interrupted finality must show itself, both as finality and as interrupture—as edging. Finality alone is not beautiful, nor is the absence *of* a goal, which we will here distinguish from the absence *of the* goal. It is finality-without-end which is *said to be* beautiful (*said to be* being here, as we have seen, the essential thing). So it is the *without*

that counts for beauty; neither the finality nor the end, neither the lacking goal nor the lack of a goal but the edging in *sans* of the pure cut [*la bordure en "sans" de la coupure pure*], the sans of the finality-sans-end. (ibid., 89)

This passage works because it is not a question of lack, in other words, of an imperfect object. It is a perfect object, but not in the sense of perfect as finished; it is a perfect and unfinished object. The tulip is not lacking anything, but it seems to have a finality and to be oriented toward a goal. This is sheer madness. If one thinks about the tulip or the horse, and, with all respect to Kant, one becomes serious, it no longer works. We can ask the question: how does the tulip have a finality without end? Kant thinks that because the tulip is not useful, therefore it is without a human goal. This can be put into question, since everything in the world has a human end. "The tulip is beautiful only on the edge of this cut without adherence" (Derrida, 88). Somewhere there must be form. The cut produces form. If not, we would have an interminable continuum of matter. Therefore, there is form. But for form to appear, Clarice Lispector says: now I stop.

"The interrupted finality must show itself, both as interruption: as edging" (Derrida, 88). The absence of goal is not interesting. There must be meaning. But not the kind that can be recovered at the level of the useful. This can be understood through Clarice's text. When reading, we should always surrender to what has hit our body. That is the moment of the pure cut, with *sans*. There is something of a finality, of a movement, of a drive but without a useful goal, without a system of reappropriation, of apprehension, of a continuum. There are a thousand ways of inscribing this thing.

To speak of free beauty, Kant uses a Latin expression, *pulchritudo vaga*, free beauty, which gives us something different from free. It suggests something vague, erring but nevertheless detached. In the passage on flowers in *Agua viva*, what could function as a finality without end?

A Finality without End: The Flowers

There are several levels. Each flower can give pleasure separately. Each paragraph may also please. Each has its own complex secret. One can say that it is the ensemble that gives us pleasure. Why? First, I would say, it is a system that casts an interruption into syntax, that is paradoxical because the syntax is precisely what links. The text puts a scene of freedom into a syntax of bound cuts (*coupures rassemblées*). This very contradictory movement starts with a meta-surprise, a kind of inventory, like a little book entitled *The Flowers of My Garden*. One never sees this in a poetic book. Especially for a French mind, repetition and enumeration are horrible. We are always asked to avoid them, and here, on the contrary, Clarice emphasizes them. There is a break with classical sensibility, with classical order, and in its place, where flowers are concerned, there comes an order that would be more primitive, not at all cultured. Afterward, there is something, if it can be said, of a breathing. It is a bouquet of interruptions, of pure cuts. There are only wild flowers, there is only *pulchritudo vaga*. It is striking because there is such an accumulation of interrupted moments. Clarice has joined the gesture to the word. She has performed it because the flowers are oriented toward gathering and binding. She has staged a finality without end at the deepest levels because the flowers to be cut are punctuated by flowers that are not meant for cutting, the wheat flower, for example. Literally, the flowers to be cut have to be cut with flowers not for cutting.

The Pitcher

I could read Clarice with the help of Heidegger's texts, especially those concerning the poet. What I am talking about, what I am tending toward, is related to the ring, *la ronde*: an overdetermined dance or roundelay that, across English and German, carries me off, toward the ring, even to that of the *Nibelungen*. I am going to work in the direction of what makes a ring, or a linking.

The ring we glance at in a passage of *Agua viva* is of glass and it broke (69). I am going to work on glass, of which I say right away that I am going to pervert, or *per-verre-tir*, it slightly. I am going to work on water—and we know who knows how to walk on water—with water on and around us, under water, in a kind of swimming that the text proposes, offers us as a gesture of reading. I am going to work on living water without a jug, in French a *cruche*, unless we are stupid, *cruches*. In fact, in a sense, women are *cruches* in an overdetermined way, and we know, especially since the German romantics that a broken pitcher is the equivalent of a broken ring.

Heidegger's pitcher, can be used for any kind of work on border needed for reading. Clarice's "things" are not unrelated to Heidegger's. And not by chance: it is precisely such a step of not-by-chance, this *pas-par-hasard*, that we can question. When I said that the pitcher, for us, was said to be broken, I alluded to a play by Heinrich von Kleist, *Der zerbrochne Krug* (The broken pitcher), but also to the fact that it is an enormous imaginary motif. The broken pitcher always refers in the imaginary to something of femininity. Heidegger does not say this because he never speaks from the standpoint of the unconscious.

I use the pitcher as something that allows me to collect a little living water. Water never lets itself be enclosed in a pitcher, the way it is impossible to enclose a text like *Agua viva*, which cannot be contained because it constantly makes us lose countenance. I will tend toward *puisement* and *épuisement*, toward drawing water and exhaustion, which in French is the difference of a simple letter, without our knowing who will be exhausted. I am sure that something related to this pouring of water can be read continuously in what we say about the text with its borders, its arrests, and its questions of interruption, and continuity.

I graft this onto my own map. For me the secret of this text is that water leads to a question of thirst. The banal expression is to have an "unquenchable thirst." In *Coração selvagem*, through thirst—that is why I point to the side of the chapter on bathing—one is on the side of water. Swimming, bathing are related to a certain thirst, to the relation between water, thirst, cutting off the water, and of the desert and drinking. Let us remember that in "Sunday, before falling asleep", eating and drinking were also taken up.

Inscription-Reinscription

Crucial in *Agua viva* is the technique of inscription and reinscription. There is in the text a tonality of return that is tragic. Clarice insists that to remember, to make something come back, is like "separating again." There is, nevertheless, each time something new. "New" is not nothing. It is very strong. Therefore there is a very violent articulation between a return, a calling back or a reseparation. All this replays the same scene of the broken ring, which is a tragic scene. It inscribes, it performs in the text as rich moments full of meaning such as "the dawn with its paunch full of thousands of tiny, clamoring birds" (58), which reappear in surprising fashion, like reminiscences with slight displacements. The latter are significant but imperceptible, almost transparent. A sharp memory is needed to note the slightest differences, which are displacements of supplements. Something is added very deftly that signifies that there is progress, that something becomes more precise, better marked.

"Who in Myself Is Outside Even of Thinking?"

Again, we take off. There is another thread. "Thinking" is born right away and becomes part of the tragedy. It is banal because everybody can do it, not banal because it is inscribed in a mode of extreme tension right away in the text. I help myself thinking to think, thinking that I think. Thinking is divided. As Clarice does this, she is in an intense wake that surprises every movement of the world as well as of the thing. To think accompanies itself with thinking thought, which helps one to think. There is always something that continues and gives rhythm to what is being produced.

"What I ask myself is this: who is it in me that remains outside even of thinking?" (55).

It is a key question in the text. In reality, there is the one who tortures her, who puts her to the question. Who in me puts me outside myself, Clarice wonders. This is the moment of the shattering of the subject. If we developed this in kind of a banal, philosophical logic, we would have: who in me is thinking, who in me is outside of thinking? What is being described here is the doubling and the division of the subject. It is one thread among others. For the moment, I leave suspended the value of thought simply to signal the mechanism. The structure is concentric. There is a system of circles. The subject tends with all its might toward something that could be called a separation, which is not really a separation, toward something that would be a limit between self and world. There is a movement that consists in probing the appurtenance to a circle, a (con)fusional appurtenance. In the text, it is constantly a question of fusion, of a fusional relation and how to disengage oneself from a fusional relation.

In a first circular instance, a little bit of subject tries to tear itself away. At that moment, it is as if one had punctured a membrane. One finds oneself in the space of something that could be perceived as a second sphere: "I exceed myself then in order to be." We can work on "exceed" or "exorbitate" in Portuguese. To exorbitate marks the orbit, the tearing out of the orbit, and the look. "To tear out of the orbit to be" is the moment of suspense between two circles, between two closures. "I'm in trance. I penetrate the surrounding air." She finds herself in a closed system, in a "dense jungle of words" that wraps around her. There is yet another envelope of all she feels, thinks, and lives.

In the question "who is it in me that remains outside even of thinking?" anguish goes through the "outside." It is like an aspiration toward a more yet to come. There is no exterior, but something that she calls freedom. It is a question of a certain freedom, not of a diffuse and useless freedom, but of what makes nondependence possible. It is separation that allows one to look at, to see the other. But the drama is that she feels—and she is absolutely right—that to think also belongs to the order of a circle of entrapment. Clarice tends toward the quasi impossible, which is to think beyond thought. Her struggle is summed up at the end of the paragraph: "Before organizing myself I have to disorganize myself internally"; and disorganization is absolutely necessary. It is positive. Something has to be dissolved in order to experiment with a first stage of freedom. The moment of freedom, an anguishing *moment-éclair*, is in any case ephemeral, a bolt between disorganization and organization. One has a glimpse of something else. But it can be effectuated only in violence.

The Oblique Life

The constancy of Clarice's unconscious (re)sources is surprising. We find in *Agua viva* what was already in *Coração selvagem*.[3] What has changed in the meantime is not the system of the coming onto the surface and on the inscription of signification, but form. What can be decanted from listening to the work of Clarice Lispector over a span of twenty or thirty years is that the whole tissue of logical discourse has become useless. One arrives on the side where one no longer has to explicate what the surprising or mysterious elements are; where one is able to let the mystery go by without accompanying it, without surrounding it with a system of presentation and excuses that is that of too great an ignorance, or too great a surprise. Yet here she happens to let herself be surprised to the point of having the need—as earlier in *Coração selvagem*—to excuse herself through a stylistic form that is even classically formulated.

I would underline what is in the register of *esquivança*, to steal, slip away, to be aloof, but by taking into account that the word is translated as *savage* afterward. I would play *esquiver* with *escriver*, between writing and inscribing. It is certainly a movement of reception, of inscription that represents the delicate relationship between *savage* and *stealthy*, aloof, as interchangeable. *Esquiver*, to slip away, defines in a precise way a certain relationship of body to body, or of self to world, which is not of the order of escaping or of lacking, but of avoiding what Lispector describes at length as a discordance, a disagreement, as a lack of (musical) harmony.

This thematics of the slight discordance and of the *almost*, which is of the order of the (dis)encounter, of the not coming to the encounter of, of avoiding the face to face, touches upon something very important in this passage: "But we almost understand each other in that casual discordance, in that almost that's the only way of bearing life at its fullest, since a blunt face-to-face encounter with it would frighten us, would stun its delicate spiderweb threads" (57).

Assustar, to shake, to disturb, and *espaventar*, to frighten, signify the vibrations of each of the bodies. This series of metaphors, which make of life a production of webs constantly weaving between the two, is related to the questioning of the violence of a face-to-face, which is always of the order of the specular. This can be inscribed in the way of a libidinal differential. A distrust in relation to the violence of the look—insofar as the law is made to take, envelop, distance, incorporate—is questioned here. Clarice approaches less in speculative fashion than through a displacement of bodies, through a system of perception. Her approach is always on the side of touching, tasting. In *Coração selvagem*, the story of the sun and of the one who sees and who does not see is the division between: I see what I see, but what I do not see, does it exist? The question is childish. But it is Clarice's question. Taking off from this primary question, we have another, that of respect, of not looking face-to-face, in a face-to-face that would be destructive. We have all that is oblique: the oblique life, a fault, an aside, a slanting, sloping, an insistence on the necessity of a coming from the side, of letting the other come, of letting oneself be surprised. This is not the space of a prevention that would be associated with the exercise of the look. If I see the other come, I anticipate and prevent. I can let the other approach, only from the side.

In the story of the terrace, Clarice tells us that there is a side of life that is like having coffee in the winter on a terrace in the cold, all bundled up in wool. The unspoken that will appear three paragraphs later is the special pleasure that coffee on the terrace in winter gives. The coffee is ordinary and not ordinary. It is a different coffee — that is what is important. What defines the pleasure of oblique life is what speaks, but obliquely.

To Eat the Fruit at Its Peak

"Only for those who are initiated does life become delicately real. And it's in the now-instant: one devours the fruit at its peak" (56).

At the moment when we are in the now-instant, we begin not being in it any longer because it is constantly the relay of that which begins to be and which, by beginning, also begins to end. It is the announcement of the interruption. At the same time, we eat the fruit at its peak, but we also eat the fruit in the time it takes to do so. We eat a fruit that lasts as long as it is being eaten. One can add that the fruit, when it is being eaten, is, gives, pleasure. One can add with Rilke that the fruit when it is ripe contains all the time it needed to reach maturation. But as Rilke said, the ripening leads to the propitious moment for eating it. What is being signaled here is that bliss lasts as long as bliss lasts. Truth gives itself for pleasure between two instants. It is the equivalent of two moments of truth.

"Could it be that I don't know what I'm talking about anymore and that everything has escaped me without my knowing it?" (56–57) does not come as a kind of leap but dwells on helping, on hearing herself think, as a moment after having given a development, an illustration of truth as delicate as she is in the now-instant. It summarizes everything Clarice has been trying to say in the preceding lines. But she says it in such a condensed, tight sentence that she wonders whether she understands herself. There is a double gesture when she says: do I no longer know what I am talking about? It is as if she followed, step by step, the oblique life. On the traces of the oblique life, she develops something; she weaves this fragile texture and arrives at the last sentence as if she wrote with her eyes closed. Her sentence wakes her up, literally. Does what I say make sense? The sentence leads back to another level of writing. That it stays inside the same paragraph is troubling. It would suffice for her to go on to the next line for the reader to have a feeling of dialogue, of a difference in the time of enunciation.

The Ring

Much has been said on the difference, on the gap, between presence and proximity. What is close is always too close and is not pure proximity. In Hölderlin's poems, we can read that, because God is close, he is hard to seize. He is too close to be easy to seize. The poetic struggle consists in having nothing or nobody precede. The name does not precede in such a way as to distance. Things do not happen before the noun, nor gods before their names. They should not be too close nor take away the space for naming. If the poet names, his naming should be obscure so that he can let the gods come, but in such a way that they have not already come. This is the problematic expression of the struggle in Clarice's language.

To come back to the ring. To attempt a reading of this passage on the ring is a little bit like forcing oneself to seize what one has to let go. One has to pretend to do a naive reading. What makes Clarice write, and what accompanies the reader all the time, has to be forgotten in favor of a reading that would listen to the text the way one listens to children who always know much more than they are capable of saying.

What this text—as well as all of Clarice's other texts—gives to read is the height of solitude. Solitude cannot be filled; it is pain itself. Clarice says this constantly. The only thing that the reader can remark with a supplementary trait—because Clarice says everything—is perhaps the origin of this sorrow:

"Mine is a new era, and it ushers me to the present. Do I have the courage? For the time being I do: because I come from long suffering, I come from the hell of love, but now I'm free of you" (10).

Later in the text, this would no longer be possible. Clarice would remark it by preceding the reader and stating it more incisively: I am not free of you since I remember the hell of love. Does saying "Now I am free of you" make one free?

"I come from far away—from a weighty ancestry. I, who come from the pain of living. And don't want it anymore. I want the vibrancy of joy. I want the sovereignty of Mozart."

And further on, she says: "But I also want inconsequence." "I want" means "I already have it, but I do not yet have it since I want it." "Freedom"? Toward the end, one reads: "Yes, what I write you belongs to nobody. And this freedom of nobody is very dangerous." This repeats the earlier passage. In slight disharmony, writing and freedom flow into each other. They limit each other.

"The ring you gave me was made of glass and it broke and love ended" (69) sounds like a popular song, or something of a complaint. Love was not enough and it is all over. The "too little" is said everywhere in this text. But Clarice pulls this "too little," which is hard to define, toward something that has become an "almost." She has pulled it to the other side of the system of values, toward the infinitely small.

Clarice's writing accompanies itself. It effectuates its own critique subtly and explicitly. "The ring broke" is also valid for writing. It is an effect of theme, but at the same time, the ring breaks continuously. The broken ring inscribes a break in discourse. Important here is the surging of the object. The object is urgent; it urges; there is the urgent surging of the object that does not speak, illustrate, and that has to do with a qualifier, with the *is*.

The *is* of the subject goes over into another domain, that of the inanimate object or of the animal. This is possible only through a double evacuation of meaning. The chair *is*, the thing *is* without meaning, without *telos*, without end, so that it can be invested by the subject; and similarly, there is an evacuation of meaning that is transmitted by the subject who speaks of the thing. What one reads in the text is how the thing receives, how it becomes the *is* of the subject. The thing is empty of itself. We can pretend to make an outline of this passage. It can be linked, articulated. The passage is composed on the general theme of the breakage (*le bris*) as a series of glass splinters, then music, then the ring, and so on. There are four moments:

1. I like objects insofar as they do not like me.
2. I do not understand; the orgy of words.
3. The record player is broken. Do I link or not? The record player is broken: the ring is broken. She was orphaned of her mother.
4. To pull out the arrow.

This composition exists. It is articulated through slight displacements. Generally, in writing, the breakages in the text are strongly marked by paragraphs. Here, they are inscribed softly inside this lengthy opposition characterized by a kind of calculated, panicked bewilderment signaled through orgy, orgasm, through a whole recurring lexical chain. *Orgia* were the mysteries of Dionysus. It is the orgy of language as being, impossible yet present, on the side of paganism. As always, it is signaled in Clarice in an imperceptible way.

On the Christian side, which surprisingly is always here, there is another index through the word "Franciscan":

"But my cook said: 'What ugly flowers.' Only because it is difficult to love what is Franciscan" (translation modified).

We are between Dionysus and Saint Francis. Saint Francis wrote, in addition to the *Fioretti*, a canticle to the sun that is a succession of salutations. This is remembered-forgotten in the text. For example, the anthology of flowers is a series of salutations to the flowers. For Saint Francis, it involved saluting creation. Clarice does not salute creation created but the creation in creation. The first element of surprise is the salute to the chair. A thing has to be empty of meaning for the subject to enter. "The chair in front is an object for me." It falls from the sky. It is in the order of evidence. It is here. Clarice salutes and discovers it. She makes it come toward her. She makes the readers see the things they no longer see. Clarice refuses the obvious. It is against the chair that Clarice is orienting herself. And a whole story is being woven around this.

To come back to the four moments once more: first there is the story of the ring that broke. The ring was made of glass. Glass is the substance of this discourse. Crystal produces music through vibrations, almost without a signified. Glass can be read like arrested water, like living but frozen water. "The ring you gave me" marks a strong continuity within the break. The whole text works on interruption and continuity, a continuity that demands interruption, interruption into which continuity flows. It can be said that this story of continuity in breaking represents the indissociable ensemble of this text. Content and form cannot be dissociated. Content becomes form; the container flows into the contained and the text weaves itself incessantly. When the text stops, there is nothing because there is no story. This continuity, this indissociation, is marked in the next sentence:

"But sometimes in its place there comes the beautiful hatred of those who loved each other and who devoured each other."

"Devoured" announces what will come at the end: the tiger. This is how, through this dense flow of words, one arrives somewhere: one is already on the way, without knowing it, toward the tiger who is waiting a few pages later.

We can return to the chair. "The chair in front is an object for me." There is a system of references that goes back to things without purpose. The autonomy of a system is inscribed here. The chair is autonomous, gratuitous. And, nevertheless, the chair is going to hang on to the quest for essence. The chair already calls me, in me, for me. On the level of the signified, Clarice manages to make this chair appear, to cut it out, as James Joyce would say, rephrasing Saint Thomas and his *quidditas*, similar to what happens on the level of the signifier through repetition such as: a rose is a rose. One pronounces the word, one uses it until it no longer signifies. But Clarice proceeds differently. Her approach is quasi-philosophical, although she keeps herself below philosophical approaches. The chair is useless while I look at it: it implies the question of the subject, of the object, of the look. This subject is not there for the moment. It is an abstraction of the human subject. She places the chair. What remains is the look. The question was already asked in *Coração selvagem* in relation to an oyster. Says Clarice: "What troubles me most is that what I do not see exists." One has to see the extreme simplicity, the extreme importance of this remark, which sounds like the questioning of a child. Children have a fantastic consciousness of what is beyond them, which they lose later on in life. They know that everything is beyond, that in relation to their small size everything is big, that there is the infinitely unknown and that this unknown does without them. This touches upon questions of life and death or of the insignificance of death.

"Useless while I'm looking at it": there comes something from the look that gets closer to the question of words, in a slow and roundabout manner and which is the question of the utterance. Does what I do not see exist or not? Does what I do not name exist or not? While I do not look at it, I have nothing to say about it. And, as Wittgenstein would say, what cannot be enunciated must be kept silent. And while we look at the chair, the whole dilemma of language comes in its place. Clarice is going to refer her speech back to a silence. She enters and exits with words of silence, like water, and at the same time, she performs it. This makes the other side, or life of the other side, appear. She says at some point that she has made a secret pact with the other side. A simple and paradoxical thing happens: if she wants to salute the chair that she only sees, from the moment she salutes it with words, there is a subject and she is taken in the salutation. There is "and." The conjunction must be as little apparent as possible in order not to interrupt the autonomy of the chair.

Then comes: "Tell me, please, what time it is so that I'll know that I'm living right now." She does not know whether she lives at this very hour or in which hour she lives, so that there must be intervention from "you." But not to know what time it is, is the extraordinary, discreet confession of an ecstatic moment. Clarice has taken off. To remain in the Franciscan mode, she inscribes this mystical experience in the least mystical, the simplest and most discreet of all possible ways. To say: I have taken off, she says: Tell me what time it is. Moreover she says: Please, because — a small detail — all the callings of the other are accompanied by a very great politeness like: May I? Please, thank you. It is mystical, without being applied because there is no belief in God. God appears between quotation marks. " 'God' is such an enormous silence that it terrorizes me." Saint Francis had received stigmata. The whole passage (on p. 69) is a stigma of this kind. The simple passage to the chair is a mystical one. "I'm finding myself in my very self: and this is fatal because only death will complete me." "Estou me encontrando comigo mesma"; I am going to the encounter of myself, it is the ring that I not only give myself but that I am. The reversal is terrifying. This is of an extraordinary power. If I form a ring with or by myself, autonomously, without you, because *I* meets *I*, nothing comes to interrupt the ring anymore; there is not even a risk of breakage. It is mortal. If you does not limit *I*, only death limits *I*. The trait of interruption can be produced only by my own death. "Tell me, please, what time it is" means, Please, interrupt the ring I form, interrupt my own conclusion. Love is no longer here to limit me in a living way. I am mortal in a natural way, that of every living being and I suffer until the end. "I'll tell you a secret — life is fatal." Life in a ring is simply mortal. "I'm going to have to interrupt everything to tell you the following: death is the impossible and the intangible." The question of interruption comes about in an ambivalent way. Interruption can be lived positively or negatively. In itself, it is always bad but it is necessary; therefore there is a moment when it turns around into something vital — but to speak, one always interrupts. The object "chair" having been evacuated, the subject literally goes into it. Without meaning. There is a residue of a subject, imperceptible, irreducible. The irreducible subject is this instance that abstracts itself and interrupts to write. If not, it could stay in the chair. This residue of subject, to hold on, not to sink again, asks for help, asks the other for proof of his own existence. Literally, what hour of mine is it? But in this paragraph we read that death is impossible, untouchable, and necessary. Death is used in two ways. On the one hand, it signifies moments of interruption of continuity. The last death is impossible since it happens in our absence. On the other, death of life, the mortal of life, is the impossible because it is not from death but from an interruption that everything can be started up again. Similarly, and the accent is nevertheless on the side of interruption, just as death breaks, love breaks at every instant and so does help.

"It's as if life said the following: and there simply wasn't any following." Clarice's subtlety reaches a point where she must say to herself: I do not know what I am saying. Everything hinges upon the colon. She says and performs it incessantly. If the colon were suppressed, one would fall into absolute rupture since what follows would not be. But if one keeps the colon, there is another precipice. There is another discontinuity. "And there simply wasn't any following." Instead of a signified, one has a signifier. Writing this way, Clarice makes the impossible of existence exist.

Clarice tells herself that she must speak, because to speak saves. But she has no words and nothing to say. There is an abyss. "What would a person say to herself in the madness of frankness?" (translation modified). There is no possible answer in such a state of frankness or candor. It is almost impossible for her at the same time that it is absolutely necessary to keep a little bit of subject to verify her mad creation, without subject, the frank creation that she herself is. To be frank is to be cut off from the world, interrupted or *être affranchi*, to be liberated. If she stays in pure frankness she is mad; she no longer has an outside; she has no longer the slightest trace of subject that can reassure her about it. She struggles with this paradox.

The terror of frankness — to be detached is terrifying — goes with darkness and carries its opposite. As if absolute frankness were already subverted by a very small system of linkage that ties frankness in something Heidegger would call co-appurtenance. There is linkage, but it is dark, intangible, terrifying. Through this metonymy one arrives at "today": "Tonight there are many stars in the sky. It stopped raining. I'm blind." First she is blind, then she opens her eyes: "I open my eyes wide and I merely see." Like the mystic, she does not see objects, she sees at the place of the origin. This is a mystical technique destined to strip the look from the already seen. It is not blindness. To be blind, here, is to begin to see.

A salutation of what has been bared, stripped in an absolute way, is put in place: "How does the naked oyster breathe?" The naked oyster is the oyster naked of the look, not looked at or an object altered as little as possible by the look of the subject. Hence, the salutation of the naked. The mystical procedure is disapplied. The consciousness of a mystical state would already be too much.

The Broken Record Player

The record player is broken the way the ring is broken. At the beginning of the text, she says: "I see that I have never told you how I listen to music—I rest my hand lightly on the turntable and my hand vibrates, spreading waves through my whole body" (5). This is related to the nakedness of music. While she listens, the music could almost be taken in by the look of the ear. The hand on the electricity of music goes through the body. "I look at the chair and this time it's as if it too had looked and seen" (70). Here the entire movement of the text signifies why the thing begins to look as if love could exist between Clarice and the chair or anything else. It inscribes the possibility of a reciprocity. Clarice is cautious. She uses "as if." She does not say, "The chair looked at me." But the possibility of a reciprocity goes with broken love, and the broken parts of love are the most naked reality. One touches upon absence of meaning. I look at the chair because I can look at the chair and it is here as if it had looked. Clarice inscribes a frank look of madness. It does not obey its own human source anymore. It is freed from a world that is neither hers nor that of the chair. But there is a look. This is one of the rare moments where Clarice succeeds—while brushing against madness—in living the instant.

But right away there is an indication of reticence: "The future is mine—while I am living." The sentence is rather ambiguous and tragic. Clarice wants the present. But she slides away at the very moment she has it. She tries to capture the present, knowing that it is going by. A sorrowful note is heard in the attempt to appropriate what cannot be appropriated. The future is mine, but the future is that which does not exist. She can appropriate all the imaginary future, hoping that she will still be alive in the next instant. This is the height of poverty and riches in relation to time and life. We live with a hope of time that includes at least the next instant. Clarice no longer speculates on time but on the next instant. But she speculates on the next instant, and that is what makes her write.

Clarice is full of humor. "Who could have invented the chair?" is an admirable and comical question. In Heidegger the question is much more pretentious, cloaked and necktied, as in the story of the pitcher concerning Rilke's poetry. In Clarice, the chair is very modest. It deals with the question of the origin of the world as a fundamental, originary question.

"You need courage to write what comes to me" (70). God does not need courage because he knows what he does. But the writer invents without knowing what. This is the question of the origin of the chair and all of creation. Clarice is a courageous God and not a sacred monster. God is dead and so is the sacred monster, the artist, the beast, the prodigy, the subject. In its place is born a "girl orphaned of her mother." From the moment she is born, she is no longer orphaned since she enters into the cycle of the egg and the hen. But she will have been orphaned of her mother in an an effect of separation from the mother that Clarice continues to replay. Here it is played out in "you."

This leads to an (earlier) passage on freedom. "I'm going to confess something to you; I'm a little frightened. It's just that I don't know where this freedom of mine will take me. It's not arbitrary nor libertine. But I am free." And this is frightening.

Then: "Am I free? There's something that still restrains me. Or am I fastening myself to it?" (25). The sentence is unclear: to a thing or my freedom. "I'm not completely free because I'm tied to everything. In fact, a person is everything. It's not a heavy burden to carry by yourself because it isn't simply carried: one is everything." This is the closed ring. I am free and not free, and my freedom is to be the question.

Birth

"I'm not frightened any more. Let me speak, all right?" (25). These are the words of someone who cannot speak. One has to look closely at the relationship to the other this implies. The coming onto the word, the passage onto a possibility of enunciation that cannot be done without the agreement of the other, is of the register of birth: let me be born. I am born thus: pulling from the uterus of my mother the life that has always been eternal. The very complex theme of several births would have to be followed. First, it resembles a human birth. But this is immediately set aside for an animal birth, in a strange description of birth. And she refers back to what has happened before. The life has been pulled out of a mother as an eternal living but in this very space, the living person has been lost. There is the incessant sliding between mother and daughter: "I'm in true birth-labor with the *it*." One does not know who is giving birth. She is born, she delivers, and at the same time delivers herself. To be born is a being born pure and absolute. "And when I'm born I am free." She is cat or child. "This is the root of my tragedy." She can already be cat. She is, as Heidegger would say, the milieu, there where everything is happening, and it is happening in us. "No. It isn't easy. But *it is*. I ate my own placenta. . . . And no one is me. No one is you. This is solitude" (26). This solitude is constantly in question: it is not a simple solitude. It is not only: the ring you gave me is broken. It is the water bag, which has been punctured, and "no one is me, and no one is you." At the end: "Look at me and love me. No: look at yourself and love yourself. That's what's right" (79). There is a relative reparation of solitude.

Let us return to God and to the sacred monster. "I know full well that I must stop. Not for lack of words but because these things, and above all the ones I think and don't write — are not said" (70). There is "not": the word is missing. It is also the necessity to mark the moment of stopping, of interruption and not the other silence, of things that are said. We will see why things do not speak and what will come in the place of milk. The passage looks innocent, but we are in real drama: "I'm going to speak of what's called experience." It is a simple word but already it is not experience. "It's the experience of asking for help and having help given.'' One is fully in the relationship of mother-origin, with the gap that there is no mother. This is associated with the things not said. In the mystical space, it is the prayer, and the prayer is granted. To pray is already to grant oneself something. But it is a mystique that demystifies. The experiences of calling, of suspending the person, of a pure call for help, and of receiving help without a subject are written. The "you" to be called is not inscribed at all. Hence: "Perhaps it's worth it to have been born in order one day mutely to implore and mutely to receive.'' The sentence is equivocal. First, despite everything, it is worth being born so that this calling will take place, even if there is no answer and everything is happening in silence. It can be a mystical experience, situated beyond language. Perhaps it is worth the pain of being born, of having been born orphaned of one's mother and to have paid this price so that, perhaps one day a mute response, of praying and receiving, will be possible. It is quite violent. Nothing is sure at all. One pain brings about another pain. "I asked for help and it was not denied me.'' By whom? One does not know. Movement has gone from not receiving to not negating. Any form of help, from the scene of birth, is not enough. From the moment a cry for help has been uttered, it already hurts, there has already been need, and also this question of help that has been granted by nobody. No one is sufficient to herself or himself. Nobody is I. Nobody is you. Here, we can read the eternal, impossible mourning of when someone else was I—an articulation between child and mother. Clarice does not say it but it is implied.

"I felt then as if I were a tiger with a fatal arrow nailed into its flesh" (71). Clarice goes into the tiger. There is real introjection. It is she who is in the tiger. The tiger, like herself, is soft with ferocity. The arrow is all the help of a wound insofar as need and truth are concerned. Truth is naked.

As in the story of the cat, the tiger is double. There is a tiger converted into a soft tiger. Also, there is she. She is the tiger to contemplate and to ask, "Who would have the courage to come close and relieve it of its pain.'' Who has courage? She is the courageous one who softly watches the fearful people. Courage has value only in relation to fear.

"And then, there's a person who knows that a wounded tiger is only as dangerous as a child. And approaching the beast without being afraid to touch it, the person pulls out the embedded arrow.'' Equivalence between tiger and child, not elimination, is shared. "And the tiger? It can't thank you.'' The value of "não se pode agradecer'' (one cannot thank) can be taken as absolute. Nobody can ever thank. One can only say thanks.

The scene of birth does not have universal value. It is not the scene of separation that everybody has experienced that produces an irreparable effect. It is for sure another story. This story goes through something that is related to the body of the mother. When Clarice Lispector is read from the beginning, from *Coração selvagem*, one notices everywhere the presence of the father and the absence of the mother. The question of birth is an intensification, a metaphorization of a situation that is read as painful. It is determining for her and recurs as one of the themes of her writing. There is a continuous emergence, a separation or a struggle of the subject in order not to lose the enveloping contact with the living. At the same time, it must be lost, during an instant, just at the time of feeling or of knowing how to live. Clarice continues to reinscribe infinitesimal autobiographical signs in sentences. In reading *The Passion according to G.H.*—and this is verified in other texts—one senses the ruptures of amorous liaisons, or substitutes for the absolute love affair. For somebody like Lispector, who has a mystical comprehension of the world, madness always threatens. At the same time, one must respond to the calling, try to go beyond the limit, and do what she says and only look. But in this quasi indistinction between subject and world, if one goes there alone—as she says in *The Passion*—one has the feeling of getting lost, or going mad. It is true that one needs to be accompanied by the other, who will be a witness, even if the *I* disappears. The other is the witness of my disappearance. At that moment, the supreme scene of the passage to the infinite is not felt like total anguish, like the fear of disappearing and of not coming back. It can be imagined that in the act of love one accedes to what Clarice calls life on the other side and, at the same time, this access to the infinite finds its limit in the presence of the other. "You" limits the infinite through which I was going. On the one hand, Clarice suffers from an originary solitude. On the other, nobody ever seems to have wanted to accompany her where she wanted to go. She has always had to come back, to exhaust herself coming and going at top speed because going is very dangerous. This is a summary from the side she calls tragic. Other moments are less tragic. There are moments of joyful pleasure where she is not human but where she is horse, her favorite totemic figure. Each time there is a cavern—related to bags of water—a terrifying fear calls for the horse. Horses gallop freely. Similarly, her dream is to drink at the origin of the spring. And that is when the horse appears. "Yes, this is life seen by life itself. . . . I let the freed horse run wildly. I who trot on nervously, delimited only by reality" (11). This dream of freedom is in contradiction with the necessity to capture, which goes through words and things. She has pleasure only as an *I* that runs fiercely as a horse. The horse, in which she invests so heavily, is associated with a noble animal.

The Sadness of the Flowers

We can drink at the source of the text. Thirst is omnipresent. One crosses some liquid spaces to begin with a text that has been lost in *Coração selvagem*. *Agua viva* is the main text that contains everything. Without the latter's water, *Coração selvagem* remains a desert.

We can take up these pages, ford them, and come back to *Agua viva*, the side of thirst and water. What will emerge from the springs, the sources—that is, what can be heard—pertains to the disquieted or inspired being. We have to study the broken ring and come back to a flattened ring, in other words, to the mirror. All this has to be inscribed in a broken circle. If I break the circle, everything overflows, under a curtain of rain that I raise. Today, it is a night with many stars in the sky. One is blind; therefore one sees, under the interminable question of questions of why such strange thirsts are surging in her. In *Agua viva*, there is a wonderful sentence: "I cut off the pain of what I'm writing you and I offer you my restless happiness" (61). To cut is a fabulous word, something a little bit like Heidegger's pitcher. It interrupts, fills, and makes overflow. One cannot not think that at the root of *dolencia* (sadness) and the English "redolent," something articulates suffering and perfume.

When Clarice says "I want to paint a rose" (45), the phrase is completely comical. Everywhere in *Agua viva* a relationship between writing and painting is motivated since Clarice goes from one medium to the other. If she writes "to paint," the verb is not metaphorical but real. Does she paint here? No. But elsewhere, tomorrow, or in fifteen pages. In other words, she has the strength to inscribe in a partially botanical discourse the desire to paint a rose. This is not performative. It performs only desire. Thus her humor, her strength. "The rose is the feminine flower" (45). She does not paint, she gives us a discourse on something else. There is a kind of organized distraction. Clarice is someone with order, and when she goes on to the next line in the text, it becomes the order of distraction itself. When she writes, "Now I am going to speak of the sadness of flowers in order to feel more fully the order of what exists" (45), she announces at the same time: "First, I gladly offer you the nectar, sweet juice that many flowers contain and insects avidly seek." This is like: "To write you I first cover myself with perfume." She says it before and we read it afterward. A break occurs. It is a game but also something on the order of libation, something propitiatory that makes the other intervene in the text. At the same time it resembles a concrete benediction: the sweet juices that many flowers contain and that the insects look for avidly. "Avidly" refers to botanical or pseudoscientific texts but also to "you." If "you" takes in some nectar, "you" is also an insect. In gliding from one realm to the other, a mutation between humans and nonhumans is brought about. But inside the natural reign, there is a gliding from flower to flower, from style to style. It glides and distracts; it turns and is comical.

The paragraph proceeds by distraction and association. There genesis appears and is all the more ordinary since one is all the time in God. In this genetic process, the proper comes out of the common. "And the Lord God planted a garden in Eden, in the east; and there he put the man whom he had formed" (Genesis 2:8). It is another way of making something surge forth. One can talk about planting, and everything of the order of planting, imaginary, real, symbolic. The garden is of interest to the reader who is planting a garden of paper, and words. An appeal is made to all the gardeners and their genealogy.

Beatitude

The story of beatitude is evident in a text like *Agua viva*. It is, in a certain way, between quotation marks from one end of the text to the other, written in a flat way in the text, as if something were always already there. Not a word fails to be a quotation of itself. If we want something primitive, something that goes forward, what can we do? Such is, as always, the question of writing. According to a convention, one always writes as if it were something original. True, everybody has but one ambition, that is, to destroy the already written, to tear from the already written something not yet written, something not yet spoken. Clarice does this incessantly, violently. She constantly goes on to the next line to break against habit.

The example is the word "beatitude" (73–75). She is talking about something, and here comes the word beatitude. Why? Because it is the name of that very thing. But beatitude carries with it a lot of old information. And when she says, I do not like that word, what is one to do since a certain state of being belongs to a given register and is marked by a given type of vocabulary. What does she do? She reverses the process. Her way of putting between quotation marks is a way of undoing what has been so heavily quoted forever. The coup of the dictionary is a little bit like the "I want to paint a rose." It is supremely clever. "Immediately afterward, I went to the dictionary to look up the word 'beatitude.' " This seems to have been the only way for her to say, Please understand me, when I say "beatitude" I do not mean to say it in the way everyone uses it. It is a detour through its opposite. She goes to get the dictionary in order to signify that when she says it, it is not a common beatitude. And why? Because she does not want to carry on the very discourse that we are using here. Anything philosophical would undermine her poetic edifice. Rarely does she have to have recourse to this kind of practice. But here, she has to do the worst. She has to go to the dictionary. She does it in her own way, almost always in a most sincere passage to the act (*passage à l'acte*) that comes as close as possible to a true spontaneity. A pure spontaneity does not exist. On this page, we have an imitation of spontaneity. She goes back through the dustbin in order to get rid of it. But she does it as concretely as possible. She stays in this kind of naïveté that is a supreme art. Why? The couple beatitude-dictionary is a very violently antagonistic couple. When one is on the side of beatitude, of the state of grace, the dictionary faints. There are no more words. It is also the limit necessarily imposed on that which faints in the without word. Beatitude does not speak. Obviously, she wanted to defend herself against the implication of religious mysticism in a banal way. Because the dictionary also goes with the coffee. "It is to tell you that I did not go to church." She defends her own mysticism, which is of the humblest, most domestic kind. Something happens in the order of beatitude or inspiration. The passage is not on the side of a coming onto writing but of a state. It is a stream of consciousness. Hence the great number of dashes and dots. Something takes place in, and gives itself the right to, intimacy.

Perto do Coração Selvagem: **Strange Thirsts**

We can go back to these lines from *Coração selvagem* in a passage where the protagonist, Joana, is leaving the boarding school (57–60). The chapter associates two bathing scenes, one in the bathtub and another in the river. It is a passage of reminiscences. When she comes out of the bathtub she is an unknown woman who does not know . . . and she forgets. Hence she remembers. The scene of the bathtub has a kind of autoeroticism, something of a constitution of a subject-body. It is a metaphor of birth. She comes out of the tub, out of unknown waters. "She glides through the hallway — a long red, dark throat." In other words, she goes back into the body that is said to be lost but found again of the mother. "Behind her the beds of the dormitory of the boarding school were aligned and before her, the window opened onto the night." This montage of reminiscence à la Joyce is associational. Of importance are: behind and before. Joana leaves something behind her, that is to say, the others. We know that they are there. She leaves the beds behind. It is violent because the girls are reduced to beds. Beds are a synecdoche of the girls. The window is Joana herself. She goes through the window. A conjunction, a passage toward the night occurs. Afterward, we are in the night and Joana is in infinite exploration. We are neither in the unconscious nor in the dream. We are in a kind of stream of consciousness. It is associational — hence the unconscious can surge. It is a bursting, a surging of the spring.

Joana is absorbed by the night. She becomes cosmic. "Above the rain, I discovered a miracle." It seems as if she could see above the rain. Now there is a rapport with above and below. The rain functions as a screen, as a cover or a curtain.

One does not get out of this rain. It seems to separate us from the miracle. But there is not one without the other, there is always *and*. Rain is also — we come from the bathtub — the presence of water. If you think of any passage of *Agua viva*, to begin with the title, rain is one of the elements of fecundation.

The miracle is double. If one reads the text, there is constantly a miracle: "A miracle divided into big stars . . ." Clarice does not say the miracle of stars but "divided into stars." In Portuguese, divided (*partido*) has to do with sharing and dispersion. The miracle is shared. But what is a shared miracle? Is it the miracle that is diffused or is it the diffusion of miracle. She adds: "big stars." And "big," in the sense of "pregnant," re-marks *Agua viva* constantly. Insistence of the word in this text is most immediate on the side of whatever is big, abundant, fleshy, and maternal.

"Why do these strange thirsts surge in me?" This expresses her desire to communicate, penetrate, absorb. What is she thirsting for? We left from the rain and went on to the stars. The light flows and she wants to swallow it, but it stays fresh and humid. Thirst can be replaced: why do these strange questions surge in me? The thirsts are the questions for which she thirsts and which make her thirsty. First question: What do they say to me that I want to understand bodily. "My God, communicate me with them." These strange thirsts are not thirsts for water. She tries to say the questions she asks of the stars and that the stars ask of her. She tries to say the astonishment of being put to the question. And every question is a question of the two.

"The rain and the stars, this cold and dense mixture awakened me and opened the door of my green and somber forest, of this forest with an odor of abyss where water runs." And she was united to the night. This is really like the *Song of Songs*. I slept while my beloved went by. I heard his voice. His voice woke me. I got up, I ran, he was not there. It goes far in terms of sexual symbolism. The lover puts his hand through the skylight and she is dripping with myrrh. Clarice's thirsts are both intellectual and erotic.

"The word shatters between my teeth into frail pieces" is extremely oral. In Portuguese, there is a system of phonic signifiers, since star (*estrela*) and shatter (*estala*) play on the letter. It is the *r* that makes the star explode. It is the infinite multiplication of stars. This reinscribes the "divided miracle." "Because the rain does not penetrate me, I want to be a star. Purify me a little bit and I will have the mass of these beings that keep themselves behind the rain." To say that one wants to become a star is to want to be bathing in the night. I want to be star, night, sperm, and matrix: a sexual totalization is inscribed everywhere. There is a gigantic aspiration. From one star, she goes to being and containing all of them. Hence the paragraph: "At this moment my inspiration aches in my whole body." And for good cause, for this is truly inspirational, an overgigantic inspiration. Clarice is absolutely faithful to what she can experience. She is at the point where she would like to absorb all the constellations and she notes: "And instead of this asphyxiating felicity, like an excess of air, I will clearly feel the powerlessness of having more than an inspiration, of going beyond it, of possessing the thing itself — and of being truly a star."

There is a certain struggle, but for the time being, inspiration or aspiration happens in the body. Yet her body cannot contain something of that size. She feels very well that this overabundance is going to turn into its opposite. And if she had to go from inspiration to act, what would she do? True, she does touch upon something here, "of possessing the thing — and of being truly a star." This is separated with a dash. It is not the impotence. It is still desire. It is positive.

She wonders where madness will lead her. In *Agua viva*, madness is frankness, deliverance. Truth is madness. Since, in *Coração selvagem*, she is a child, she asks: where does madness lead? But it is truth that appears here. A few lines later it is opposed to naked reality. The division is very important. It will renew itself incessantly; truth and reality do not go together. "Does it matter if, in appearance, I continue at this moment in the dormitory, the other girls dead on their beds, their bodies immobile? What does it matter what really is? In truth, I am kneeling, naked like an animal, next to the bed, my soul in despair as only that of a virgin can be. The bed disappears little by little, the walls of the room retreat, fall down vanquished." She wants to communicate, make love with the universe. She wants to undo walls of the soul and of the body. And then, there will be liberation. "And I am uncaged in the world." The same process can be found in *Agua viva*. It is always the same question. How does one go from the self to the world and through what transposition? She feels in the world, free and fine like a doe in the plain. It is absolutely biblical. "I dive and then I emerge." That is also the technique of *Agua viva*. I interrupt, I enter, and I exit, cut. "Distracting my tired thirst to rest in a goal." She has a paradoxical thirst. Generally, thirst feels like the ordinary thirst, a thirst that wants to be quenched. But Clarice's thirst needs to continue being quenched. It gets tired from being stopped. It is an infinite thirst, a thirst that needs to be satisfied. She needs strange questions. "Where have I already seen a moon high in the sky, white and silent?" It is against a kind of thirst but also an allusion to a primal scene. "I am fooling myself, I must come back." This, as in *Agua viva*, is a sentence of being out of breath. There is a moment when she is beyond anything that could be expressed. She feels that she has to come back. But she defends this excessive moment. "I don't feel madness in the wish to bite the stars, but the earth still exists. And because the first truth is in the earth and in the body. If the luster of the stars hurts in me, it is that distant communication is possible; it is that something almost similar to a star trembles inside of me." Joana aspires toward the high and the low. When she takes a bath, it is in water from below. When she talks about biting the stars, it is in the mode of refusal that says that the stars are too high to bite. She tries to bring back this roof, this mixture of rain and stars that is the milk of man to the body of the earth. The first truth is in the earth and the body. She relates to stars because she has stars in her. Her relationship to symbolization or sublimation remains very corporeal. She refuses to the stars the status of something that one cannot bite into. She expresses a desire to bite into the breast. At the same time, this *sortie*, this exit through the window to the stars has a vital meaning for her. It is an evasion in a necessary and dangerous mode. When she says, "I must come back," she comes back to limit herself. "When I surprise myself in the back of the mirror I scare myself. I can hardly believe that I have limits, that I am cut out and defined." She does everything to prevent an interpretation that would be directed narcissism. "I almost forget that I am human." Without a mirror she would be dispersed. She would be a star. "I forget my past and I am with the same freedom of finality and of conscience as a thing simply alive. It also surprises me, with my eyes open onto the pale mirror, that there is so much in me beyond the known, so many things always silent." She maintains her strangeness when she looks at herself in the mirror. She does not need the mirror to recognize herself. The mirror is necessary because it limits. It is a mirror that must seize and arrest. It is a kind of Lacanian mirror, but it frames something strange. What she sees in the mirror is something of the other. She does not see herself, but she surprises herself with open eyes in the pale mirror. She has interrupted, she has cut or blurred the source of the image that looks at the onlooker. She does not look at herself. There is a kind of look that circulates between her and the rain, between her and the mirror. One wonders where the paleness of the mirror comes from. The mirror is going to be a well for another secret. Its shiny surface is the impassible mystery. This mirror is going to be her little sky, her domestic space. "Fascinated I plunge my body in the bottom of the well, keep all the sources silent, and, somnambulant, follow another path." The well would be the mirror. But it has come about unexpectedly. It is a sentence, a look that frees her body from the superficial image. She is the young girl, so to speak, as flower.

What did this mirror do? During a necessary but brief instant, it has limited her thirst, which is not a simple thirst, to absorb what she calls the mass of being. It is a thirst that exceeds the self, is generalized, and spreads into the world. But she also thirsts to absorb. This is inscribed from the beginning in the "why," through the question of the question: why do these strange thirsts surge in me?

In rereading Derrida's little text "Qual Quelle: Valéry's Sources," in *Margins of Philosophy*, one can recognize a similar theme, written from a masculine border. The difference is obvious. One of the words that makes up the title in the text on Paul Valéry is source (*Quelle*), as in Clarice. Also inscribed immediately is, of course, division, or *Qual*, the German torment. One recognizes the torment of *Agua viva*. It is double. There is excessive disquietude. Clarice says: I am making a mistake. I have to stop. When she arrives at the limit, the disquietude brings about a return of quietude, which in turn is going to be disquieted simply because nothing is more disquieting than tranquillity. And thus, from disquietude to appeasement of disquietude, which in turn becomes agitated again, she throws herself back to the stars. In her question about "why" the whole paradox of this agitation is evident, since "surging" is the word that would express the appearing of the water, of the spring. In fact, thirsts surge like springs. They are springs. If the thirsts are springs, the springs never need a rest; if not, one would die of thirst. It happens very often that thirst is restful. Then one dies of thirst, and to die of thirst is the question of *Coração selvagem* as well as of *Agua viva*.

The Mirror and the Portal

The portal and the mirror (62–65) are a symmetrical *X* whose two lines must meet. They are supposed to be immobile and fixed, but movement and passage prevail. As Clarice says, "At the same time that I live it, I hurl myself into its passage to another instant." She throws herself in the movement of the text from one page to the next, from the portal to the mirror. The two pieces are inseparable. "That's how I saw the church portal I painted." We are already in the space of the portal-mirror because it cannot be known whether one has seen the portal of the church to be painted or the portal of the painted church. "Symmetry was the most successful thing I did." Symmetry has been lost and found like everything else in this text. "I have lost my fear of symmetry, after the disorder of inspiration." Something has happened. "My symmetry in the church portals is concentrated, successful, but not dogmatic. It's suffused with the hope that the two asymmetries will meet in symmetry, that as a third solution: synthesis." In Portuguese, *perpassada* gives hope that the two asymmetries will meet. It is a troubled symmetry in movement, in waiting. Complex and agitated, it tends toward something. In the passage, trouble and torment abound. Clarice insists on saying, "No, what's there isn't exactly tranquillity." A painting has to be agitated in struggle but not symmetrical.

The thing is standing upright, despite the torment inflicted upon it. It is something of the order of Christ. Matter is riddled by the hope of something. The densest, most compact colors are tormented by their opposites. What torments them is "the lividity of something that though twisted, is upright" (translation modified). A metaphorization, inscription, and incarnation of torsion, or struggle, take place in what it takes for the thing to be a thing. In another passage, she had said, "I work only with losts and founds." And, "I'm little by little. My story is to live. And I'm not afraid of failure. Let failure annihilate me, I want the glory of falling. My lame angel who becomes disdainful, my angel who has fallen from Heaven to Hell where he lives relishing evil." This is picked up in another passage: "My crosses are twisted by centuries of mortification." We can think that those are the crosses of her painting, but they are in fact her own crosses, her own passions. We can believe that it is the work of painting. But it is essentially her own crucifixion. The cross is also going to appear graphically, like a sign of the unknown, the letter of the crossing, of the articulation, of the violent encounter in its symmetry, of a violent encounter. "Are the portals a prefiguration of the altar?" Question. No answer, only the silence of portals follows. The portal frames, contains, even prefigures the silence. The temporality extends between an already, a not-yet, and a future anterior. A speech made in advance, a warning, is itself a part of the tension that continues to carry away symmetry through hope. Silently, portals say more than the portal. This is how the greening has to be read, the greening as something that participates in this kind of immobile movement, as an insistence called intensity at the end of the paragraph. It is truly a passion.

The "dense" and "tranquil" colors are disquieted by old bronze and steel. There are very few colors. Clarice speaks in colors, but colors are not in view. When there is color, it is not "green" but the alteration of color. The whole is amplified by a silence of things lost and found. This picks up the theme: "I work only with losts and founds." These things that are lost are to be found. This deals with the coming and going that meant simply that nothing can be found that has not been lost. Everything begins by being lost. This will take on its full significance in front of the mirror. There clearly it can be understood what it means "to find," but on condition that it has been lost.

The portal of the church is already the altar. This will lead back to the mirror that is already a mirror. Everything in this text can stand for everything because water is everywhere. Living water is unlimited. It is impossible to limit a drop of water, except when you drop it, so to speak, at the moment of the fall. To find is to lose. To find, to feel that one has found, is to arrest, to lose the movement of what lives. That is where the story of the absent Christ takes on its complex value, that is not only absence of belief in God, but absence as a value of inscription of the value of presence through absence. He is named. A Christ is here, absent. He is the epitome of presence. If he were present he would be absent on the first glance. The absent Christ announces his other in the absence of self in the mirror.

In a passage of "Qual Quelle: Valéry's Sources," the originality of Clarice's work can be seen in relation to a problematic issue involving originary division. When I say *I*, I am divided into *I* and I say *I*. This is what Hegel, who is interpellated in Derrida's text, gathers under the name of *Qual*, the torment in relation to God. In the Hegelian dilemma it is said that God, who is infinite, is tormented from the beginning (something that is in any case unthinkable). He is disquieted and goes outside himself through disquietude—and that is history or the *sortie* of this originary point. God goes outside himself, from the point zero. The fact remains that the infinite is pushed to add to itself something finite. That is the beginning of the whole negative process of the dialectic. The source is put to work by the negative, or is divided by itself. It is even cut off from itself. Such is the *Qual*, the torment. Now in German, *Quelle* means source. *Qual Quelle*, a tormented source. This is the general and banal dilemma, and also that of Paul Valéry in Derrida's context, which joins the general philosophical dilemma of the absolute origin, often designated as source. Derrida begins at the origin of the world: "I—mark(s) first of all a division in what will have been able to appear in the beginning."[4]

The nonself is for the self. Clarice Lispector's enterprise consists in leaving the nonself alone. This is her supreme endeavor. It is logical, although we have the impression of a caprice. She works capriciously all the while she leaps from one point to the next. We go from the portal to the mirror and, if we do not work systematically, we may think that the mirror is being called forth through the symmetry with the portal. But the episode goes much further into what she calls the thing, the nonself, and its deliverance. She tries this experimentally with the test of the mirror that, by definition, is where the self finds itself as self, at least as the saying goes. She tries a movement of liberation from the mirror.

Before jumping into the mirror, she says a last word: "I create the material before painting, it . . . " It is impossible to know where the gesture takes place. It is left in supsense, but an answer follows: " . . . and the wood becomes as indispensable to my painting as wood would be to a sculpture." What gesture of painting calls for the wood? a support? a frame? What follows is: "And the created material is religious." "Religious" has to be understood especially in a material-spiritual mode that links and props. The portal will take on its whole meaning only when it will have become mirror. It should be noticed that "coagulated color" indicates how color is something organic. "Coagulated color, violence, martyrdom are the beams that hold up the silence of a religious symmetry." In the addition of the finite to the infinite, or the struggle of two asymmetries to make up a symmetry, everything comes together to make up the silence of a meditation or the very locus of meaning.

Yet another break occurs: "But now I'm interested in the mystery of the mirror." I am interested, I am inside, in this mysterious milieu. How is one to speak of it? "I search for a way to paint one or to speak of it with the word." In fact, she is trying to get out of it in order to be able to talk about it. She is looking for the point of articulation. Does the mystery of the mirror speak? If it is mysterious, it cannot be talked about. That is the point of articulation, the point of breakage. At this point of interruption the mystery ceases to be completely mysterious. The question of the enigma of the mirror is also the question of the enigma of the relationship between self and world. We have to pay attention to the question of the subject, which was not that of the Lacanian mirror but, on the contrary, that of *Coração selvagem*. Clarice is going to go there with all her philosophical strength and with all her poetic ruse. This passage smacks of ruse. In Lacan, there are no ruses. There is a mirror in which we look at ourselves. Here it is a mirror in which one does not look at oneself. The question of usage, which is not raised in the text, can be asked. If one refers the mirror to something that is not of the order of its own mirrorness, or of the mirror that serves to mirror, what will there be? The ruse—which is going to be stated—is that this mirror is going to be like water a few pages later. The text mirrors constantly on all sides. There is crystallization. There are facets. Elsewhere, it mirrors in the fashion of the mirror through the question, "A mirror?" The text mirrors its own question. What is a disaffected mirror?

The text is an illusion. The reader is not given an answer but is sent back the word: "A mirror? . . . " "What is a mirror," is the answer. The text asks us constantly what it is that we are talking about. "The word mirror doesn't exist, only mirrors exist, since a single one is an infinity of mirrors." The word "mirror" does not exist, only *a* mirror on condition that it be unique. It is like God. It entails an infinity. A unique mirror is infinitely divisible, but mirror is always plural. "A mirror is not made, it is born." Clarice puts her cards on the table. She violates received opinion insisting that a mirror is created. The entire textuality surges forth from this mirror. "Not many are needed for the sparkling and somnambulant mine." A mirror is always double. Two mirrors are the source of all mirrors. It is a question of seeing the mirror without being seen, of surprising the gaze in the mirror. But this mirror has dimensions. Two mirrors are sufficient, and one has all the mirrors of the world. The other mirror can be the absent eye. The mirroring of two leads not to three but to the infinite. One reflects the reflection of what the other has reflected. One does not leave the space of the mirror, but there is no other, no self. Birth is to be understood from this hard water, the mirror, which is a phantasm. The mirror opens the space of succession: "And I can scarcely talk, from so much silence unfolded into others." She can no longer speak because one can do so only if, as in the classical dilemma, the constitution of the subject takes place through division with a subject of enunciation and a subject of the utterance. Only if one accepts the *coup* of the source constantly dividing itself. But who can speak if it is silence that is mirrored in silence? And if nobody looks into the mirror? There is something of a double, there is doubling but no self. There is not one source divided by the word. There is the infinite, that is, an infinite possibility of words that barely speak.

"Like a cat with its fur standing on end, my hair stands on end in the face of myself." In order to see oneself there has to be a point of origin of the look. The look has to be outside, exterior. There has to be a simulacrum of exteriority to see onself. Clarice calls this "extraordinary." It is extraordinary and goes out of itself. That is where the necessary break intervenes in the paragraph. If one admits the interminable emptiness of the mirror, obviously without end, there is nevertheless something ruseful at work in the passage. A *coup* of magic. The simplest magic in the world consists in breaking a piece of mirror–and the mirror of which Clarice speaks is unthinkable because it is a written mirror—into an infinite mirror. To see onself one has to break off a piece: "And it's a magical thing: anyone who has a broken fragment could go with it into the desert to meditate." We can go into the desert with a little piece that draws a limit. It is the repetition of the interminable mirror, which is a written mirror: "Its shape isn't important: no shape succeeds in circumscribing and altering it." The mirror depends on the other. The mirror is what mirrors itself. Clarice always considers the mirror as not framed except when it is broken. It has an infinite capacity of mirroring. Every piece is a whole, but to say, "To take away its frame or its contours and it spreads, as water pours," is to open the big faucet, to acknowledge that she takes the mirror for water. And one goes off on the side of the mirror, as the water starts to spread. It is closed and frozen again in the question: ''What is a mirror?'' We can understand this mirror that gets broken from time to time—even better in its repetition—that is the very story of the mirror. The ring of the self had to be broken by another. But the mirror is a ring that is not broken by another. It is also glass. Glass refers the reader to all the stories of frozen water, of transparence, and of vibration. If the mirror is to be a pure mirror, it must not be looked at, because it would be a mirror of the self. One has to mime the famous walk of the crab that approaches the mirror from the side. It manages to see before being seen, to surprise the mirror when it is alone. Who surprises it? Either it is nobody and is a phantom that does not touch upon its solitude. Or it is somebody who does not manage to see the mirror. ''Only a very delicate person can walk into the empty room where there's an empty mirror, and with such grace, with such absence of self, that the image does not register.'' One finds here the absence that already was that of Christ, in the covering of his tracks. ''As a reward, that delicate person will then have penetrated into one of the inviolable secrets of things: he saw the mirror as it is.'' It is the paradox, the sign of inscription of play with the mirror, because if it is penetrated, it opens into nothingness. Inviolable secrets remain inviolable. Clarice has penetrated the sacredness of that thing. Literally, she has seen the mirror strictly speaking: ''No, I haven't described a mirror—I have been one. And the words are themselves, with no discursive tone.'' She does not describe in the sense of circumscribing. I cannot circumscribe the mirror, I have been it. This does not mean I have been mirror. It means I have lent my being to the inscription of mirror in the text. I gave myself to the mirror. I mirrored myself. She lets the words mirror themselves but without anybody to pronounce them. When she talks about the mirror, she talks about *agua viva*, about living water. A few paragraphs earlier, we read: ''And he discovered the enormous, frozen spaces in himself, interrupted only by a block of ice here or there.'' There is a displacement toward something that freezes. We are between two types of matter, light and water, as the mirror is discovered at its natural origin, that is, the block of ice.

The Beautiful Man

The extraordinary passage on the beautiful man (52) begins precisely without touching him. First, there is what could be called a halo or aura, figured by the ellipsis. This moment is going to be told in a style of necessary delicacy. It can almost not be told, because probably nothing of what can be called ''happening'' happens here. An encounter takes place that is not even an encounter. We are constantly in the space of the almost (*à peine*).

To work on style, on language itself, I will take up again the work on this murmured narration. I would have to invent categories and a genre, not of narration but of something specific. I first take something that happens in language in order to stay in the most extreme delicacy. If something happens, it will be in this nonlocus that is first of all language. In order to cheat a little, I will read Flaubert at the beginning of *L'éducation sentimentale, the* manual of French narrative. Frédéric, a young man of eighteen years, is taking the boat from Paris to Normandy. Flaubert describes the scene on the boat:

> These, apart from a few well-to-do people in the first class, were workmen and shopkeepers with their wives and children. As it was the custom in those days to put on one's oldest clothes for travelling, nearly all of them were wearing old skull-caps or faded hats, threadbare black jackets worn thin by desk-work, or frock-coats with buttons which had burst their covers from too much service in the shop. Here and there a coffee-stained calico shirt showed under a knitted waistcoat, gilt tie-pins pierced tattered cravats, and trouserstraps were fastened to list slippers. Two or three louts, carrying bamboo canes with leather thongs, glanced shiftily from side to side, while the family men opened their eyes wide as they asked questions. Some stood about, chatting, or squatted on their luggage; others slept in corners; several had something to eat. The deck was littered with nutshells, cigar stubs, pear skins, and the remains of sausage-meat which had been brought along wrapped in paper. Three cabinet-makers in overalls stood in front of the bar; a harpist dressed in rags was resting with his elbow on his instrument; now and then one could hear the sound of the coal in the furnace, a burst of voices, or a roar of laughter. On the bridge the captain kept striding from one paddle-wheel to the other, without ever stopping. To get back to his seat, Frédéric pushed open the gate leading to the first-class section of the boat, disturbing a couple of sportsmen with their dogs.
>
> It was like a vision:
>
> She was sitting in the middle of the bench, all alone; or at least he could not see anybody else in the dazzling light which her eyes cast upon him. Just as he passed her, she raised her head; he bowed automatically; and stopping a little way off, on the same side of the boat, he looked at her.
>
> She was wearing a broad-rimmed straw hat, with pink ribbons which fluttered behind her in the wind. Her black hair, parted in the middle, hung in two long tresses which brushed the ends of her thick eyebrows and seemed to caress the oval of her face. Her dress of pale spotted muslin billowed out in countless folds. She was busy with a piece of embroidery; and her straight nose, her chin, her whole figure was silhouetted clearly against the background of the blue sky.[5]

The scene is as far removed from that in Lispector as possible. In Flaubert's text, people are designated by their waste. In both texts, we have the same view from what could be called an absolute masculinity on the one hand, and an absolute femininity on the other. What I retain in Flaubert's accumulation of human detritus is "It was like a vision." It is not, "And I saw him all of a sudden and it was a man." "It was like a vision" is an isolated sentence. There is a moment of extreme violence in the text. The sentence, detached on the page, produces the effect of a vision. There is a kind of rupture in the homogeneity of the chaos. There is irruption, and this irruption is attenuated, tempered by *comme* (like), because Flaubert is the author of analogy. He does not say it is a vision. There remains for us, naive readers, a vision or the promise of a vision. 'She was sitting in the middle of the bench . . . he could not see anybody else.'' There will never be anybody in Flaubert. There are just visions, sometimes with large straw hats. The vision is repressed under its *comme*, its like, with its system of ribbons, benches, and headbands. The reader is to hear what kind of a bench it is about.

Now we can read about the vision and its value in Clarice. It begins with this precaution of ellipsis. The construction of the sentence, the inscription of vision, is given in the very first words: " . . . I noticed him suddenly." "Him" marks the violence of the irruption, the surprise and the performative. She who saw, saw. What matters is the surprise. Only afterward does "and it was a man" appear. It can be taken literally, as something realistic: On the one hand, the him (*o*, in Brazilian) can function as cataphora, to announce what follows with exceptional force since, as pronoun, it should come afterward. It comes before the noun as the effect of this *coup* and in the very general relation Clarice has with nouns, even if they are common. Touching upon the dilemma of the *it*, the sentence begins with a white space, a not seeing, a seeing that is not seeing. It is not going to be Flaubert's repressive dazzle. It is Clarice's nonseeing that is a sublime way of seeing, an effort not to see violently. It starts with spacing, with a sudden nonseeing, a dazzle that is not blinding and is remarked by the grammatical system. The effect of surprise is such that for us, the man who is going to emerge seems to come out of the sentence. A sudden vision occurs in such a way that the locus from which one sees comes afterward: "It's not that I wanted him for myself, just as I don't want for myself the child with the hair of an archangel I saw running after the ball" (translation modified). Here, there is a little of Rimbaud's technique. One is not governed by the grammar of the sentence, but one reconstructs grammar according to reality. One does not know who runs, the archangel or the child.

"I just wanted to look." That is Clarice's motto. To look absolutely is not to look at anyone or at anything, but to look purely.

"The man looked at me for an instant and smiled calmly." His calm is explicated from a classical colon: "he knew how beautiful he was and I know that he knew I didn't want him for myself." A very simple and very complicated sentence, it designates exactly the source, the origin, of the smile. This smile is benediction itself. It is a smile "that comes from," "the origin of which is." The colon is important. It marks a detachment, an independence. It is pure smile. The smile has as origin: I know that you know and you know that I know. It is this kind of circulation of knowledge that is the height of felicity. It is the happiest thing in the world because I know that you know, and this is absolutely unique. We can make of it the economy of Clarice's discourse. And on the trace of this discourse that does not take place, what comes . . . is the smile.

"He knew how beautiful he was" can be understood as an epiphany, as the moment of revelation. It should not be taken at the level of vulgar narcissism. It would be vulgar narcissism if there were not the following sentence: "I know that he knew that I didn't want him for myself." What happened in this silence-smile, in this smile-silence, is less a narcissistic scene than its contrary, or what allows the man to be beautiful. It is the opposite of the story told in Heinrich von Kleist's *On the Marionette Theater* about a boy who did not know that he was handsome. The narrator tells him that he is handsome and looks like a statue. From then on, the boy loses his beauty. Here, it is the contrary. The nonappropriating look gives the man the pleasure of his own beauty. This pleasure is marked in "how beautiful he was." He fully indulges in pleasure because no implications of seduction or castration are at stake.

There follows a development explaining this: "He smiled because he didn't feel at all threatened." It is the fact of feeling no threat that allowed his smile. Then follows the explanation: "It's just that beings who are exceptional in any sense are subject to more danger than normal people." They are subject to the narcissistic dangers of taking themselves for somebody, or of being taken for somebody.

Something extraordinary happens: the crossing of the street. The moment when the world can take place in this genesis of strange beauty, the movement in the street, of the taxi is inscribed. When there is ecstasy, an epiphany to describe this smile-look, a beginning of movement takes place. The sentence is banal: "I crossed the street and hailed a cab." At a first level, this is realistic. It is also metaphorical. The cab, by definition, functions as metaphor. We are in transport. She was ravished. She took herself a means of ravishment. She does not take the man; she takes the taxi in which she is going to retreat. Her position in the taxi is one of retreat. Clarice works on distance. We are into something light and detached: "cab" and "breeze" happen curiously and lightly. There is a change in subject. We were between her and the man; we were in fascination and now we are in the breeze. Fascination is undone: "The breeze ruffled the hairs on the back of my neck." This happens in the middle of the paragraph. In this text where the center is peripheral, the complement becomes the subject. The breeze takes on an extraordinary value since it comes in the sentence at the same level as personal subjects.

"And I was so happy that I curled up out of fear in a corner of the cab, because happiness hurts," has to be read in its apparent strangeness, its heaviness. It is the transport of fear, ravishment. It is positive fear marked by "No, I did not want to.'' I did not want to touch. I wanted to leave intact, virgin. The remark on the economy of happiness that is typical of the type of felicity, of happiness inscribed by Clarice over and over, is completely on the side of excess. The Portuguese sentence with its *dói* cuts the breathing and associates happiness and pain. ''And all this caused by the sight of a beautiful man.'' ''All this'' and ''beautiful man'' in their gathering double the force.

Clarice writes, thinks, where the incomprehensible begins. If she had understood, she would have destroyed. It is essential not to understand, and her not wanting to understand is on the same level as her not wanting it. All this was taking place, but it was not hers: ''I didn't understand any of that.''

''I crossed the street and hailed a cab.'' Crossing the street, one goes from the extraordinary to the ordinary. ''And all this caused by the sight of a beautiful man'': this sentence frames what had happened: ''I felt a joy of creation.'' The first sentence in a certain way speaks the creation of creation. It is a question of a chain of creation, continuation, continuity: ''I continued not to want him for myself.'' She continues to be in the position of desiring a not wanting that makes her creation possible. Something defines without definition between wanting and loving (in Portuguese, *gostar*, to have taste). There is a disinterested love and an interested love. Clarice has an interested love for people ''who are a little ugly and at the same time in harmony, but in a certain way he'd given me a lot.'' The ''but'' means: I like people who are a little bit ugly but I do not like this man. ''But in a certain way he'd given me a lot with that smile of complicity between two people who understand each other.'' In Portuguese, ''understand'' is ''hear.'' ''Who hear each other'' implies a mutual silence. The movement of the taxi is a way of letting things be where they are, in their incomprehension. It is the indication of an end or of a displacement, of the putting into freedom, of the abandonment of the moment. That joins the whole dilemma of the incomprehensible that one finds a few pages later around the sentence with a pure cut: ''Since I understand nothing — I therefore cling to a vacillating, mobile reality.'' It is on the condition of not understanding anything that I understand what is outside me. This is the condition of a kind of praxis that undoes the self, the subject in Clarice. There is no *I*, no understanding. She says. I do not understand, therefore, between parentheses, I am. I do not understand, therefore the other is, therefore there is the other, there is the other who besides can also be me.

Silence

With a leap we go on to the next paragraph: ''The courage to live: I leave hidden what needs to be hidden and what needs to spread out in secret.'' It is a kind of *Nachträglichkeit*, of aftereffect, located very far from what has just happened. To live is to live without understanding anything. This does not mean not to understand anything at all but to live while understanding that there is something incomprehensible.

"I fall silent" is Clarice's technique of the performative. In Brazilian, the sentence is more powerful. There is an absence of the *I* in the verb. *I* is kept silent, suspended, on the page, in the air. Maybe it is the "I fall silent" that has presided over this scene without words. It is also a definition: I do not understand anything, therefore (I) am. It is another way of saying: I am, I keep quiet, I keep quiet this me, this reflection of myself on myself that would prevent me from hearing the other in order to signify the force of silence, or of falling silent, she inserts white spaces in the text.

"Because I don't know what my secret is." There is something violent and absolute in the construction that has all possible temporal values. There is no explicative relation with what follows. One is not in a causal system. There is "I fall silent," period, absolutely. On to the next line: "Because I don't know what my secret is." This is dependent on and independent of "I fall silent." It looks as if the sentence should depend on the preceding sentence, which may or may not be "I fall silent." Yet "I fall silent" performs the act of an active silence that takes place between two secret moments: "I leave occult that which needs to be left occult and needs to irradiate itself in secret." It is an absolute "because," with a cause that has been lost. It signifies also: there is no beginning.

"Tell me yours, teach me about the secret of each one of us. It is not a defamatory secret. It's simply that: secret." It is an absolute sentence. There is no formula. The secret cannot be told since there are no words for it, although it can be taught.

"I think that now I'll have to ask permission to die a little. Excuse me, will you? I won't be long. Thanks." In Brazilian, *obrigado* is more ambiguous. I am obliged to you not to stay. I come back to you. Allow me to leave, I owe it to you as a favor not to come back. And then I have nothing to say anymore.

In the next paragraph there is ellipsis. The story started with ellipsis, but it is not finished. "Thank you. . . . No. I couldn't die. Will I end here this 'word-thing' by my own voluntary act? Not yet." The ellipsis is here but not at the end. The story is in suspension, started in suspension and continues, and there is another one that starts in suspension, and continues. It starts with a "No," which is never totally negative. It is the negative of the negative and comes instead of another silence. There was a silence at the beginning, ellipsis, and then: "I noticed him suddenly." There is a silence, then "No," which can be either no to silence or no to something that comes afterward. Everyone should have this kind of silent encounter. But something more somber could also be added. True, it is only in silence that this can happen, between two silences, because God only knows what the man would have said if he had started to speak.

(Non-)intelligence

In *In order not to forget*, Clarice says that the greatest effort of her life was to become intelligent so that she could understand her nonintelligence. She implies that intelligence has to be used to understand nonintelligence. This is related to the two types of knowledge, to the law, to the apple and to the door about which I spoke earlier. The title "Human Work" is the smile of the angel of Chartres. It is terribly ironic. Inscribed first is a "maybe" that has a double value. The whole declaration is under the sign of "maybe." It stays in uncertainty, the transparent trait between intelligence and nonintelligence. To understand nonintelligence, I had to become intelligent. One could produce philosophical tracings around this assertion. It is not really a paradox, since a paradox is already something too rigidly fixed. This would be the greatest effort of life: the strange sensation of becoming intelligent. One starts from nonintelligence, not to become intelligent, but to understand nonintelligence. This presupposes something of the order of intelligence of nonintelligence opposed to a nonintelligence of nonintelligence.

This is a serious play on a seemingly paradoxical utterance. The supreme intelligence is intelligence of nonintelligence and is related to two kinds of knowledge. A simple sentence is extremely complex. Of course there is also a stupid intelligence—animal, brute, forceful, humorous. She does not write about it here. Intelligence is everywhere.

The second part of this discordant text is in parentheses, which signifies a retreat of the second utterance in relation to the first one: "(One uses intelligence to understand nonintelligence.)" In "The instrument continues to be used," things cannot be picked with human hands. In other words, intelligence incessantly contaminates nonintelligence. This raises the question of the pure and the proper. A pure nonintelligence remains a nonintelligence. It exists as a field in which we cannot have pleasure. If one approaches it, all that is powerful and pure in the spot is lost. Clarice feels such regret that she has to put it in parentheses.

The sensation that precedes thought is nonintelligence. To understand it, an intelligence must be invented that is *agua viva*, or living water itself. But once Lispector writes *Agua viva*, she no longer has clean hands. That is the drama of writing, of thought, since at the same time it is its only possibility. There is no choice. Either one stays in nonintelligence that is a kind of hidden treasure, which does not give pleasure, or one goes toward intelligence but pays the price for having done so. There is no other way. Either one stays completely outside, or one approaches and while attaining it, one hurts and is hurt by it.

1980–81

Notes

1. Clarice Lispector, *Agua viva* (Rio de Janeiro: Artenova, 1973). Translated by Elizabeth Lowe and Earl Fitz as *The Stream of Life* (Minneapolis: University of Minnesota Press, 1989). All quotations are from the English edition. Modifications have been indicated.

2. Jacques Derrida, *The Truth in Painting*, trans. Geoff Bennington and Ian McLeod (Chicago: University of Chicago Press, 1987), 87.

3. Clarice Lispector, *Perto do coração selvagem* (São Paulo: Francisco Alves, 1963), 57–60. All translations mine.

4. Jacques Derrida, "Qual Quelle: The Sources of Valéry," in *Margins of Philosophy*, trans. Alan Bass (Chicago: University of Chicago Press, 1982), 275.

5. Gustave Flaubert, *Sentimental Education*, trans. Robert Baldick (New York: Penguin, 1979), 17–18.

Chapter 3
The Apple in the Dark:
The Temptation of Understanding

I

The Apple in the Dark[1] is the lengthy story of a man who flees civilization, thinking that he has murdered his wife, and of his encounter with two women on an isolated farm in the Brazilian countryside. It can be read around questions of sexual difference and of different libidinal economies. The hero of the novel is called Martim. Martim is tuned into a mode of continuity-discontinuity with two women, Ermelinda and Vitória. In the last and most important part of the book, everything takes place between Martim and Vitória. In appearance, Martim is a man of failure and Vitória is the woman who rightfully bears her name. But for those who know how to read, the situation is reversed. Failure is victory and victory is failure. It can be said that victory as failure comes back to a man and that the apparent victory as failure is that of a woman. So, what is Clarice Lispector's position in this?

In the last part of the book, the question of passing the line of difference is continually raised. What do masculinity and femininity mean on a libidinal level? If one does not read carefully, one can say that it is the man who understood the other, who was capable of otherness. But I shall continue to say femininity is more capable of otherness.

In the nuclear passage of all these pages (335–46), something emerges: "A few hours before, beside the bonfire, [Martim] had attained an impersonality inside of himself. He had been so profoundly himself that he had become the 'himself' of any other person, the way a cow is the cow of all cows."

It is while being most himself that he begins to be other. All this, of course, takes place in the space of the unconscious: "But if beside the bonfire he had made himself, right then he was using himself. Right then he had just attained the impersonality that makes for the fact that as one man falls, another rises up—the impersonality of dying while others are being born, the altruism that makes other people exist. We, who are you. 'What a strange thing. Even now I seem to be wanting to reach the tip of my finger with the tip of my own finger—it's true that with that extreme effort I grew, but the tip of my finger is still unreachable. I went as far as I could. But why didn't I understand that the thing that I could not reach in me was already other people? Other people, who are our deepest plunge! We who are you just as you yourselves are not you.' In that way, concentrating very hard on the birth of others, in a task that only he could carry out, Martim was there trying to give body to those who would be born."

The scene is one of masculine birth. But the metaphor and the bodily labor cannot not be borrowed from the real other, here the woman. The ineluctable presence of the maternal, the matrical is reinforced in the unconscious effects of the next paragraph:

"Slowly, he finally came out of his quietness. 'I can count on you,' he said to himself, groping, 'I can count on you,' he thought gravely; and that was the most personal form in which a person can exist. We, who only have any value as long as we are whole, like money. Martim was even ashamed of having been personal in a different way. It was a dirty past, his; it had been an individual life, his. But it also seemed to him, as he forgave himself, that he had had no choice, that it had been the only way in which he had learned to be other people. Underneath we are all so much alike and the children of the same mother."

As the mother appears, little by little Martim says to himself: I think about my mother. In fact, like all of Clarice Lispector's characters he is continually haunted by the father. But here, the mother imposes herself. She comes back incessantly from the beginning of times, from a genesis that would be linked to love. Love comes back to the mother.

In all of Lispector's texts, there is a poignant element. In *The Apple in the Dark*, Martim has left the conventional world of the known. As the reader is led to guess, he was able to accomplish this only through a gesture of rupture, in his case a crime. From the beginning to the end of the text we do not know what it is. It is only at the end that a sentence escapes from him: "I killed my wife." Shortly afterward, the reader realizes that this is not true but that it is of no importance. He had to accomplish a break in order to escape the ready-made, the world of likeness, that is to say, of death in life. What happens in the last pages is terrifying. Again, it reminds us of Heinrich von Kleist's *On the Marionette Theater*, in which, after a passage to the infinite, after a fall and a return, there is a reconstruction, but outside the world of imitation and reproduction. Concretely, in the novel, Martim is apprehended by the police. This is but a metaphor. It illustrates the question Clarice also asked in *The Passion according to G.H.*: If I leave the world of the known in order to find the life of the unknown, what do I become? Such a move is prohibited by society; similarly, Kafka meditates on going to places from which there is no return. Those who go beyond the socially and culturally legitimate and acceptable space are alone. And absolute solitude, one can say in epilogue, leads to madness. It may be morally intolerable insofar as saving oneself alone may not be a way of saving oneself at all. In any case, it inevitably leads to the question of the other. In *The Passion according to G.H.*, to this question of breaking out of the repetitive closure of imitation, Clarice answers: I can only do it on condition of coming back to look for someone who will cross to the other side with me. That is how it begins. She comes to get the reader and leaves again. Throughout the text, she repeats this trajectory to the point of ecstasy.

In *The Apple in the Dark*, the same dilemma exists but with differences. It resembles that of another of Clarice's stories, "A vingança e a reconciliação penosa" (Vengeance and painful reconciliation). Martim exited the world of the known, but painfully so. He felt guilty for having left a world of guilt, and at the same time for being so violently and uniquely innocent. He lets himself be caught, taken back by the ordinary world. Emblematic scenes show how he is caught by four hands. He is apprehended by the police, the law, the mayor, and the police inspectors — by all the representatives of the social establishment. And they are represented through their hands. He is a giant, for good. But he lets himself be taken back little by little by the ordinary world, to the very last detail. The supreme sacrifice that can only be understood in the negative is that no real reasons for the crime were available. In the ordinary world thousands of reasons explain why a man would kill his wife. Given the nature of his crime, one could think that Martim is a real man. In fact, everything is reversed. A close reading shows that he is the most feminine of all the characters.

Martim has enigmatic reasons for his gesture of absolute rupture that cannot be explained. Since Clarice cannot stand bloodshed, Martim's gesture goes largely beyond ordinary rationality. A man kills out of misogyny, or because his wife had a lover. All that was not true. But if he started to say that he did not do it for ordinary reasons, who in a court would understand? Martim lets himself be understood in order to be readmitted in the ordinary and stupid human circle, out of a great feeling of humility. Little by little, he accepts letting himself be interpreted. He makes an admirable effort to resemble the misogynous, imbecile murderer who is recognizable. On condition that he be a true criminal, he can be forgiven. Martim's trajectory, similar to that of the protagonist in *The Passion according to G.H.*, but with a different modulation, leads him around the world so that he can see that it is open on the other side. He can enter Paradise. At that moment, he discovers that he has arrived there alone. He accepts abandoning the

Paradise of which he is the author and coming back to our little burning hell, out of love for humans who hate him as they should. It is as if this giant, in order to become humble, had to shrink himself from six feet to four feet. It is only in his dwarflike stature that he can be understood. Generally one reads like a dwarf, and it is hard to imagine a transforming trajectory like Martim's.

An admirable machine is put in place, a kind of reductive or interpretive machine. There is a small exemplary detail. Martim wants to be readmitted among men as a criminal. First, he fails. Then he wants to be recognized for his good will. He wants others to recognize that he gave himself up. He says to the dwarfs that he could have saved himself but that he had been waiting for them. It is a way of saying: I love you. What does it mean for dwarfs to be loved by a giant, or for a criminal to ask to be loved by the judge? He says that his love consists in being caught, judged, and executed. It does not work. He is told, obviously, that if he did not save himself, it was because he suspected that he was completely encircled. He realizes that he will never be able to enter their little universe. So he lets himself be reduced, interpreted. The most clever of this small world proposes that Martim's argument revealed his desire to pay his debt to society, that is to say, to be less harshly penalized. He is being confronted with the ordinary logic of reductive reasoning and has to learn again to calculate according to this order.

The Apple in the Dark is a tragic book. It represents, in Clarice's writing project, a lesser stage than that of *The Passion according to G.H.*, which was written at a later date. In *The Apple in the Dark*, the anguish of absolute solitude is so strong that Martim accepts the destiny of smallness. But *The Passion* accepts passion. It accepts total isolation and the danger of madness.

In *The Apple in the Dark*, Martim is not completely himself. It is not as plenitude but on a border that is made up of others, of nobody, that he has an extraordinary movement of birth: "In that way, concentrating very hard on the birth of others, in a task that only he could carry out, Martim was there trying to give body to those who would be born."

Clarice Lispector uses the word "parturition" for birth. Martim is being born and gives birth simultaneously at the extremity of himself. He gives place, body, and existence to the other, but others have also given him that which, had he stayed alone, would not have been accessible to him. The others while being born become body for him. It is from the others that the possibility of feeling the tip of his finger will be given to him.

In Clarice, one never arrives at a place, one always strives toward it. That is why the marvelous little text, "E para lá que eu vou" (That's where I'm going), says it all. There is only the path, a movement toward what cannot be an arrival, in the same way love cannot be free. The world wants us to love everything, but an arbitrary self prevents it and opposes true love. In *The Apple in the Dark*, Martim muses: "Oh, people are so demanding! They eat bread and they are repelled by those who pound raw dough; they devour meat but do not invite the butcher to sit down at the table; people ask for the process to be hidden from them. Only God would not be disgusted by his twisted love.''

Clarice attacks our hypocrisy of survival and our idealism that make us close our eyes and ignore the process. Martim therefore is in a hurry to go back to prison. He needs to rest, to be isolated again:

''Out of fatigue then, with the quick balm of vision, he took refuge among the thick plants of his plot of ground, which must now be peacefully getting ready for night among the running of the rats. 'I am going to the devil,' he then said to himself, looking at the men, nauseated at being a man. The peaceful plants were calling him. 'Not to be,' that was a man's vast night. 'Even if it's not even the intelligence with which one goes to bed with a woman,' he thought, deceiving himself, and so deep that he really did not understand what he had meant by it. His desirous thoughts went back to the plants of his Tertiary plot, with a longing for the black rats. A softness made up out of sensuality dragged him out of the struggle; it gave him a nostalgic shamelessness, a wandering melancholy. He still tried vaguely to stand up straight and make himself over: 'I'm a Brazilian, after all, what the hell!' But he could not make it. That man was sated; he wanted refuge and peace.

''But in order to find that peace he would have to forget about other people. To find that refuge he would have to be himself, the self that has nothing to do with anybody else. 'But I have a right to that!' he justified himself in a tired way. 'What the hell! What do I have to do with other people? There's a place where, before order and names, I am I!' ''

And wondering whether this might be the real place in common with what he set out to find, he adds:

''Then why fight? Inside a man there was a place which was pure light, but it did not show itself in the eyes or cloud them over. It was a place where, all tricks aside, one exists; a place where, without the least pretension, one exists; . . . To be honest, long before we were aware of it, dogs were already loving each other; in short, by the right of having been born, we have the right of being what we are. So let's take advantage of it, let's not exaggerate the importance of other people! Because there exists in a man a point that is just as sacred as the existence of other people. Let other people take care of themselves! From birth a man has the right to be able to go to sleep peacefully — because things are not as dangerous as all that, and the world won't come to an end tomorrow. Fear may have confused reality with desire a little bit, but the dog in us knows the way. 'What the hell!' ''

This is a stage. One is not yet at the end of the road. *The Apple in the Dark* is a text-refuge of the common place, before order and naming, our common and solitary earth, where we would, once again, arrive in an easy place. What is solitary is easy. For us, the other is always a rat. In ''A vingança,'' Clarice had written about how her easy happiness was interrupted by the presence of a rat. The interruption had led her to a meditation and the acceptance of a world of rats and nonrats. Her rat, a common occurrence in her bestiary, and one that links her to major texts like Freud's, is a phallic rat. In the feminine, this rat becomes not a she-rat but a fear of being born. In "A vingança,", she states: "My fear, is to be born." The message is clear. It is only from the moment of having gone through labor, only after having been scandalized at length by our own selves, that we will cease to scandalize ourselves at the world. Put vulgarly, it could be said that it all has to do with mechanisms of projection. In fact, these are analyses of our deepest narcissistic insufficiencies. We cannot not be scandalized by ourselves. A scandal may be something positive, but in any case it is a slow labor. One should get used to it not on the mode of repression, but on the mode of acceptance. It must be an active process. To be born is active. It is the beginning of a labor. Once one is born, one has to be born over and over again. It is an absolutely incessant activity. It is to be born or to give birth incessantly. And it has to be said the way Clarice says it marvelously and without cheating: the process is exhausting. For Martim, it is different: "Who can tell whether jail might not be just the place where I'll find what I want?"

Prison is a kind of luxury of unemployment. Martim makes his statement in a tone of calm violence. But of course, prison is but a grotesque little cell from where he has to give birth to himself, in order to be free, and to invent freedom incessantly. Fear consists in having to leave, or go out of prison. This is symbolic, but in reality it is also true. Leaving prison is, once again, not to be afraid of being judged, not to be glued to the image, but *to make* oneself.

Doesn't love himself: love each other
Don't love each other: love each other

Such utterances can be made up. They are the very condition of love. It can also be said otherwise with the scene of love shifting onto a level of comprehension with all its dangers. My reading could be entitled: the temptation of understanding. Temptation has to be read in a strong sense, such as the temptation of Eve. "To understand" can be replaced by a concrete equivalent that is the temptation to take or to absorb. To maintain the space of love is always a process, because there is no love but in the relay of love. One could juxtapose another remark next to what I just proposed:

Do not understand each other: understand each other.

Out of necessity, in noncomprehension, there is always a part of comprehension. To say to someone "I do not understand you," may signify I want to understand you; I do not want to understand you, go away; I want to but cannot understand you; or I am trying to and am about to understand you. The supreme statement of love would be: I do not understand you. I do not want to understand you. I love from not understanding you. And love is the explosive, painful tension between not understanding and wanting to understand, between trembling at the very idea of understanding while passionately wanting to be understood and fearing above all any type of comprehension.

The temptation of understanding is always good and complex. If we think in terms of this relation to the other that is always present in my readings, obviously we are only tempted to understand the incomprehensible. The incomprehensible alone propels the drive to understand. But if we have the courage to say the most subtle things we feel in our relation to the other, we quickly arrive at some very paradoxical statements that resemble those one finds in a negative theology where God is defined negatively as being neither this nor that, and for good reasons.

This is still why, in a trembling, intense space, I am going to gather a certain number of remarks. One could recall Kafka's *Letters to Milena* and Tasso's *Jerusalem Delivered*. I put side by side the couple of Trancredi and Clorinda with the two couples of *The Apple in the Dark*. Decisive for a reading of Tasso, aside from the sexual indeterminacy of Clorinda and Tancredi, is the question of otherness. Of importance is the metaphorization of love as struggle. Tancredi and Clorinda meet only while fighting each other. Rinaldo and Armida, the other couple, the classical heterosexual couple in love, do not fight, they seduce each other. When saying that, I am not on the side of war. In their scenes, Rinaldo and Armida, as if under a spell, constantly fall on each other, in both the forest and the garden. One is taken, caught by the other, seduced (*épris*), they embody seduction, (*épréhension*), not a desire to take (*préhension*). But Tancredi and Clorinda are engaged in this tragic and mortal struggle that could not be otherwise because, with its cultural and political determinations, the text does not allow anything other than a pure struggle up to death. This struggle, contrary to what we might believe, when it is being symoblized, is the very condition for conservation of love.

The Apple in the Dark is a most deceptive book. It is presented like a novel, but it is the opposite. It is a mystical path of such density that it becomes perhaps even more unreadable than *The Passion*. The book is double. In *The Apple in the Dark* there are two couples, Martim and Ermelinda — whose name is not accidental — and Martim and Vitória, the main couple. It is in the latter that Clarice gathers the maximum of information. She writes the subtlest treatise of love around them. She writes as closely as possible to a place of enunciation, close to the heart, to passion. The strange story betweeen Martim and Vitória is about victory of failure and failure in victory. Martim and Vitória are two beings who struggle. Martim carries the path of genesis and the love story. The entire text inscribes between Martim and Vitória a mad form of love. Most strikingly, love is never a question between the two. They share so much love that the word is never pronounced.

Martim and Vitória miss each other, in the way that I said "love each other." They try to reach each other with the same intensity with which they try to avoid each other. They constantly succeed in missing each other. Here I am only summarizing what is not explicated thus in the text because words completely close off the gap of love. One can follow the protagonists' mad trajectory in their itinerary of missing each other. From paragraph to paragraph, they accompany each other the way one musical instrument accompanies another. They accompany each other while verifying that they are afraid of each other. They move in parallel fashion while constantly verifying their fears. They confide in each other without understanding. Now, since human paths are not mechanical, there are possible variations. One accelerates while the other decelerates; one goes straight while the other turns away at the risk of hurting the other. The struggle to keep a harmony is constant. They attempt to make minute rectifications of the slight gap between them. Without this gap, one would fall onto and crush the other. When they are too close, a moment of rejection ensues. At the moment of extreme closeness, when the reader thinks that nothing will separate them anymore, one of them feels like throwing up. They constantly miss each other, which means that they never miss each other. The story has to lead to a separation that is marked from the beginning. *The Apple in the Dark* is a possibility, a moment, a version of *The Passion according to G.H.* Martim and Vitória stay in the space of what can be called the nonpossible.

Clarice inscribes "E para lá que eu vou" in yet another space, where a strange mixture of possible and impossible options pervails. But Vitória and Martim stay in the space of the nonpossible, which means that they are no longer the most representative couple of a love story. Theirs is one of many types of relations.

As for Ermelinda, she is the one who wants to make things possible. In her need to love, she goes from the possible, from the desire, to its realization. From the moment she accomplishes exactly what she wanted, the possible exists no more. Everything has been realized. Martim, this fabulous being, wants to realize the impossible. He is the first version of G.H., drawn up before Clarice decided to reduce her protagonist to something even more essential: to femininity itself. Martim does precisely achieve the impossible. He maintains the impossible in impossibility.

Clarice's text could be placed side by side with Kafka's, especially with his letters to Milena. His story with Milena is the most tragic. Biographically, it is situated at a moment when Kafka is free to play out his life between death. Afflicted with tuberculosis, he is already allied with death. In his situation, the defensive factor of the citadel of his soul is completely other. The same can also be read in some of Dostoyevsky's novels, in relation to protagonists who are condemned to death. An exceptional situation changes the ensemble of the relation to the other, to weather, to life, to the limit. Kafka is already on the other side, hence beyond all limits.

His relation to Milena, of a burning intensity, resembles a flight from beginning to end, and certainly much more so than with Felice. In the last letters Kafka dreams that he is burning with Milena. He is sending an additional dream to Milena, the way one would send somebody to the stake. He sends the burning stake that is none other than himself. In his dream, one burns in the other. It cannot be known who burns the other. A true dream, it summarizes the question of destiny, of the fatality of this relation that was too burning from the beginning not to be destined to reduction to ashes. This is not the destiny of every love; rather, it is the destiny of excessive, devouring passion. The good love, the kind not given over to consumption, is rather on the side of water, on the side of *Agua viva*.

In Kafka, there is also the inscription of a calling. In the Bible, different episodes deal with calling. The best-known episode has Jonah refuse to hear the calling of God. Like a madman, he is constantly running, in order not to hear this calling, that is, in order not to hear, as Kafka puts it, what he has already heard. Thus, with all his might, he does nothing but answer God's calling. If I displaced the reading in the direction of a story of sexual difference, it would really be the law that he heard. He tries to run away back to the bosom of the Mother. But since all this takes place in the Bible, even the whale, the most bellylike of all bellies, the most motherlike of beings, does not keep him. Jonah's movement is exemplary because such a strong calling, as Kafka reminds us, is the real calling. It calls upon Jonah to go out of himself. Nothing could be more terrifying. Here the calling comes from the other, but from a very strong other. Jonah tries to escape outside of himself by going back into the belly of bellies.

But it does not work. It is not a love story. Since it concerns God and Jonah, it deals with obligatory love. To be sure, Jonah must love, but what would be the calling that does not force him to throw himself into the uterus of the whale? It would be a pure calling, which asks for love not as a due but as infinite freedom, including the possibility of not loving. It would be a calling for nothing. That can be placed side by side with another text by Clarice Lispector, "A repartiçao dos paes" (The sharing of the breads). In the latter, the tomatoes are there for nobody. The kind of love that would not force us to seek refuge in the belly of the whale would be one that calls for all and for nothing. It would be on the side of grace.

II

This is where we can insert Clarice's short two-page text, "E para lá que eu vou".[2] If "A repartição dos paes" could have been her Bible, this text could have been that of her secret. It performs at the same time that it describes. It is a text that announces love; it is but annunciation, or the very secret of writing. Here a movement is oriented toward something and at the same time suspended. The movement is marked by expressions: "beyond"; "at the extremity of"; "at the tip of"; "at the edge." An inscription is made of an entire system, of a certain type of space and of a relation to space.

"Beyond the ear there exists a sound, at the extremity of the look an aspect, at the tip of the fingers an object—that's where I'm going.

"At the tip of the pencil the trace.

"Where a thought expires there is an idea, at the last breath of joy another joy, at the tip of the word magic—that's where I'm going.

"At the tip of the feet the leap.

"It seems like the story of someone who went and did not come back—that's where I'm going.

"Or am (I) not going? Yes, (I) am going. And (I'll) come back to see how things are going. If they continue magic. Reality? I am waiting for you. That's where I'm going."

The secret of this movement is in a coming and going. How can one come and go, if not by going to the very end of the going, to the extremity whence the return begins? At the limit of such a going is the infinite. There is no coming back unless one has gone around the world. There is something vertiginous in this text, which contains, as Shakespeare would say, the infinite in a nutshell.

The important words are "magic," witchcraft, which touch on a local, regional and a worldwide space. The theme of transmutation is involved. In a French linguistic space, it could be called, as in Rimbaud, verbal alchemy.

From the beginning, Clarice treats of the impalpable. She shows right away, through typography, that the text is thrown into the beyond. "Beyond the ear" reminds us of singing. "At the extremity of the look an aspect" points out the colorlessness. "At the tip of the fingers an object" invites a first reading that would be a kind of humble word for word. Then one reads the following sentence: "At the tip of the pencil the trace." There is a first displacement from the tip. First, there is a series of parallels and then one sees the pencil. One lets go of the pencil until it calls us back because, finally, it is here again. As a reader, I resisted this kind of calling to the very end. I worked the text over by noting my own resistances and then said to myself that I was bordering something without wanting it to stop. It was the very question of writing. That is the strength of Clarice's text. It is rather secret, yet almost transparent.

Clarice writes in order to dissolve through a certain chemistry, through a certain magic and love that which would be retention, weight, solidification, an arrest of the act of writing. That is why she ends by dropping the subject pronoun and saying: "What am I saying? Am saying love."

We could say: no, she writes it. But that is precisely what she gets away from. In a leap, she tears herself away. Only, it must be said that she does not do it out of denegation. She performs it analytically by dissolving the thing: "And at the edge of love are we."

To write such a text, we have to take complete liberty in relation to the police we have inside us that make us write grammatically, correctly, and which make us justify ourselves permanently, place the subject where we must and wipe our feet at the door. Clarice's text is so hard to read because it is so light. To read it, since it is about taking leaps, we must be able to jump, for example, from verb to verb, or from here to there. The subject "flickers" (in English in the text— Trans.). It is the truth of a palpitating subjectivity that is here, there, incessantly. We may wonder what kind of a state Clarice was in when she wrote this text. She must have been in the ultimate state of grace where she gave grace to herself, made grace of herself, but to the point of being the moving locus of this trans-mutation.

Clarice does not say: "I leap." She performs it in a moment when she literally cannot use words, without a feeling of raping the finest thing of life. But she must jump. What comes about in terms of punctuation shows that it is a text of silence. It is a text that lies the least in relation to the stakes of living and writing. It allows for otherness, the very otherness of writing to be both silence and si-lence of writing. To make a space for this silence is an infinite art and, in this short text, it is made through the art of typography, through paginal setting, through the space of paragraphs. It is a little text without breath that has an un-heard (*inouï*) bodily rhythm, and the sentence without sentence that came to me was: a writing of silences.

The title of the text is fabulous. It comes to me in terms of a song. To write songs is the most difficult task in the world. I do not mean to write words to music, but to write words that become song. This is the very secret of the sen-tence. The infinite has to be put into three words. In tension, in vibration, it has to be infinite and open. In lower case, the title is an open, yet finished, sentence that gives direction. Rilke said that God was a direction given to love. Clarice's text is in movement when we encounter it. We have to jump into the arch of the text and follow the direction shown to us. "I'm going" is fully active, absolute. At the same time, "that's the way" is vertiginous. What is the question? Clarice tells us incessantly that she does not know. Rather than telling us, she shows us. Something takes place. Before that, there was no place. It is the movement of going that will produce a place, that will make it possible for something to take place. There is no "ground" from which to read, on which to tread. As with the witch, she who invents or produces with her magic is and does not exist until the end of a text of which she is most likely the instigator. Clarice is, after all, a witch. She discovers herself being a witch. Between her movement of emergence and of suspension where a thousand adventures occur, I happen upon this first sentence: "Beyond the ear there exists a sound, at the extremity of the look an aspect, at the tip of the fingers an object—that's where I'm going."

An indication as well as an inscription of a beyond are made. The beyond is there, or rather here. At the same time, since it is beyond, we are not there. "I'm going" toward this beyond. This is the mad movement of this text that incessantly goes toward itself. The first sentence has three beats, three strikes. The text is inspired, powerful, and at the same time very tightly constructed. Clarice is diabolical. She has an extraordinary mastery of the text that seems to be like a bubble. In the first sentence, a masterful coup takes place. Three beats, three departures, three beginnings: "Beyond the ear . . . at the extremity of the look . . . and at the tip of the fingers."

The reader takes three paths. The text can be read horizontally or vertically. It is a text that traces its own way (*démarche*). Clarice's movement goes into certain directions, by mutation, metamorphoses, by displacement of the body, or displacement in space. The sentences communicate a certain movement, a bodily movement and, from time to time, they leap and bound. When one works on language like on a piece of leather, this type of textual movement—that is, of advance or progress—is called metonymy. It is being communicated as if it were desire. It catches on fire. It ignites, starts breathing, and, in a certain movement, going from one point to the other, it begins sliding. The sentence begins and ends with the body: "Beyond the ear . . . that's where I'm going . . . to the end of the word."

I am on the path of the word and of its beyond, I let myself follow the word: "At the end of the word there is the word. I want to use the word *tertúlia*."

If I am following the path into the beyond, at the extremity of the word, I'm going toward "my poor name." In a series of beginnings, the third departure, like the others, is effectuated from an extremity: "At the edge of I, am me."

Again, we take off. For those beginnings to take place, we have to come back in order to leave again.

A key in the sentence enables us to come back to the beginning: "At the tip of the pencil . . . "

Each organ, so we find out later, has the virtue of tracing. It is not *I* who is writing; it is each organ that traces. Each organ is pencil and the pencil itself is taken in this chain of organs as an organ.

The text is organized around the movement of going, in a passage from the intelligible to the senses.

"Where a thought expires there is an idea." To "expire" is a key signal. The text goes to the verge of infinite loss but is immediately sublated. Here we are on an intellectual plane whereas, right before, we were on that of the senses. In the same paragraph, we go from one to the other through the pencil in the same paragraph. In this movement, each step, each paragraph, is planted. Aside from that there is nothing.

"Where a thought expires there is an idea, at the last breath of joy another joy." This is perfectly beautiful. It is the alliance between the last in a series and the first in another. Thought copies an idea. One can give this text the right not to answer. Its poetic side will not give any reason. But the rhythm in three breaths may be the rhythm of the body, of song.

There are plenty of unexpected coups de grâce in this text. Then comes the sword: "At the tip of the sword magic, that is where I am going."

The sword cannot be commented upon. It is going to be there in the text with some other violent and surprising elements that seem to be heterogeneous. The *coup* of the sword is the metamorphosis of the pencil. If this sword were not the sword-pencil, it would hurt. Potentially harmful, the pencil nevertheless inflicts a wound, just as we wound the text by talking about it. I make the sword heavier, so that it can be saved. It is given back to its double potential of being wounding and magic. I take a leap because the text leaps. Onto the next line: "At the tip of the feet the leap." This return (*coup d'envoi*) went from the ear to the path of the body, from high to low. The space that is going to be figured is one of extremities. It is as if we jumped into this text, with our arms and legs stretched out, and as if, swimming in emptiness, we traced the beginning of another space, of the space beyond. The astonishing thing is that the space that I am approaching is right here. The paragraphs are reversible: Am I going there or am I there, before or afterward? Do I take a departure from the beginning of the sentence, or from the sentence and its dash? Because it is constructed on this mode, "E para lá que eu vou" always follows. There is repetition, which indicates continuity of movement, but each time she repeats something, she is further.

First there was a trace, then the leap. We can note that in the constructions: "At the tip of the pencil the trace," "at the tip of the sword magic," and "at the tip of the feet the leap," the verbs are missing (*sautent*).

Comes the sentence: "It seems like the story of someone who went and did not come back—that's where I'm going."

There is an enormous jump. One goes from the feet to the story. It is through a jump of this kind that the story is made. The indication of this secret in the sentence is performative. It could be said that the story is being shown in the present. The story is only of what has already taken place. But nothing took place. There is no story, only its announcement; that is the allusion to the possibility of a story that cannot be told.

It is the story of someone who went away and did not come back. A story is defined by narration. But here there is a story beyond a story. There is a story that will not be told because the carrier of this story went away and did not come back to tell it. It is completely paradoxical. What is suspended, rendered transparent, is the story of the story in Clarice. She constantly insists on not wanting to tell stories. This carries the refrain further: "That's where I'm going."

Through insistence on the impossibility of the utterance the construction can be reversed. One could substitute, for example, a dream. But that too is deceptive. The dream is not at the place we assign to a dream, nor is the story at the place we assign to a story. The text is written in such a way that the movement of going always follows. What immediately precedes gives the signal for departure. At the same time, the departure cannot but be in this repeated utterance of:

"That's where I'm going."

The next leap comes with the

"Or am (I) not going?"

The text, like a dance, leaps in this way:

"Am going, yes."

There is perhaps a disturbance in the movement of going. It is the nonreturn that brought about this leap. Clarice writes the story that would resemble someone who went away and did not come back. But she is someone who went away and did come back. The enterprise is to come back to write almost the nonreturn. She tries to write what is not written, to tell what is not told, to make the story about what has no story. That is where we enter into the drama of the text: "Or am (I) not going? Yes, I am going. And (I'll) come back to see how things are going. If they continue magic."

This is the second magical trick, the first having been the sword. In reality, the photograph can also be magic in its technical form. "Reality? I'm waiting for you."

Perhaps we wait for an interpellation, as if Clarice had called on reality, at the level of a ceremonious address. At the same time, she is waiting for what she is going toward. Reality comes afterward.

Something is being inscribed, between word and name; it is the story of this being I-me who writes the text, or sings it. As one is carried off, very rapidly, one arrives at the family. One has to hold on to the metonymy: "At the tip of the word is the word."

The sentence calls for a word. And a word arrives like a bird plummeting in the text. It alights with quotation marks like a little bird. The word is detached, liberated from its familial obligations through its appearance. It appears only as word. It is a word that gives pleasure. I have taken it to be a signifier, a verbal thing to be used. Clarice opens the curtains of language, and, suddenly, a signifier that she likes appears. She works on a signifier freed from the family of language. Yet, its signified is on the side of the family. The family is pulled toward *tertúlia*. It is the family reunion that brings about the family, the way magic conjures up the witch. It is the power of the word.

"I want to use the word *tertúlia* and I don't know where and when." This is Clarice's declaration of faith. *I do not know*. At the same time she can only use it in the freedom of not knowing when and where. But *tertúlia* calls for the family: "At the edge of the family am I."

This is banal as a construction. The inversion is important. *I* has to be on the edge of the sentence. It makes of *I* someone slightly outside the family.

"At the edge of I, am me."

There is a displacement, from border to border, from relay to relay. But we do not enter because we stay at the edge of the circle. I read it as a jump, as an anacoluthon, or a break of classical construction. From *I* to me I jump: "It is toward me that (I) am going."

There and *me* are parallel. They can be exchanged. The closest *me* is the one furthest. The progression is important: "And from me I go out to see. To see what?"

The text is full of questions that Clarice asks of herself. Why questions? It is a play of genius. First there is a question as a point of departure, a rhetorical question, that comes from an inscription of what is not yet known about whence the answer will come. "To see what exists." She does not know what since she has to go and see.

"After being dead it is toward reality that (I) go." Now we begin to understand: reality, I am waiting for you. Since reality would be afterward, it is also something that exists after what she calls death, a going out of the self.

"Meanwhile, it's a dream." Clarice speaks of ordinary life. Ordinary life is not working. The dream dreams us, implacably and fatefully. The dream is fateful. It is that which announces. Perhaps it is an unconscious dream, although Clarice never uses such words because she is stronger than that. After the dream, everything becomes real.

Movement toward reality is what constitutes reality. Clarice speaks of reality as "afterward." It is death not as deadly or as obligatory passage, but as abandonment of self that gives access to the real. The dash is the very figuration of the jump. Clarice speaks of the afterward from before. It is still to come.

"And the free soul searches for a corner to accommodate itself." Once the threshold of self has been crossed, there is a vertiginous freedom that frightens. The soul needs to reduce its own freedom, to anchor it. Clarice remains human. She is used to her former dwelling.

"Me is an I that (I) announce" closes the meditation on the passage from *I* to *me*. Clarice localizes the instances in a way that is different from what we are used to. The entire text says that she considers the self, *me*, as the innermost instance. *Eu, I*, is a grammatical subject. Most readers have different analytic or mental habits and tend to consider *it*, rather than *me*, as the innermost of the subject. When Clarice says, "It is toward me that I'm going," it is not the me, self, as outside but as inside. The self has to be restituted in Clarice's specific dilemma.

"Me is an I that (I) announce." She does not know what she announces because she constantly goes toward what she is, although she does not know. An intimate space must be opened.

"(I) do not know what (I) am talking about. (I) am talking about nothing. I am nothing" Clarice says it while trying to say it; she is performative. She will know it only after having said it. It is always the process of "that's where I'm going." While she says it, she continues to go beyond herself, "there." One is moving very slowly toward the inscription of what could be writing, toward what language is going to trace and what does not yet have a name. Why? Because we are afterwards. We can say, "(I) am talking of nothingness. I am nothing."

"I am nothing" is the necessary passage where she is equal to a nothing that allows her to continue.

"After death."

Undoing of self, loss, are accompanied by a thought of real, concrete death: "After being dead (I) will grow and (I) will disperse myself."

The two movements are contradictory movements, but they are the same. Dispersion may be a kind of growing.

"And someone will say my name with love."

But Clarice nevertheless touches upon the dilemma of a posthumous writing. It comes about with the mentioning of the name: "It is toward my poor name that (I) am going."

Morally, this is very strong. She does not see herself as being famous, to the contrary; it is from infinite poverty, from an absolute nakedness, that love will be revealed. Her name, having nothing anymore, is impoverished of everything. There remains of her the other, a chance, a possibility of being called with love by the other. The sentence must be read as desire. She goes to her poor name as a sign of poverty, as a remainder of the self, in order to be called, and to be able to call in the direction of love: "And from there (I) will come back to call the name of the loved one and of the children."

In these propositions, we approach something of a definition of the very secret of love.

"They will answer me. At last I will have an answer. What answer? That of love."

This is an answer as gift. From absolute poverty, from the name itself, there emerges the possibility of a gift. The answer is the other name of love, of gift, of the purest gift. It is yes. A simple answer. The gift without limits. The gift is simply to say the name or to call, and remains the only answer she can have. Everything else will only be questions.

"I love love."

In love, there is love. From the sublime, we arrive at something that seizes us, but is, color: "Love is red."

This little sentence is childish and secret. A French memory would think of Rimbaud's use of color. When color begins to run free in the emotions, in passion, it inaugurates the most archaic libido. How does a color play with the other and alter it? We may not like having green glide into the eyes, hence have our eyes colored with jealousy. Again, I read a movement from the inside to the surface.

"My secret is to have green eyes and that no one knows." We go through red and green, through the color of jealousy of the one who, in the text, implores, needs, and cries. But at the end of the lament, the lament becomes song, and at the end of the song, the words are carried off by the wind. There is no reappropriation, no incorporation but this kind of formidable spacing of the body, situated beyond appropriation where everything is carried off through wind and movement.

"I am at the edge of my body and (I) wither slowly." We are back again at this strange surface, at the border or at the locus of the active "go," intense and quick. We jump and take a rest until the next and last time: "What am I saying? (I) am saying love."

From there one can hear that everything is but a way of saying love. Everything that has been said is only the edge of saying love. Love can only be said from the limit of life. Earlier she had said: "(I) do not know what (I) am talking about." And there was a repercussion later: "(I) am talking about nothingness." At the end of the text, the following utterance appears: "(I) am saying love."

Nothingness and love can be put side by side. Clarice discovers herself saying love, something that can be said only from the edge of nothingness. She surprises herself, saying love, nothing that can be said. But love traces a border: "And at the edge of love are we."

She makes a border with love. What is beautiful is the verb in the plural: "are." Love is a kind of communion. The text ends with us. In a text where there was nothing but dispersion and detachment at the end, everything gathers in *us*. Again, the Portuguese construction puts the subject at the end: "At the border of love are we." It is as if *we* came out of *are*. Being elaborated from the beginning is that *I* goes toward *we*. This does not mean that *I* has arrived. *We* is on the edge, is the edge. We have to continue. It is a vertiginous situation. At the limit we could think that this last act of transmutation is the trance of the *I am* to the *we are*: *I-am-are-we*.

The force of this text is signified by the final *we*. Its center can be situated around the sentence: "It is toward my poor name that I'm going."

Then we leave again and we arrive at *we*. The verb of being, *are*, is a kind of rest stop while during the whole text, we leaped ahead, carried off by the little sentence: "That is where I'm going."

This is one of Clarice's densest texts. *The Passion according to G.H.* is infinitely longer. The density here is due to condensation through transmutation, and the rapidity of transmutation.

The femininity of this text is inscribed in scenes of risks. It is a text that leaps, lets go, loses, lets things be lost, does not hang on, does not hold back. I think that the phenomenon of transmutation goes well with a certain libidinal economy. It is a text of border, written from fear, after fear and after loss.

It is the same process of incessant leaping, of letting go of the border, that traces the path of love in *The Passion according to G.H.* or in *The Apple in the Dark*. It is not a state of being, but a path that is not followed step by step but leap by leap, always from one extremity to another, and always into the unknown, into the void. The goal is the movement *toward*, not the arrival.

III

The theoretical space in which I am placing my readings deals with different libidinal economies. We can put side by side — and I do not say oppose — what would rather be in the way of discourse, for example, an ordinary telephone conversation, as coming from a rather masculine economy, with a kind of retention, an organization linked to apprehension, to the fear of losing with something that would be closer to flow, to a kind of fluid or to echoing sounds. The two types of communication are not separated. They are always present in different degrees, in different quantities, in the same message.

The miracle of the fluid that Clarice gets across is neither metaphor nor nonmetaphor. Clarice continually links the human and nonhuman and nonhuman matter and through that matter that fluid circulates. How does fluid circulate? In a certain way, it would be an intimate, internal, and liquid metaphor of the telephone: how is life being communicated? Imagine a telephone that lets fluid pass rather than words. That is what I want to work on in *The Apple in the Dark*, between the man with the roses and the victory in defeat. I want to work on the mystery of supreme communication, almost at the level of blood — of a living whole, with another living whole which is that of an incommunicable mystery.

We have to be careful when we read Clarice Lispector. In *The Apple in the Dark*, for example, we should not be fooled by the fact that, in this text, there are characters who are men and women in a strictly novelistic sense. The generic term is deceptive and the economies of giving, of exchange, of communication do not correspond to the apparent sex. We cannot not see that someone like Martim — the man who carries the text and reconstructs the world — is not Adam. He is full of Eve. There are moments when he is Adam, for example, at the beginning. But since he is an Adam without God or Eve, he can become Adam only from the moment when Eve constructs him.

As for the women, there is an enormous gap. When we read the text with a little distance, we can see Clarice Lispector's position in relation to these problems. The text is heavily invested, impregnated with her own libidinal programmation. One sees how much, for example, on the side of Ermelinda, there is a woman with an economy said to be feminine. At the same time, she is the hysteric, the classical woman. Vitória, however, has a violent rapport with castration that is very subtly analyzed. She is almost a woman. She is a woman in the sense of a person who would be capable of a feminine economy of spending, of risk, of flowing overabundance. But she cannot get there. In *The Apple in the Dark*, the moment when one is on the border, on the verge of jumping off, it is impossible. The only leap that will have taken place is Martim's. And Martim jumped before the text began. It is a tragic text, not at all triumphant like *The Passion according to G.H.*

All of the protagonists in themselves feel a wonderful temptation to free an economy said to be feminine. Again, I cautiously use the words "said to be feminine." This temptation is everywhere in the text. But they do not lose themselves joyously in it. It is rather trembling with fear and going backward that those who accede to it right away move away from it again.

The way the title borrowed from James Joyce, *Coração selvagem*, said everything, the way the title of *The Apple in the Dark* says exactly what is at stake in this economy. It is Eve in darkness. The apple plays as if it is that which would come in place of light and is the luminary of this darkness. We are not in the space of darkness, of hell, but in that of Paradise. It is with closed eyes that one sees better. This light does not emanate from a sun but from the flesh of the apple in one's hand.

IV

In order to proceed while giving myself over to an economy said to be feminine, I continue metonymically and, from the apple to the hand, I tender you this short text by Clarice: "Tanta mansidão."[3] Clarice writes about being at the window and watching the rain.

Maybe the text is the very writing of rain itself. Something that simple. It is this barely writing the rainy aspect of rain that one could call, in our vocabulary, an emanation of femininity. It is a capacity to make a nonviolent, nonexclusive difference. It is pure, internal difference through affirmation. The one that is expressed in: "The way rain is not grateful not to be a stone."

The rain is so much rain that it suffices to itself as rain. It is the power to recognize this that one could call femininity. It is a space where recourse to opposition does not need to be made to mark difference, at least with the paradox that the way one remarks, out of pedagogical necessity, something that does not want to be remarked, which is not to be remarked. Because there is writing, Clarice is constrained to re-mark what is not remarked. The rain is not remarked. It is writing that marks it as rain. The paradox of writing is to have to go nevertheless through the shadow cast by the negative in order to make the affirmative emerge. Clarice's technique consists in ending by saying: "Rain is." But in order to say that, she proceeds in a way that resembles a negative theology. She begins by saying: "Rain is not a stone." We are obliged, the world being what it is, to go through the negative in order to bring about the affirmative, not the positive. The positive would refer us back to the negative. One needs all of rain in order to inscribe a sentence that would have no sense without the rain, without the non-stone: "Am a woman, am a person, am an attention, am a body looking out of the window."

"Tanta mansidão" is difficult to read. It is barely a little shower. In "E para lá que en vou," Clarice gathers not only a philosophical treatise on extremities but also a mass of cultural referents: the most immediate and the most marked of Brazilian and universal culture. Here, there is only rain and it is difficult to think, to write, to read rain.

Etymologically, in mansuetude, there is hand. In Latin, *mansuetudo* is a double word. It is a word full of otherness, full of love. It is composed of *manus* (hand) and *suescere* (to accustom, to tame). *Manus suesco*: I take with the hand, I appease with the hand. The trajectory of this word is astonishing. It has reached sublime heights since one never talks of mansuetude where it emerges, at the point of contact between the hand and the other body. Mansuetude is the way in which, with the hand, I tame the other body. The text is of infinite mansuetude. I only speak here of communication. When one is in the space of mansuetude, there is mansuetude. A little bit like in *The Passion according to G.H.*, communication is done between *I* and *me*. It is a scene of intimacy. There is no other human. The question must be asked constantly of Clarice's texts, because she is often alone. At that moment, many difficulties are resolved, which still does not mean that it is easy to communicate with oneself. No more than with rain. This is one of Clarice's lessons.

In *The Apple in the Dark*, the question of mansuetude, of the rapport between hand and body in relation to the other, living, present, different, is agitated, tormented, flamboyant. But the position of the person, of the being, which allows communication to take place, is that of mansuetude. One should have a mansuetude equal to the other, when the other is a human being.

In Clarice's unpublished fragments collected and edited by Olga Borelli, we can read: "When I look too much for a meaning, I do not find it. Meaning is as little mine as what exists in the beyond. Meaning comes to me in breathing and not in words, it is breath" (translation mine).

To look for meaning already situates us in exchange. For example, in a dialogue with someone, we punctuate constantly with more or less aggressive remarks of the kind: What did you say? I do not understand. We are looking for a meaning. An excessive search prevents the meaning from happening.

V

Choosing night as Martim's partner, Clarice raises the question of solitude, so omnipresent in her texts. Clarice always works on several moments at once: night as a generalized other and the moment when night becomes personified. The following passage of *The Apple in the Dark* (273–361) unravels the story of the other, or a story toward the other. At the beginning there is chaos, a nocturnal chaos. In the slow construction of the text, a process leads to human night. It is from the moment one attains human night that one enters into great fear. From the moment one has to go toward the other human as night, one begins having a terrible fear. It is a question not of understanding but of letting oneself be understood by the other who is not always as soft as night.

One does not eat the apple because it is a question of being eaten. In this whole passage, everything is about being absorbed or not; of how to let oneself be absorbed without being destroyed by the other. A question of incorporation is being played out in the scenes between Martim and Vitória, about how to give oneself to, or how to give oneself to be understood, or to give oneself not to understand the other, how to risk oneself to the other human. There is a moment when Clarice says that it is not loving that is difficult, it is being loved. And that is Vitória's question. It is the story of the apple. Vitória represents the great passion of not being loved. She knows everything about love, but what happens again and again, and what starts up like the very destiny of this woman, is the fear of being loved. The most dangerous, the most vertiginous experience for the human being is the experience not of loving but of being loved. To be taken in by the other without dying of fear and besides, from the moment one accepts the risk, the danger of being loved, to have to give back as love this being loved. That would be the real process of love. The exchange is situated between being loved, which is already in a movement of return, and loving. It is to be capable of being loved. To be able to love the way the other loves means to abandon all claim to one's own truth, which is always wrong anyway. True alteration is to let oneself be thought by the other. This is what is happening in the last part of *The Apple in the Dark*. In the first two parts, there is the staging of the first darkness, but there is a succession of dark spaces. We sink into the very heart of darkness. The apple, which is at the place of light, is perhaps the heart.

The question of sexual difference is constantly being raised by Clarice. There is an astonishing part in this passage where she enumerates three types of *confusions*. It is a word that looks light and familiar. But it is not. It is the very intricacy of passions. The scene takes place between Martim and Vitória. Vitória is talking. She is in one of these great moments of interminable monologues. She is alone. She arrives at something that could be called the paradoxical extremity of purity and she falls. There are admirable passages punctuated by Martim's inner reflections on how Vitória bores him. This can be taken at the banal level of comedy, but it is the opposite. It is the very rejection one finds in any relation to the other. Without this rejection, we would fall on the other, disappear in the other. Martim says to himself: "That confusion, of a woman who's afraid to die—could that be it?" (translation modified).

There are three types of *confusion*. One is that of the woman who is afraid of dying; another is that of the woman who is afraid of living. One could think that one is represented by Vitória and the other by Ermelinda. In fact, things are reversed. A third confusion is that of a man who does not want to be afraid. These three confusions inscribe the entire issue of libidinal economies. The fear of dying is linked to the fear of living, and the fear of living is already brought about by death. Only the women are on the side of fear, the fear of living, the great negotiation between life and death. The man does not want to be afraid, and that is the definition of a masculine economy. The position of the man is, of course, the weakest. Why? Because what is being signaled is the man's fear of being afraid. It is inscribed at the level of the textual unconscious. Martim, who himself is the carrier of this analysis, stumbles and cuts his own sentence. He remarks his own utterance with a phantasm of castration: " . . . 'and the confusion of a man who . . . of a man who did not want to be afraid?' "

All this is suspended by a system of question marks. Clarice writes a nontheoretical text, leaving it up to women to illustrate what would be the most feminine possible, and to men what would be masculine. But of course we can displace it all.

Fear is related to a phantasm of castration. This is what analysis has shown us, and it can be read in this passge. I could replace it, in Clarice's text, with loss. The dark space would be that of the unknown, of this other who can be translated as femininity. Yet I would prefer to say simply "other." Fear is related to a possibility of loss. All depends on whether the situation is lived positively or negatively. On the side of masculinity, it is inscribed negatively. When Vitória claims that she is afraid of losing herself, she is on the side of masculinity. On the side of femininity, the possibility of loss may be considered as positive. It is inscribed as need. The feminine may be said to be in need of need. Need is marked by a plus, as in *The Passion according to G.H.* It is linked to having. On the side of masculinity, need is lack. That is what the text continues to say, incessantly.

The erotic *stakes* are enormous. Clarice throws out the kind of signs one could find in Faulkner. A preliminary scene with Ermelinda is going to be played over several times (165–70). It consists of variants and repetitions of a scene to be played later. One has to be constantly translating to see what the sexual scene really is. Of importance is the terrible and comic scene with the shoes, which is closer to a symptom than comedy. Clarice does not lose herself in the silliness of sublimation. She stays where love stories do take place, near the body and the unconscious. Two beings never reach each other in the way of Tristan and Isolde. In Clarice, protagonists burn themselves while en route; they fall down and do all kinds of things that signify: I do not want to. The more one wants, the more one does not want to. That is what Clarice signals. Otherwise, there would be neither love nor desire. Ermelinda, to meet Martim, had put on a pair of shoes that she had taken out of the trunk. And the shoes are too small. They are hurting her. At the end of her wait for Martim, she thinks only about taking off her shoes. But if she took them off, she could never get back into them. It is a displacement of a movement toward the other. But Ermelinda enclosed her feet in the shoes. She fetishizes her feet in a way that is more than significant. Martim, who comes toward her from the other side, does not have a problem of shoes. For him, it is happening at the level of the hands and of the eyes. He comes with his ax, step by step, as he is in the habit of doing. Martim's pace is both masculine and feminine. His ax is masculine and his walk feminine.

"The flowers were illuminated from within and the red roses were trumpet-blare; from far off Martim saw the girl as a dark patch in the air."

There follows a dance in space that inscribes both proximity and distance.

"From not so far away, he saw her standing in the sun" (translation modified).

Everything is happening in distance. Martim is not closer; he is not as far; he is always far.

Since Ermelinda lives in the imaginary, she foresees and apprehends. However, Martim who has done the kind of work we know from the beginning, is somebody who first sees matter. From an originary chaos, he reconstitutes little by little a human form, because he no longer cheats at this level:

"The garden was lengthened by two or three cutting shadows that the clothesline laid upon the ground. The motionless sun kept the plants heavy, in a watchful silence where anything could happen." What happens? Everything: Martim.

"Martim kept coming closer, with the ax in his hand. The things were waiting, deserted. But the honeysuckle was quivering the way a lizard does before he dies."

Once again, conjunction, transformation are the predominant order. Transmutation is taking place in the inside of the thing and of the signifier that names it. Lizard is feminine in Portuguese, a little animal in the feminine, whose little tail, nevertheless, is representative. Here we may think of Freud's famous reading of Wilhelm Jensen's *Gradiva*. It is like a little lizard, or like a little Ermelinda before she dies.

"Then—looking at the bright, motionless roses and walking toward them, as if looking and walking were the same perfect act, looking at them and what there was red about them—a wave of power and calmness and listening passed through the man's muscles."

As in *Agua viva* and *The Passion according to G.H.* there is an inner movement. To look and to walk are the same gesture. Martim sees the young woman and looks at the roses. There are incessant slippages. Immobile, he looks at the violent roses. The immobile has been transferred from the sun to the roses. Everything communicates, erotically. An opposition emerges between the powerful and the calm.

"And a man walking in the sun is a man with a power that only one who is alive can come to know."

The repetition of "man" reduces him to a brute mass of muscles. It is only little by little that the distance is attenuated. Upon his arrival, something emerges: "From afar he saw her standing in the sun, a woman's face hardened by lights and shadows, with splotches of light on her dress."

The text follows the look and proceeds metonymically. Martim constructs his vision by alternating soft and violent juxtapositions:

"With interested eyes he asked himself how can it be that a person can put so much into another person. And he thought that because, while he had been working, it seemed that in a short time he had transformed the simple girl into something vague and enormous. Only when he got closer did he discover to his surprise that the girl's face was really cold and colorless. In some way that discovery reconciled him to the fact that she was just herself and not the repository of some great hope."

Martim shows respect for the reality of this unknown person. He only touches the surface. He is at the moment of the look. His remark about the excessive repository of a hope means just that. It functions as an obstacle to a violent projection or penetration. The trajectory is one of looks. One kind is barred by images and is a look with screens. The other lets things happen. It lets the appearance of a person happen, without apprehension or prevision.

"Without any disillusion then he saw her exactly as she was." This is a negative labor. But one look goes toward the other: "And she, she looked at the stranger."

Ermelinda is on the side of strangeness, Martim of exactitude. We are at the stage of two looks moving toward each other. What is going to happen between the two occurs on the level of the body, with as little symbolization as possible. These are stages between looking and touching. It is the inverse of the exchange with Vitória, which is all in words. But both experiences are partial. Because the total experience is made up of words and body.

In a letter Clarice Lispector wrote in Bern when she was very young, she quotes some of Kafka's aphorisms that she had affixed on her wall:

"There are two capital human sins from which all the others are derived: impatience and sloth. They have been pushed out of Paradise because of their impatience, they will not go back there because of sloth. But is there not but one capital sin: impatience?"

And another: "To swim against the current only helps in very rare cases that have to be recognized; if not, it is to keep oneself afloat, to glide on top of it that must be the politics of a man who wants to profit from the mystery of the currents" (translations mine).

In *The Apple in the Dark*, impatience and running water are crucial, as in *Agua viva*.

"And it seemed to [Martim] that the murmur of the cold water among the rocks also ran inside her."

Water runs like words, protean, but necessary and refreshing. The secret is a murmur between two sentences as if between two rocks.

"Not that he was in love with her": The sentence marks a reserve, the very reserve of love.

In the scenes between Vitória and Martim, a little paragraph is echoed at the summit of an encounter (279–80) that consists of a struggle. In its course, Vitória incessantly tells Martim to surrender, which he does. He then catches himself in one of these moments of virtual and terrible struggle. What Vitória is saying is of mad violence. She is surrendering a secret or perhaps a nonsecret to Martim. What is it? Something that she precisely cannot say; it is a kind of double-bind: if she utters it, it will be annulled. She wants to but cannot say that she is a saint. If she told Martim her secret, she would give herself up entirely. To reveal oneself to the other is the greatest aberration, a real surrender, a sacrifice. If Vitória said, "I am a saint," she would sacrifice herself. She would effectuate her own sanctity. She is on the verge of saying it, but she stays on the edge: "I came here to build a life, to make my life."

To say this is aggressive toward those who are situated in the space where this dialogue takes place. Martim finds himself the depository of a gigantic secret:

" 'What is it all about?' she asked vigorously. 'I'm only taking advantage of your freedom! What's it all about, can't you tell?' she asked with great severity.

"She did not know exactly what she was referring to, and he understood without knowing exactly what she was referring to" (279).

This type of communication that takes place without knowledge or words is perfect communication. Words always have a violent, explosive space that goes beyond thought and meaning.

"But if it were not that way, how poor our mutual understanding would be, our comprehension made with words that are lost and words that have no apparent meaning; and it is so hard to explain why one person was happy and why the other one despaired—we do not keep in mind the miracle of words that are lost; and for that reason it has always been so worthwhile living, because many have the words been that were spoken and that we scarcely heard, but they have been spoken."

Only a rigorous reading will allow us to approach the secret that is revealed here and passes through words. It is at no point a question of silence. There must be speech. Speech has to flow like water. Speech must flow with such protean fluidity that a positive incomprehension can emerge, in something beyond mutual comprehension. Comprehension comes about through loss and loss becomes gain. The last sentence associates the necessity of living with risk, happiness, and the trembling risk of speech. Words have been poorly understood, but joy or despair goes through such a misunderstanding. Neither joy nor despair can run this risk of misunderstanding and loss.

"For an instant neither hesitated to understand the other within their incomprehension." It is the union of two mysteries who do not try to destroy each other.

I am jumping to a passage that may be the very summit of the book; it consists of a short sentence Martim utters after the hundreds of sentences pronounced by Vitória:

" 'I do not believe a word you said,' he said."

In a typical conversation, an interlocutor would commit an act of hostility through this type of sentence. But here, Martim redeems and saves Vitória. She did not say: I am a saint, yet what she said was equivalent to it. Earlier she confessed: "And suddenly, as if she were regurgitating her soul, she shouted with the pride of her fifty mute years."

At the end of this regurgitation, nothing remains. After having vomited one's soul, one is entirely given over to death. Vitória confessed. She surrendered, she abandoned herself by betraying her secret. To give away one's secret in its nakedness is to take the risk of death and is tantamount to giving it to someone who will be unable to receive it, will almost annul it or to turn it into derision. It is like a crossing of the seas. We can think of the death of Virgil and his inaugural barge. Vitória finds herself in this barge, thinking that she has died: "But as if before I had died I had received communion" (288).

She talks about the crossing of life and death in the past. She reenacts this passage, in the present, in front of Martim. She reenacts perhaps exactly this communion before death. If someone hears this, Vitória will be left only with a silence not full of millions of unspoken words but empty of everything she has said. That is why, in a kind of supreme divination, Martim answers: "I do not believe a word." Through this sentence, Martim gives back to Vitória all of her words.

The episodes with Ermelinda are infinitely less anguishing. There one is in the space of the gaze and one goes toward the other. The other cannot come: "And she, she looked at the stranger. Before that the girl had had within her a kind of silent heat of communication from her to him, put together from begging, softness, and a kind of confidence." In the way that there is the cold murmur of water with Vitória, there is warmth of communication and noncommunication with Ermelinda. It is not in, but *from*, the words that something emanates. There is a paradoxical economy, which is that love stops where it begins.

"But face to face with him, to her surprise, love itself seemed to have ceased. And thrown into the situation that she had created, feeling herself all alone and intense, she was held there only by determination. The way she had spent a whole exacting week getting ready for a dance, and just as then, left waiting, had taken a taxi and gone to the dance: exactly what she had wanted.''

Ermelinda is someone who precedes. She spends everything, just before: ''Ermelinda was sad and surprised. And just when he was finally right in front of her, she looked at him with resentment, as if he was not the one she had been expecting, and as if an emissary had been sent her with a message: 'The other fellow could not come.' ''

Ermelinda can live only in strangeness in a minimum of distance without that she loses herself absolutely. It is a moment in a long development that finally ends in an act of love. But this love is composed of many moments of nonlove. Clarice Lispector's strength is to have the moments of nonlove appear in love. It is not on the same mode as Vitória's story. It is a possibility of love among others. Ermelinda's structure is full of imaginary forms. Living with images, she attains reality only with difficulty. She precedes with images. She has a lot of trouble attaining reality. Symptomatically, she puts on shoes that are too small at the moment when she needs to put her bare feet on the ground. She advances by retreating. She cannot do otherwise. It is by going through ''no'' that she is able attain ''yes.'' Why? Because all the imaginary needs to be destroyed. She has to reach the point where she can cancel it. Being capable of proceeding only by deception, she goes from deception to deception up to the point where something naked will be produced. First, she has to dispense with a simulacrum of love in order to attain real love. In the message about ''the other cannot come,'' it is not the other who cannot come; the one who comes is the one she did not fabricate. But her fabrication is awaiting him unbeknownst to her: ''Why did she not tell the man the truth, then, and go away immediately? She felt the truth as a weight upon her heart, and she did not know what it was—even though she had been thinking more and more, as if all of her was the sleeping heart itself. Why then, if she was to open her mouth, would this one truth not come out in words? Ermelinda did not even part her lips. Not wanting to lie, she would say to him, 'I don't love you.' ''

She has a desire not to lie rather than to tell the truth: ''But she seemed to know something else: that she did love him, she did love him.''

Beyond the truth of not lying, there is another truth so true that it eludes speech. The text is situated in one of these incomprehensible spaces where a story cannot take place. A kind of vibration is produced by the shock between what is living and what is speaking. This is what is at stake in the writing—rather than in the telling—of stories. Most people, however, do tell stories. If this scene were real, it would be hard to imagine. One can hardly say to a person with whom one consitutes an ensemble of love: In order not to lie, I am telling you that I do not love you. Fear is precisely what produces fear. If one does not want to lie, one says terrible things. But those are also the most beautiful. In reality, and if by chance one happens to be at that level, it would be surprising if the other person were there at the same time. If one knew how to read such a text, one would learn tolerance, pardon, and patience.

There is a rapport between these passages and "E para lá que eu vou" that also takes up the question of limits. The sentence in this title could be taken as the very movement of distancing from the self. The last sentence had said it in its entirety: "What am I saying? Am saying love. At the border of love are we."

The work of love is linked to this double movement of going toward the other and of going away from the self. I am also going toward the other as if toward myself. It is only at that limit that the other can appear. To go toward the other is what *The Apple in the Dark* entails; that is its whole technique, which consists in surrendering to the other while letting oneself be called by the other. Martim is being interpellated first by forms and colors. The other, simultaneous movement is that of a distancing of the self. It is difficult to surrender to the other, to go to an encounter with the other, and to succeed in encountering the other. Even if the other is strong enough to attract you, you also have to do the work of a detachment of the self. Often, one goes toward the other that one imagines one sees. But to love consists in discovering more and more the unknown person and to arrive in the place where, as in *The Apple in the Dark*, one can truly enter into the incomprehension of the other. If one follows "E para lá que eu vou," and goes in the direction of the other, a moment ensues when one cannot continue to advance step by step. One has to take a leap. That is love. But that is precisely what Vitória cannot do. The moment one jumps is the moment one realizes that something cannot be solved by staying in the same place. At that moment, one has to accept the unknown of life. Afterward comes the truly unknown. The other will be there or not. It is a matter of life or death.

We can return to Martim and Vitória and to the story of poetry. It is situated within Vitória's nonconfession to Martim. Vitória, from Martim's words, "Afraid? Yes," is slowly carried off by an irresistible need to talk. This is her way of not confessing something to herself, of avowing without avowing, something that could be love for Martim, a love triggered by a kind of inexplicable jealousy for Ermelinda. There are various moments in this episode. They could be scanned in rather comical fashion. But it is very serious. Every time Martim is about to return to work, Vitória calls him back. The organizer of this *fort-da* is Vitória. Martim is the spool. Vitória makes her confession after Martim is leaving one more time. He turns around and she calls him back: "Again he stopped. And again he went back over to her. But this time he stopped farther away from the woman, as if he knew that in a little while he would start to go and in a little while she would call him back: Therefore he stopped halfway."

The confession is a kind of self-discovery for Vitória. She does it on a mode of determination of symbolic identity. Following a moment of comical interpellation, she does not say that she is a saint but worse, that she is a poet:

" 'What would you say—I wonder, what would you say, with that way you have of sneering at other people's lives—what would you say if I were to tell you that I'm something of a poetess?' she shouted.

"Martim looked at her with such surprise that she became paralyzed. A reddish color spread over the woman's startled face.

" 'Well,' he said, laughing suddenly and shrugging his shoulders. 'I wouldn't say a word.' "

This prefigures what will come out later as "I don't believe a word." Martim always chooses the position of not speaking. But it is not pure nonspeech. He says that he will not say. He allows the other to say anything she likes while he says that he will not say anything. It gives Vitória a chance to say:

" 'Everything in the world interests me and I study the open book of life. And my inner life is very rich,' she said, and she shook her imprisoned hair as if it had been turned loose in curls.

"Martim took a quick look at the tree, as if he and the tree were exchanging a furtive glance."

As in the passage with Ermelinda, this can be read as a symptom. To shake your hair while it is tied in a knot is precisely Vitória's way of speaking. The description is of an infinite cruelty. Martim feigns not to see what is only too visible, that is, Vitória's lack of shame.

Then comes the important paragraph on poetry:

" 'I even started a poem once,' she said, frightened, forcing herself to go on because she thought that talking consisted in saying everything, and at the same time she saw herself slipping into nothingness with her shame being sacrificed uselessly. 'The poem began like this: "The queens who ruled in Europe in the year 1790 were four." ' —He was going to know everything, and she would not have anything left . . . 'But the poem wasn't going to be about queens, you understand?' —but she knew that he did not understand, she knew that there was only success and failure, and that between them nothing existed, and that because of that she would never come out of her limbo to prove that through the phrase about the queens the poem would take its subtle drive; and since she knew that she would never prove to other people the infinite beauty that can take flight with a simple phrase, then she, who believed only in success, did not believe in the very truth of what she felt; and there she was, all tangled up in the inexplicable phrase of the poem, and after she had said it she had been left with four queens in her clumsy hand. 'It was just for the sake of beauty!' she said with violence.

"They remained silent. The woman was breathing heavily. But what she could not tell him, what she could not say, was that she was a saint. Opening her mouth several times in agony, she tried to, but she could not. That, that could not be told to anyone."

In this scene of violence, a vocabulary, or a semantic field is drawn around shame. The "forcing herself to continue" brings about "she saw herself slipping into nothingness with her shame being sacrificed uselessly.'' The vocabulary pertains to rape. Except that she is the one who puts herself into a position of being raped. She evaluates poorly her attempt at giving herself. The gift is lived like a gift inviting rape.

The appearance of the four queens is important. At the end of the paragraph, the reader is left with the four queens in the left hand. The question is: what remains of poetry? Reference is made to a card game. But who wins, loses? There is the metaphor of play.

Violence is everywhere in the paragraph, especially in Vitória's revelation. She does not tell her life. Worse, she says that she is a poet. Poetry is located in the various levels of violence, but sanctity she cannot say because it is beyond her strength to do so. She will manifest it otherwise. Why is the supreme revelation the supreme loss? Because the secret, the greatest treasure, can also be lost, for example, writing. That is where the strongest prohibition is found. The incongruity is heightened by the fact that it is happening on a farm.

To say is to lose. Vitória first believes that speaking consists in saying everything. That is the problematic of speech. She thinks she must say everything. Therefore she cannot stop speaking. From the moment she starts reciting her poem, the way the little girl recited a poem to her father in *Coração selvagem*, the mystery of poetry is lost. Vitória senses this the very second she speaks. She tries to save her poetic queens by saying something that is quite true: the subject of poetry is not the subject of poetry; there is a true subject and a false subject. The true subject of this sentence is not the queens, it is beauty; it is the story of the lost words. But beauty does not exist. It cannot be communicated. It is the miracle. Having uttered this sentence, given her relationship to failure and success, Vitória is bound to lose. She has said the unspeakable, and she is left with four queens in her hand. This is of great metaphoric violence: she has incurred the risk of trying to signify what is beyond speech. She does not succeed because she lives only in terms of success and failure. Martim's incomprehension deprives her of herself. If Vitória were not somebody who has to prove something to others, she would not be deprived. She would say her sentence and this sentence, and what would become of it would be of no importance. But she is with the other in a relation of struggle and of play, where she needs to win or lose. She loses. But she has left her queens. Why? Because she went from the scene of poetry, which is a gratuitous and inexplicable scene, to a scene of play with the other.

In a certain way, this paragraph has a double beginning. Several levels of communication are engaged. There is a whole geography of the text that is projected onto an intersubjective space. She says: ''I even started a poem once.'' She does not finish her poem. She begins twice: she begins a poem that she had already begun; she also begins to speak. The two beginnings are cut. A terrible scene of sacrifice ensues. This man was going to know everything and she would be left with nothing. If the other knows, nothing remains for her. If he does not, she would be left with nothing. What is left? One would have to look at Jean Genet here, and at his work on remains. The dilemma of the rest, of the remains, is always related to castration. It is possible for everything to remain. But not for Vitória.

We know what "the subtle drive of the poem," or "the infinite beauty of the sentence," is about. By definition grace and beauty cannot be proved. They can only be lived and felt. Since she lives in a dilemma of proof, of success and victory, she loses grace. She loses it to the point where she does not believe in herself anymore. It is not even Martim who is at stake.

She loses the grace of poetry. She does not venture to the following level, that of sanctity, which is the problematic of *The Passion according to G.H.* The repetition, "she could not say, she could not say," must be read as a mark of impotence. Stated once, the sentence would be equivocal. But a double repetition is the attempt of failure. The failure goes so far that she is in agony. She should have taken the risk of speaking. Afraid of losing sanctity the way she has lost poetry of her own doing, she does not dare.

We can evoke the myth of Psyche, which is also a story of daughters, such as *Beauty and the Beast* or *The Apple in the Dark*. The story is caught in the schema of a relation to the father. In an exchange of hostages the daughter becomes the equivalent of the father. The analytic stakes in the Oedipal story between father and daughter are manifold. Contrary to Clarice's story of *Beauty and the Beast*, in the myth, a mysterious being marries Psyche. That being fulfills her but on condition that she not look at him. It is a story of obligatory blindness maintained in darkness. There again, we find questions of darkness and truth. Psyche cannot see the truth of the one she loves.

The schema of transformations taking place at the last moment in the narrative, through the sacrifice of a woman, is well known. It can be found in many of the Grimm tales, but in the story of Psyche, her husband is Love himself. He is the most beautiful being in the world. Of interest is the displacement of hidden beauty into manifest ugliness. And there is also the question of the father and of Psyche as a person. This structure can be read both in *Beauty and the Beast* and in *The Apple in the Dark*.

In *The Apple in the Dark*, the turning point in the exchange between Martim and Vitória comes when Martim takes up: " 'Afraid? Yes,' he said patiently as if he were talking to a child."

During this mute dialogue between the two, in this confrontation—it is a question of head and figure—what is manifested in the insistence of the word is the paradoxical struggle to repress fear, as if, in a psychoanalytic register, in a resistance to transference. Vitória speaks in order to repulse, but by repelling, she makes it happen. In her movement of rejection, there is a kind of calling. It is as if—and this is performed in the text—by pushing it away, she made something come closer.

What is of importance is the linking between the words: fear and she; fear and yes. Afraid? She, Vitória, who directs the farm with a virile hand. Then, there is an accumulation: afraid, she who was a he. She was ordering this man around. There is a formidable ascension. It takes the form of a struggle against a man. She constantly tells herself: I am more man than he is. During her entire ascension she accepts neither being loved nor being a woman. She is more man than her father, since she is courageously going to dilapidate her father's heritage. She is a hyperfather. But this ascension is followed by a fall. We are already on the descending slope when she says: "Waiting for an uncertain day when this domain would be the greatest in the region, and then she would at last be able to open the barriers" (translation modified). There is a passage to the infinite, but nothing is certain since these are only phantasms. What barriers would she be able to open? Those of the domain of the unconscious. Vitória plays everything in relation to her father's death. But if she pushes to the infinite of the imaginary, what will happen? At the infinite of the imaginary, there is reality. It is: will this day come? No. What does this mean? The sentence does not mean much of anything. And "open the barriers" means even less. One goes over into the imaginary because, at that moment, what would open is she. When there is, "Her whole body revolted," it is not against the masculine incomprehension that her body revolted but against the opening of the barriers. Here, the body appears but everything closes upon itself right away. One goes from the body that has appeared and retreated to: " . . . her whole being got ready for a gesture that would make her own indignation explode."

Before, nothing was big enough, now nothing is strong enough: "Afraid! She looked at him in surprise, bitter. What did he know about her, this man?"

Through her own glance, she undoes the individual. On the one hand, an ascension toward mastery is entailed, on the other, a negative, reducing portrait. This is very clever on the part of Clarice, since now Vitória confronts Martim: "How could he ever understand her courage, he whom she now confronted without any fear. She perceived for the first time how stupid his face was" (translation modified).

This means that she does fear him, since she remarks that she does not. All of a sudden, she discovers him. Without discovering it she discovers her own stupidity, which consists in thinking that because he was an engineer, he was intelligent. She remarks her own stupidity, but without saying so. She had fallen into the trap of mastery. She thinks to get out of it, but she falls back into it even more. She falls back into it while saying to herself that she had never wondered if he were intelligent because a title is enough! The symbolic is put into question: "But when one looked at him nakedly, how stubborn and crude he was!"

She covers with words what she sees only too well. And he says: " 'Afraid? Yes,' he said patiently as if he were talking to a child.'' He wins right away. He reestablishes the father-daughter rapport: ''The repeated insult made her tremble and this time her whole being got ready to strike back with an insult.''

Clarice is on the side of the face and the figure. The face, the traits, the surface give in:

''Afraid . . . her mouth twisted with sarcasm.

''But instead of that, the features of her face suddenly gave way. She could not take anymore.''

In these formidable stakes of castration, she loses face but not for very long:

''Afraid? Yes. Afraid? Yes.''

She takes the expression back into her own account. And in a single blow, she regains fear. Very passively, she lets herself be taken over by fear, when all of a sudden she remembers that she had possessed fear. And she takes back that fear: ''She remembered how being afraid had been the solution.''

This is an enormous coup of mastery: '' . . . and how her courage from then on had been one of living with fear.'' She remembered the supplementary degree. Then comes an immense and astonishing passage, which opens with: ''Afraid, yes!'' She takes on fear, adopts it. She affects it with a positive sign.

''What do you think that means? Afraid, yes. Listen then and take it if you can; take it if you're not afraid.''

The scene is reversed. There follows a long autobiographical narrative during which she tells her life story. One can see how everything is linked to the father, but especially through the following sentence: ''Listen if you can . . . ,'' she addresses herself at the same time to Martim and to nobody. Her confession is really addressed to nobody:

'' 'I took care of my old father over the years, and when he died I was all alone . . . ' The woman stopped herself. When her father had died she had suddenly been all by herself and on her own.''

This kind of compact, biographical monologue, an immense gush, is heightened by the mute confrontation of the preceding scene. Here, there is a flow of words. And as she speaks, she vomits fifty years of silence. Fifty years are condensed into three pages, in a mininovel, an immense analytic biography replete with interventions by a third person, which are of the deepest, most analytic, kind that she could not utter in the first person. Shifts back to the first person are made, and then again to the third. While reading this passage, one should have in mind Clarice's story of *Beauty and the Beast* set against the background of the mythic story of Psyche. These are stages in Clarice's writing. She asks herself questions of life and death:

''And with the clumsy impulse of those who start late and no longer have the skill for it, she had wanted for the first time to try what she called 'living.' ''

Here the question is of destiny, of the grace of living, of life's value. Before that, the opposition was with the domain that could extend infinitely. Here, to the contrary, we are in something that is more restrictive. And the restriction is felt more and more at the level of the place. Vitória goes to the island, then to a hotel that becomes smaller and smaller. At that moment the important crossing of the water in a boat intervenes: " 'I went to be by myself and to concentrate.' " She is going to concentrate, literally, as if she were going to the center of the world.

" 'And I left everybody and I took a ferry with my suitcase. But once on the boat, once I was on the boat . . . ' "

She is leaving with her sex on the boat:

" 'I had that ill feeling that I recognized, this ordeal, this almost good but dangerous sensation' " (translation modified).

This opens up a traversal of femininity and, for her, it is catastrophic: " 'As soon as I had stepped on that boat that was rocking wildly, everything touched me and made me sad, curious, alive, full of curiosity—but wasn't that just what I wanted? Wasn't that just what I'd gone to look for? It was, but why was it that I refused to realize that it was happening? Why did I look at everything with my head held high, making believe?' "

After this incredible crossing, she finally arrives at her island and there follows the whole story on the island. There are all the elements of this trajectory spanning from the infinite back to the exiguous dimensions of a cell: " 'I didn't know anyone on the terrace and I didn't let any of them guess that it made my heart beat faster. I left the bag in my room' " (translation modified).

All this activity stands in contrapuntal relationship with an exit into the night, toward an encounter with the sea: " 'But outside the hotel the whole beach was glowing in the dark. Beautiful, all white with so much sand, with the dark sea— but the foam . . . .' "

At the heart of the text, a wedding scene takes place: " 'I remember that the foam was white in the dark, and I thought that the foam looked like a piece of lace.' "

Everything is here, but Vitória cannot take it: " 'Then I hurried back to my room and quickly turned into the daughter of an aged father because it was only as daughter that I had known calm and composure, and only then did I realize the security I had lost with the death of my father; and I resolved that from then on I wanted to be only what I had always been before, only that.' "

Vitória seeks nonpleasure. She quickly returns to her room in order to have pleasure. What does she do in the room? She smoothes her hair with a brush and she takes up a book. The book is her antiapple. She pretends to read because she knows herself: " 'I even sighed comfortably in bed with the book in my hand, the book I had never thought I would open on the island.' "

She knows the clichéd question: What book do you take with you on an island? She marries the book she reads, not the one she writes. But the moment when she begins to read, since God is waking, all the lights go out: " 'I knew that I was not reading, but I never let myself be convinced that I was making believe; and it had not been reading on an island that I had come to find out there. I tried to ignore the fact that God was giving me exactly what I had asked Him for and that I—I was saying No.' "

God gives her his hand one more time, since he makes the lights of the hotel go out. This is a supplementary test. Vitória was going to say no to life. Instead of making love, Vitória chooses to read the book. She is so much afraid that she takes the book. The moment she hears herself say a mute no, God turns out the lights so that she does not have to hear herself say no. She has another chance. She hears the ocean:

" 'But I also knew that if in that very moment I did not pick up the calm thread of my previous life, my balance would never come back and my things would never be recognized by me.' "

She proceeds as daughter of the old father:

" 'And that's why I pretended to be reading. But I could hear the ocean waves; I could hear, I could hear! It was then that, all at once, all the lights in the hotel went out. Just like that, all at once, without any sound, without any warning, nothing. Only the next day did I learn that at nine o'clock at night the lights were turned off to save electricity. The lights had all gone out, and I was left with the open book in my hand; I was left in the dark as I had never been before.' "

As with someone who wants to read, it is for the first time that she undergoes this experience of total obscurity. The second time, it was the night before she told this story that sheds light on everything:

" 'I was left in the dark as I had never been before. Only last night was I left in that dark for the second time in my life—like that, with that simple way of being in the dark.' "

The insistence on *darkness* is repeated three times:

" 'It was very dark as if I was trying to find the hotel and did not know where it was; the only thing I could touch was the book in my hand. The fear, the fear that you accuse me of, would not let me make one single movement, but after the surprise had worn off—then there burst forth what I had only barely kept back until that instant—the beauty of the beach, the fine line of the horizon, the solitude to which I had come of my own free will, the rocking of the boat that I had thought pleasant . . . ' "

All her femininity explodes:

" ' . . . and also the fear of the intensity of joy that I can reach—and unable to lie any more, I cried as I prayed in the dark, praying as I said . . . ' "

Vitória addresses her prayer to the Father. And what does she ask him: " 'Never this again, oh Lord, never let me be so bold, never let me be so happy.' " Do not let me feel like having pleasure. Do not let me be happy. Do not leave me any possibility of being a woman: " 'I don't want grace, because I'd rather die without ever having seen it rather than see it just once!' "

An inverse crossing follows. She takes her boat again, in the manner of Virgil's barge of death, in order to go home, to her old father. She accompanies this trajectory with a perfect analysis of why it was necessary for her to go back and withdraw into the arid bosom of castration. Otherwise, she would have to experience pleasure and she would die; she would be in a humid space that she fears more than anything, she who thought she had vanquished aridity.

" 'When I was sitting in the ferry the next day I thought that I had died.' "

She is saved and she thinks she is dying:

" 'But as if before I had died I had received communion.' " She is not mistaken:

"Martim was pale. Oh, what he would have given to insult that naked and shameless face."

And he responds: " 'I don't believe a word you said,' he said." And he annuls her great narrative because he saw something quite unbearable in it, that is, the spectacle of such a choice of death. His desire to hurt her is a desire to reach her as woman.

The question of fear, which is a fear of living, is completely linked to the symbolic, to the recognition of oneself as the daughter of the old father and to the book of reading. At some point Vitória had said: "I am a poet." The question of reading and writing is always present. Vitória missed herself or did not miss herself. She prayed God to take away from her the courage to live. God, give me fear: it is the summit of a paradox. Give me fear because I am afraid.

Vitória moves constantly between fear and courage, between aridity and humidity. She knows that danger lurks under aridity, but humidity is what instills fear in her. When we first encounter Vitória, she has amnesia. Then, little by little, scenes of youth and adolescence emerge. These scenes are humid, of a disquieting humidity, like that of a fruit. Vitória goes up to the very point of evoking happiness.

A progression into the depth of quotidian life follows and all the way up to the very depth of surface. On the one hand, the symbolic is completely articulated, while, on the other, orality prevails (292–300). Vitória has a drop of perspiration on her nose. She humidifies herself while she speaks. At the end of this immense exchange between Martim and Vitória, Martim says to himself: Why am I so afraid of this woman who has wet armpits? She is a woman, she is human. She has a drop of perspiration on her nose:

" 'I will tell you what happened . . . I wore a blue dress.' "

This is her virgin dress:

" 'And we ate in restaurants so many times enjoying ourselves and getting to know the restaurants.' "

That is what she knew of pleasure:

" 'It was the first time that I had ever done anything like that.' "

And she covers herself more:

"Martim took his dirty handkerchief out of his pocket and wiped his face. The woman saw that he had not understood."

Vitória and Martim make love incessantly. They do not stop. It happens in every possible way, with slight displacements.

"She stayed there for a moment with an unraveled look, reduced to remembering herself alone as in the restaurant." Here she thinks that Martim fails her. In fact, he does not. From time to time they stop, exhausted, then they take up again:

"And how her mouth glowed at the sauce as it poured out, giving her a touch of repugnance; how in those days it had seemed to her that one had to exult in what was ugly; and then, with a feeling of nausea that she suddenly had not been able to separate from love, she had admitted that things are ugly. . . . It was surprising, it was horrible, as if it had been a wedding."

This is her first wedding. The second wedding is with Martim. As often in Clarice, the most beautiful thing is the least visible:

"At that instant the woman trembled.

" 'Maybe the food was too heavy?' he suggested."

This may seem like comedy. But no. It is not true. He insists repeatedly. And little by little, the woman accepts.

" 'It's quite possible,' Vitória said in anguish — 'it's quite possible that the meat was very heavy indeed.' "

" 'Why did you not go to a stomach specialist?' Martim asked."

The reader feels like laughing. But here, one has a great proximity. It is quite serious, high and low at once, the way that everything is beautiful and ugly at once. In what could be called incomprehension, there is nothing but comprehension. Vitória simply cannot accept being understood. She runs away in reverse, convinced that Martim does not understand her. She advances in this amorous relation on condition that she thinks that the lights are out and that she cannot read the book.

There follows an episode of total blindness:

" 'As I was saying, it was because of that that I came here. It was a mistake. But I've done so many other things for the same reason that I can't explain it!' she said simply, perplexed."

And here is the key:

" 'It is as if something that should happen is waiting for me; and then I try to go after it, and I keep on trying, trying. It's something that happens, that keeps on encircling me, it's something that owes itself to me, it looks like me, it's almost myself. But it never gets close. You can call it fate if you want.' "

This is what Henry James explores in *The Beast in the Jungle*. It is the same story. She never speaks of this event that encircles her and which is happening. She *is* there. Her destiny is here:

" 'Because I've tried to go out and meet it. I sense this happening as if it were some kind of affliction. And it's as if, after it happened, I would become someone else,' she added peacefully.' "

This sublime passage ends with an episode that is the first model of the supreme event she is waiting for:

" 'But once' — she said serenely — 'once while I was waiting for a streetcar, I got so distracted that when I came to, there was wind on the street and in the trees and the people were passing by, and I saw that the years were passing by; and the policeman signaled to a woman that she could cross. Then, do you understand? Then I felt that I, I was there — and it's the same as if what was going to happen had been there . . . I don't even know what was going to happen, because almost before I felt it, I had already recognized it — and without even giving me time to know what it was called, I had somehow fallen down on my knees before it, like a slave. I swear I don't know what had happened to me, but my heart was beating, I was I, and what had to happen was happening.' "

She cannot even give it a name. But here, she is in her island:

" 'Oh, I know that I was very frightened, because being on the street had nothing to do with my father, or with my life, or even with myself; it was something as isolated as if it had been something that had happened — and all the while, in spite of that, there I was surrounded by the wind, the streetcar passing by, with my heart beating as if it had just had a thought. That was one of the times when I had come closest to what I'm used to calling "my fate." I could feel it the way a person feels something in his hand.' "

At that moment, Vitória becomes beautiful and Martim sees it happening. The event is here. But at this moment Vitória has to be in the street. Some of Clarice's other stories also take place in the street. To be in the street is the most difficult thing in the world. The most beautiful film would be: something that takes place in a street with the wind blowing and a train passing by.

1981–82

Notes

1. Clarice Lispector, *A maçã no escuro* (Rio de Janeiro: Paz e Terra, 1978). Translated by Gregory Rabassa as *The Apple in the Dark* (Austin: University of Texas Press, 1986). All quotations are from this edition. Modifications have been indicated.

2. "É para lá que eu vou" (That's where I'm going), in *Onde estivestes de noite* (Rio de Janeiro: Artenova, 1974). All translations mine with the help of Claudia Guimaraes.

3. "Tanta mansidão" (Such mansuetude), in *Onde estivestes de noite* (Rio de Janeiro: Artenova, 1974). All translations mine.

Chapter 4
"The Egg and the Chicken":
Love Is Not Having

Chickens play an important role in many literary works. In Joyce, for example, the bizarre author of *Finnegans Wake* is an egg that has been laid by a cackling chicken walking along the text. It is an adoptive chicken, F.W., and is presented among other things like a gigantic letter. The letter plays on the signifier "litter," as both litter and waste. Joyce enjoys putting into the text a chicken that explores the litter. It discovers an immense letter, that of F.W. The question of the chicken and the egg is everywhere, since the chicken in F.W. discovers in F.W., F.W. Lacan loved this text and in fact cackled about it at length on the topic of literature as waste.

There is a chicken in *Coração selvagem* and in many other stories by Clarice Lispector. Often her chicken stories are addressed to children. These children are adults, that is to say, the readers, who never really know whether they are the egg or the chicken. There is no chicken in *Agua viva*, but a tiny egg that refers to an immense egg. Our task will be to look for eggs and work on the relationship between eggs and chickens. This goes back to what comes first, the chicken or the egg, the question of origin. In Clarice, the question is latent, in a comical or serious mode. She inscribes the question of life and its origins. I say inscription in order to speak more concretely of something that belongs to a literary text. It is something that would be grafted, scratched, or ingraved on something like a black board, a monument, or on something of the order of a textual surface.

Clarice's texts, like Kafka's, are not narratives. They contain a secret, a lesson. But this secret and this lesson are dispersed in the verbal space in such a way that the meaning cannot be apprehended at a first reading. Discourse is that which arrests and gathers meaning. I recall the technical word "disseminated" (introduced by Jacques Derrida), which referred metaphorically to a handful of grains thrown on the ground and which represent food. To have meaning—and a chicken—the grains must be gathered and picked up by the chicken. Obviously, dissemination is also a sexual metaphor that refers to semen and masculine sexuality. It is a metaphor of expansion, of spending, with the implication that if it is not gathered, it is lost. In this light, reading consists in a double movement. One has to let the text disperse itself. That is its movement as well as what makes it differ from television, which is pure discourse. At first sight, a text is not readable. It cannot be summarized. It is free. It diffuses and spreads. One of the texts closest to textuality is *Agua viva*. It is living water, water full of life. It cannot be contained or taken drop by drop. *Agua viva* is an immense flow, a river in which all the objects of the world—a church portal, apples, chairs, a woman, a man, a foot, the universe—swim and float, along with a small egg.

With Clarice, we cannot speak in terms of genre. Some of her texts are presented as novels, others contain miniature narratives, micronovels, but nothing like the generic novels we once knew. We are now speaking of writing, of fiction. These words must be dusted off a bit. When we speak of writing—a term that has become part of a classical discourse on literature—it is in order to eliminate old notions like representation. A text does not aim at representing a reality that can be coded, but shares visible affinities that are those of the unconscious in life. Often, Clarice's texts are introduced by scholarly introductions that explain the text in detail, give rules for reading. When texts are treated like commercial objects, the question of writing no longer pertains. It so happens that Clarice's texts try neither to represent nor to express, which does not mean that representation and expression are eliminated. Rather, in order to work as they do, they take up inscription. They let effects of reality, effects of life sift through in a mode that is infinitely more faithful to our experience than that of classical literature with its procedures of psychological inscriptions.

With its title reminiscent of a fable, "The Egg and the Chicken" is something completely different.[1] The experience could be artistic, creative, religious, mystical. Or it could be a quotidian experience of love. The quotidian is supernatural. To read something that is not mechanical, but something living that has been symbolized, an active reading has to be invented that is not rendered mechanical by the application of external categories. One has to be as close as possible to an analytic reading. It is from an analytic position that one has to listen to the text at length: one has to listen to what is said between the lines, to the silences, the breathing, the hidden as well as the revealed words in a text, to the living reality of the text, its repetitions, anomalies, grammatical curiosities. A text has to be treated like a person, with its mystery. We must have in our relation to the text a position both active and passive, one of patience. One has to accept what one accepts from a person: not to understand. It is there that the very question of meaning is posed. A text becomes meaning. "The Egg and the Chicken" has meaning but in the plural. It has many meanings as well as nonmeaning. All its contradictions have to be accepted. This is important, especially for interpretation. A bad analyst hears only what he wants to hear. This does not mean that there should be no interpretation. But there is enigma. There is not simply one word for the enigma. The enigma is complex and infinite. It can be received but not reduced. It is hidden. La Fontaine once said that one should not kill the chicken, or there will be no more golden eggs. The text is a chicken that incessantly lays golden eggs. The text will not cease to lay golden eggs unless one makes an incision to go in and see what is in its belly. The meanings of a text are like the eggs: they are to come; they are in preparation. For an egg to be, one has to give the chicken a chance to live. It has to be given time to eat. All this is to say that if there is interpretation, it is not through the theft of the egg but out of love for the chicken.

One has to work on the surface. This surface is not hidden, it gives itself to be seen and as part of a mystery. The textual surface is in a vital, organic relation with the inside, like with a living thing. The textual surface gives itself to be seen with the effects of its meaning from the inside. It always has to be remembered that the life of the text is produced by a quantity of small units, and of a general ensemble, which is the text. What is explicitly stated in the discourse of the text, is only part of the signifying group. There are other meanings that are produced by the surface. The text could also be considered like a painting, a musical partition. Because a text is printed, one often forgets that it is mobile. It is in movement. One should always bring back the movement of the text, the fact that meaning runs along it like music that reaches us only once it has been fully played. Nobody is going to cut a symphony into little pieces. It is the ensemble that strikes us. One cannot read two pages of a text that one has not read entirely. Like the paleontologists, we can take a page and reconstitute the text. But one has to have great skills. It is like reconstituting a body from a tooth. A text has to be read in its entirety. It is only afterward that one can look at one of its fingernails, as in times when we are in love. To read, one must have already read, in order not to be unfaithful to the entire life of the text. Once the text has been read in its entirety, we can examine a finger, a smile, a page, a paragraph or three words, while knowing that it was taken from an entire body. Then, the second time around, to read without betraying, one can pay attention to every smile in the text. But the smile and the laughter are not part of a personality. If one takes a picture, one will not hear laughter. I am speaking metaphorically on purpose. When reading a text, one should not forget that it is constituted not only of what anatomy teaches us, but of many expressions, analogies of the expressions of a human being. Mysteriously, this crosses over into the linguistic matter that makes up the text, from one letter to another, from one sound to another. It is there that the most refined work is to be carried out. That is also where works in translation become a problem. It is necessary to go to its very source, in order not to lose part of the reality of a text. We have to perform this act of listening to something that is not simply contained like a bird in a cage, or in a phrase. But we also have to perceive a different kind of a text in the text itself, made up of all the combinations of audible and visible forms. That is where one can speak of a textual unconscious. A text says something very different from what it is supposed to say or thinks that it says.

Egg Writing

The beginning of "The Egg and the Chicken" carries a strong inscription of eight *o*'s:

"Olho o ovo com um só olhar [I take in the egg at a single glance]."

Something is happening in Portuguese between the egg and the look. It is of the order of the *o*'s. On the second page, there are four or five paragraphs that begin with *o*, *ovo*, the egg. A series of eggs is laid.

"O ovo é óbvio [The egg is evident]."

The question of evidence is raised in this text. It is also a question of the stolen egg, as in Edgar Allan Poe. By definition, the egg does not fly (*voler*), it is always stolen (*volé*). The egg is always stolen when in fact we should think of it in terms of a flying egg. Clarice writes a defense and illustration of the egg.

The text is constituted, very visibly, by a series of sentences. Each sentence forms a whole that has to be analyzed. There are paragraphs. A survey of the ten pages (*survol*) can be made to see that the text is presented like an ensemble of rather even masses, of paragraphs. Here and there, a sentence is detached, short and visible, which explodes the continuum. The title is presented as having different values, as the title of a fable, or a chapter from a book on natural sciences.

The first sentence is short in relation to the enormous paragraphs that follow:

"De manha na cozinha sobre a mesa vejo o ovo [In the morning I see the egg on the kitchen table]."

This beginning sentence has multiple entrances. There is a series of entrances. I enter five times in the kitchen, through five doors. I begin to make way toward the egg. These are semantic hallways. There is a kind of logic of perception that would be a grammatical logic of language. It recovers this series of entrances in the text and one can follow a whole tracing of time, of space. On the table, there is a system of placing, of seeing the egg. The text brings us in a few steps to the egg and tells us about this movement. It is organized by aligned doors that all lead toward the egg.

"Olho o ovo com um só olhar [I take in the egg at a single glance]."

This second sentence is composed of a series of *o*'s and very small words that gravitate around the egg. The entrance to the paragraph is "I take in at a glance."

We have to work on glance, on look. This kind of description is that of the anatomist of the egg. Something is posited and annulled: "I immediately perceive that I cannot be seeing an egg." The egg slides between the sentences. At the moment I see it, I do not see it. There is an eclipse of the egg that has to be analyzed as an eclipse of the possibility of seeing. From the first sentence, we are in the present tense. What kind of a present is it? Which morning? Where are we? What is the impossibility of seeing? The egg appears and disappears, turning between tenses, between the present and the eternal present. It is the lesson of the egg as well as of the look. It is a lesson of love and of reading. I look at the text with one glance and see that it cannot be seen. I can look at it, I may have read it and, at the same time, I have not read it. Also we are going to see the invisibility of the egg. We have to work on the unreadability of the text. Clarice says: I see that I do not see. In other words: I see.

At the beginning, the egg is at the end of the sentence. One moves toward the egg, which is posed at the moment of its disappearance. The egg only gives itself to be seen in a single glance. If I try to see the egg, it escapes me. There will be an incessant dividing between looking and seeing. The egg does not lend itself to a "look," and in order to "respect" the egg, one has to give it a quick glance, which allows it to manifest itself in its invisibility.

From one egg to another, we arrive at God. We leave the egg and we do not arrive at the chicken, but at something more-than-chicken. When I read a text, I page through it. I look at its first, its last sentences. I treat it like an egg. I take it. I turn it around. I look at its big end, its small end. All we have to do is take an egg in order to see that this text works on evidence in the most obvious way. After having seen an egg, one has not seen anything. What is beautiful is that the egg contains, puts into the world, more than an egg. There is God and there is love.

Clarice enters in five ways at once. This is also the way she is going to envelop the egg. The textual process consists in turning the egg around incessantly. It is a starlike process. The egg is put into orbit. In this essay on the egg and on vision, what is the obvious is at stake. The egg, like the world, is obvious.

"Como o mundo, o ovo é óbvio [Like the world, the egg is obvious]."
That is to say, invisible. The question is similar to the one suggested by Rilke's Abelone in *The Notebooks of Malte Laurids Brigge*. The visible is invisible. We absent that which is present: all that which is in the egg, under the egg, beyond the egg. There is also the surface of the evidence. The first sentence recalls that of Kafka's "Before the Law." In Kafka's story, the man from the country appears before the law. Everybody thinks that this is evident. Nobody wonders what the door of the law means. As if the evidence of writing were the law, as if one had received an obvious blow, a *coup d'évidence*, in the eye.

Another remark on the shell of Clarice's text: the paragraphs are composed by sentences separated or joined by hyphens. They are not ordinary paragraphs. Typographically, one can see the traits fall down, one by one, in a cadence. For us, it is something of the order of separation. I put down and take back. Sentences are suspended through hyphens, which mark moments in the text. At times they indicate a step-by-step movement during which the egg is placed.

The paragraph begins with the egg. I see the egg; I do not see the egg; it exists; it does not exist. This type of utterance parodically resembles the lesson of things. The egg is an oval object. All of a sudden, it happens: the chicken. But it does not arrive that easily because an egg has great difficulty in laying a chicken. A great effort of the text begins with:

"The egg is the soul of the chicken."

Only with difficulty does the chicken begin to come out of this complicated situation that has the chicken laid by the egg. One begins with the soul. There is an inverse process of gestation and of a putting into the world of the soul by the body.

As readers, we have to do work in an oval form. In my opinion, all stories about eggs are stories of love. A mathematician would probably see only geometrical lines in this text. I prefer working on the geometry—of passions. The text is incredibly complex, and the word "love" appears only late in it, perhaps in order to correspond to the time of gestation. If the text is a chicken, it needed time to lay that kind of egg.

In painting, there are thousands of phantasms of eggs. In Hieronymus Bosch, for example, broken eggs are everywhere. They are subjected to all kinds of violence and are really anti-eggs. What, then, is an egg? Clarice's text answers the question without breaking it. Why are eggs rare in literature when they are the most common thing in the world? The egg looks hard although it is not. We could go on and on about the materiality of the egg, about what it can represent at the level of the unconscious. It is a form that presents itself as having to be nonviolated.

We will see what kind of a relationship we can establish between the egg and a certain form of writing. The egg is a model of a modern text. How can one read the egg, what does it mean? The exemplary egg writing for me is Clarice's story, but other egg-texts come to mind. There are also negative eggs, black eggs, such as Maurice Blanchot's *The Madness of the Day*. When I say egg-text, I think of a certain form, of a certain sign. The egg-sign of Blanchot poses a problem. If one tries to place his egg, one has great difficulty in doing so. His is an egg that rolls, that cannot be placed, except if we are Christopher Columbus, but then we know how.

Thanks to the egg we will speak of all the problems concerning that space, of the evaluation of the unlimited world of passions, of the unconscious, and of the technical evaluation of the text, its production, its writing.

I will begin with a few fragments, with some feathers of a chicken named Clarice. These are small feathers that I have torn out of *Para não esquecer* (In order not to forget). It is entitled: "Escrevendo" (While writing). Writing opens onto time in movement, onto something in the making. If I say "while writing," I am already writing in writing. The play of the text has begun a long time ago. Any subtle text is some kind of egg, an object that can be placed only with absolute caution, like an egg on the table. It is hard to put an egg on the table. The very gesture calls the table into question. It has to be placed as if it were a feather, or then, in the way of Christopher Columbus, who "uneggs" the egg. The egg, like the text, escapes any desire of fixing, of positioning, of immobilizing. The property of the text is to be in a continuity without interruption.

The text has to be read in its entirety and then reread. From the beginning:

"I no longer remember where the beginning was, it was in a manner of speaking, written all at the same time."[2]

This remark is easily recognizable for readers of modern texts. But what is the relationship with a text that has a lost beginning? One never knows if it is the chicken or the egg. Yet a text is always here in its entirety and comes forth all of a sudden. Even if, afterward, time is needed to write it, is a living being.

"Everything was there, or should be, like in the temporal space of an open piano, in the simultaneous keys of the piano. I wrote looking carefully for what was organizing itself in me, and only after the fifth patient copy, did I start to perceive."

Clarice indicates that the position of writing effectively precedes writing. To write, we might say, is to follow writing, to copy oneself. One precedes and one follows, that is the mystery of writing. It is only in the aftereffect things fall into place and fragments of meaning can emerge. This means that the unconscious is at work, and such is Clarice's position, like that of every true writer. When one reads something like "The Egg and the Chicken," one gains a marvelous feeling because the text is so powerful and precise that it makes sense only in the aftereffect. The text is an athletic exploit, or the flight of the egg and the flying egg. During the flight, one does not know what will happen to the becoming of the egg. It has to be a very powerful egg to make such a long and strong flight.

"My fear was that, out of impatience with the slowness that I have in understanding myself, I would be hurrying to bring about a meaning before its time."

If I mark this sentence down, I have to hear that something has to be understood in me. It means that I have to understand myself, I have to envelop myself. There is an egg in me and I do not have to hurry its birth. I also have to undertake the astonishing trajectory of my own comprehension, of entering into myself and being my own egg.

We constantly have to deal with the succession egg, chicken — with something that could be called the relaying or the sublation of one by the other. Stated incessantly in "The Egg and the Chicken," it could be expressed in a serious or comic mode. In Hegelian terms, it could be called the dialectic of the egg and the chicken. In this text a strange theme of death takes up a sort of sublation of the self or the chicken. It comes back in the expression: "how the egg is the sacrifice of the chicken," that is to say, how one is radically transformed by the other, how a girl-chicken, becomes a woman-chicken or a mother-chicken. Something has disappeared. There is no death in nature. It is the human being that has an imaginary rapport with death. In "While Writing," Clarice tells the story of a woman who answered "and I thought I was dying," to the doctor who informed her that she was going to have a child. It is a moment of life as productive and positive loss.

I could read the two texts side by side in relation to the question: what is a text? Meaning is perceived afterward, in the aftereffect. While making the tour of the egg, a certain meaning becomes perceptible. A text has to be considered like a living organism. But every fragment has a meaning, like a spark of fire. And the spark does not make the fire, even if the spark has taken off from the fire. It is the very strong insistence of the unconscious part of the author that disengages the latter from a position of mastery. This is what can be called the textual unconscious. A quantity of supplementary effects is produced by the fact that the text is made with language and that language always speaks several languages. Language can carry a discourse, and in "The Egg and the Chicken" too we find a line of discourse. But while carrying on this discourse, or following an idea, many side discourses produced by language proliferate. While following the law and going from one point to the next, language plays the role of Little Red Ridinghood in the forest. On all sides, there are stories that take place in a sentence, that detach themselves, circulate from one paragaph to the next. They are told in this forest of language, through signs that detach themselves.

Distance in Relation to the Text

"The Egg and the Chicken" plays with eggs, with *o*'s. It is a textual basket full of *o*'s. The *o* and the *a* are elementary sounds. They are also the first sounds. One cannot overlook the surface. It inscribes many graphic and phonic effects. "The Egg and the Chicken" concerns the technique of distance in relation to the text. How does one turn around the egg at a certain distance? How does one find the distance that allows us that, on the one hand, it cannot be understood, since Clarice says that if one does understand it one makes the thing disappear—and that, on the other, one does not let it get lost into oblivion. It can be neither understood nor forgotten. One must find the proper distance.

The text is written in a singular manner, through a kind of distancing. One never seizes the egg. One never arrives at it. The egg remains unseizable. Then you have it and then you don't. The play of this gap must be accepted, and constitutes the challenge of this text. It is a text that constantly breaks with its object and then comes back to it. The truth of the egg is in the incessant return of the egg. At the end, we watch it come.

With the first sentence, one is already inside the aura of this text. The text writes in a kind of incessant coming and going, of entrances and exits that approximate the egg. When we enter into the kitchen, as time and space, we have the morning, the table, and the kitchen. The egg is placed and we fly around it. But since we are not equipped for that, we have to alight upon it from time to time. The text proceeds by flying, leaping, by taking rests. There is an extraordinary work on dispersion, on opening eyes wide, on the formidable spacing that can be in the trajectory of a look. Be it a short or a long look. The distance covered by the look is the distance covered by light.

"Like the light of an extinguished star, the egg, strictly speaking, no longer exists." The egg is, so to speak, the end of the egg, but we do not know very much about the beginning of the egg. The "egg, strictly speaking," no longer exists, but the egg exists. When the light arrives, it arrives long after the origin has disappeared. But at the moment when the reader is told that the egg, strictly speaking, no longer exists, the text opens to say: "Egg, you are perfect. You are white."

An extreme violence is folded in these declarations, which cancel each other. The "now" of the egg no longer exists, but the egg is here. It is here in space and time; we do not arrive at the egg at the same time as it is here. These are paradoxes that produce rather surprising effects of this text, which the story of the star allows us to read.

"When I was ancient, I was the depository of an egg." There can be—if we imagine ourselves in the perspective of astrophysics—we have a perception of light that left millions of years ago. I want to signal the real and imaginary trajectory between the table, the very simple plane on which this text unfolds, and the sky. One goes incessantly from the table to the sky and back again. At the metonymic level, a propagation is made through the *o*'s and the *a*'s. The egg and the chicken make their way through the text, and from *o* to *a*, one goes to the last sentence. The window (*janela*) is a system of *a*'s that opens to let the egg enter. A textual relay exists at the level of the letter and of the phoneme. Something circulates, and the egg is always suspended on a table subjected to mutation by metonymy. There are propagations of movement from origin to origin, from the chicken to the star. It appears with brightness and disappears like the twinkling of a star. At one point, the moon appears: "The moon is inhabited by eggs."

Imperceptibly, through writing, Clarice succeeds the chicken. There is also a moment where the chicken is Clarice, and she is chicken, the identity brought about by the text. However, a little while before, she was the swallower of eggs.

"The same as the egg, in the immense metonymic movement," sometimes is taken in an exchange with celestial worlds, sometimes is a kind of star, when it lands on her shoulder. One wonders if it is not of another nature than the egg, "strictly speaking," maybe chicken, maybe angel. One does not know. It is a word. At certain moments, it resembles an egg the way we think it in everyday banality. Sometimes it is not the edible egg, but the drawn egg that enters into our space.

"The egg is originary of Macedonia, it is the drawn, oval egg." Each fragment of text between hyphens is a beginning because the text is written "to the chicken" springing from one grain to the next. Even if a certain number of paragraphs were invented, nevertheless a progression is evident. The first page is organized by the look. From a certain moment on, Clarice ceases to be the chicken attracted by the worm, for example. She begins to leap about madly; though still bound by the *o*'s and the *a*'s, she is brought back to the table and the egg. The more the text advances, the greater the distances become since it is a starred text. From egg to egg one arrives at God, but God is also an egg. One makes an infinite egg journey to the supreme egg, which is the cosmic egg.

We can land in Macedonia, which used to be Thrace, hence Orpheus's country. Perhaps, by landing in Macedonia, Clarice makes a distant allusion to the Orphic tradition, which said that the world was first an egg, the Orphic egg. Most cosmogonies propose the world as egg: the Chinese think the world is first a kind of egg; the Egyptians propose it as egg and eye.

The text subverts philosophy, but also the world of legends. Subversion here is of the order of a kind of freedom that literature allows itself in relation to the philosophical referent, which lingers like something more theoretical, but never as a vast enterprise, like the freedom of the egg. The text writes the triumph of the egg. The egg comes in through the window, but where is the chicken? The chicken arrives very slowly through the *a*'s, pulling itself by the *o*'s. It comes in toward the middle of the text. Clarice tells about the sacrifice of the chicken. The mother is the locus, the means of the son. Mother and son are everywhere. It is the story of the son, but since it is a human story, although it goes through the chicken and the egg, Clarice questions the *real*, cackling chicken and its way of living. When she goes from the chicken to the chicken-woman, when there is egg and chicken, Clarice wonders what may be the real chicken, that is to say, the woman. She takes up her problematic relation to the egg, to the child, to production in a way that becomes human. Other conditions come into play. The triumph of the egg touches also upon the question of writing: "Out of devotion to the egg, I forgot about it. My necessary forgetfulness."

But the remembering forgetfulness, not the forgetful forgetfulness, remains, and it concerns love: "Suppose I were to make the sacrifice of only living my life and forgetting about the egg. Suppose the egg were to be impossible. Then — free, delicate, without any message for me — perhaps once more the egg might move through space right up to this window which I have always kept open."

I, as woman: "And as day breaks, it might descend into our apartment. Serenely move into the kitchen. Illuminating it with my pallor."

Whose pallor? maybe that of the dead star? of the moon? of the chicken? of the woman? There are all kinds of eggs here: there is a fantastic egg, a philosophical egg—there are a thousands of eggs. And then there are the eggs in the frying pan. There is day. The world arrives with the sentence: "As with the world, the egg is evident."

There one sees very clearly the equivalence between the world and the egg. The more it is obvious, the more invisible it becomes. At the same time, Clarice works on the signifier. The egg is *ovo* + *b* + *i*. In *óbvio*, evident, there is an obvious egg and another that is not obvious as the sentence tells us.

There is the egg of the chicken and the egg of man. There is the egg of woman and of the egg. The egg of the chicken, the egg of the woman; the egg of the star are eggs that form a living ensemble. They are eggs with full forms, while the egg of man is a flat egg. It is the line of the egg, not a full egg. It is not the egg full of eggs, but rather the circumference of the egg: "drawn by a man in the sand."

Clarice touches upon the origin of writing, the lost origin, but it is not only an allegorical scene. Writing is here in order to keep. What one does not know, what writing does not keep, is the origin because there is no origin. Everything is origin. In this scene, the egg is traced in the sand, but it is the contrary of writing. It is writing that is lost. It illustrates the frailty of the written egg, of the flat egg drawn with a stick.

"The egg is invisible to the naked eye." From egg to egg, the reader goes up and down and comes onto God who is invisible to the naked eye: "Perhaps the egg was once a triangle which rolled so far into space that it gradually became oval—Is the egg essentially a vessel? Perhaps the first vessel modelled by the Etruscans? No. The egg originated from Macedonia. There it was calculated, the fruit of the most painstaking spontaneity. On the sands of Macedonia, a man with a rod in his hand designed it and then erased it with his bare foot."

There is a mass of information. I want to link the naked eye with the naked foot. The theme of nudity keeps recurring. The chicken was considered to be a disguise of the egg, a cloaking of the egg. The sands of Macedonia bear echoes of a dissemination, a dispersion, a masculine inscription. Macedonia will always remain for us the carrier of the name of Alexander. Old Thrace was considered a barbaric country. The rod, banal as it is, accentuates the phallic side. It could be a childhood scene about an egg that can be erased. Nothing but a sign of an egg remains as perhaps a primitive sign that of the origin of writing. We can imagine writing to have been born while someone was playing in the sand. The most elementary shape might be that of the egg. The gesture of erasing can be read as a miniature phantasmic episode or as something serious, the way the text requires it to be. It is contrary to what the woman and the chicken do. They spend their time trying to protect the egg so as not to erase it, not to forget it so that it cannot be erased.

This scene has to be linked to a previous one: "The egg is still the same egg which originated in Macedonia." There is insistence and survival of the egg:

"The chicken is the most modern of tragedies. She is ever uselessly up to date. And she is continously being designed anew. The most appropriate form for a chicken has still to be discovered. While my neighbour answers the telephone, he absent-mindedly designs the chicken anew with his pencil.''

One can wonder why there is this attraction of a man and a pencil for an egg and a chicken. At the same time, they are objects of writing. In the next paragraph, we can read about what in the space of femininity escapes the trait, flatness, manipulation: silence, the cry, blood, the inside. But here, it is the exterior, the flat, the erasable.

The text has a precise grammatical structure even though it has a thousand meanings. It is almost like a shattered eggshell. Not everything combines, although everything can be. First, the grammar begs to be remarked. But second, two major themes of reflection are at play, and so there is a set of philosophical problems and a multiplicity of subsidiary questions—fragments of the main questions—that are brought about by the form of the text. For example: "To the egg I dedicate the Chinese nation.''

One could, like the man in the text, erase this sentence without interrupting the narrative. At the same time, the sentence carries a wealth of meaning. Tiny utterances, micromonads, a quantity of tiny eggs next to large eggs of meaning, are stated, making up a text constituted of an enormous cluster of larger and smaller eggs. One can pick up a thousand little details that organize a whole, for example, the story of machines. The text is like a picture, an enormous countryside full of elements, and in this gigantic textual machine, little machines figure as ornaments, although, in fact, they are not ornamental. Everything is integrated into a vast system of meaning. There is an egg that becomes, one day, chicken. Psychoanalysts talk of *Thewoman*. Lacan talks of *Thelanguage*. Here, we can distinguish the chicken from *Thechicken*. It is chicken only for some time. The egg is almost all the time *Theegg*, and only from time to time, grammatically, goes over to the side of an egg. We can speak of the shell of the egg, in knowing that it cannot be distinguished from the egg without being broken. I can put the egg in parentheses and replace it with the thing, the other. The structure of the relation between the egg and the chicken allows Clarice to work in a more immediately readable way than if she worked through a relation of mother-son, or mother-child. When, for example, when Clarice says; "The chicken does not know that she loves the egg,'' she shows in a more analyzable fashion something that would be obfuscated if she said: "The mother does not know that she loves the child.'' And when she says it, she does so positively. It is necessary not to know what one loves.

"The Egg and the Chicken'' is the passion according to the chicken. The author is in the same passionate state as in *The Passion according to G.H.*, in a journey undertaken in proximity to a vital experience. The difference between the passion according to G.H. and the passion according to the chicken is that the former progressed orthogonally, step by step, chapter by chapter. The trajectory went from self to cockroach. A space of perhaps three yards had to be covered. Three yards divided into a multiplicity of tiny movements of thought that are inscribed slowly, minutely in the text. The book has time to develop between the moment when Clarice opens the door to the room where she had first seen the cockroach and the final moment when something is happening between her and the insect. In "The Egg and the Chicken," something of the same is at work yet with a difference due to the object of contemplation, of meditation. Instead of the trajectory between self and an insect reaching back thousands of years in history to the originary cockroach, the text opens with the egg as always there, on the table, so that the position of the egg is such — as with all eternity — that the subject is not even an entering subject. In *The Passion according to G.H.*, one enters, one sees Clarice advance, open the door. In "The Egg and the Chicken", due to the function and the form of the egg, no such process is possible. Instead of the kind of slow mobility of *The Passion according to G.H.*, there is something of the order of gravitation. It gravitates and gravidates. Let the egg be! It engenders a text that is written in a system of phrases, a linking of phrases, which turn around this little essential object. It is not the same curve that is described here. Wide or narrow curves can be described with a big or a small pencil. Clarice does not proceed by chapters, according to an order of an infinitely multiple trajectory, but rather sentence by sentence, or by small packages of sentences. The reader falls into a kind of vertigo. The sentences are short. They are here one after the other, in a paratactical model, without coordination, without subordination. It is not the procedure of other texts, like *Agua viva*, where everything flows like water. Here we proceed by leaps, without coordination. For our minds so used to linking, the effect almost bothers our reading habits because we have a feeling that the logic is interrupted, which is not at all true. There is only a certain type of reasoning that is erased. This paratactic type of progress is like medieval reasoning. The effect is one of naïveté when we read: "I see the egg — the egg does not exist — the egg does not have a self — love for the egg cannot be felt either."

This progression, sentence by sentence, without coordination, produces effects of discovery. Each sentence discovers something, and from time to time, interventions occur. They are comic. One enters the sentences through formulas like "it is necessary," through something that resembles a recipe.

"It is necessary for the chicken not to know that she has an egg." This utterance is received like a law. It mimes a natural law by producing effects of necessity. One has the impression of being in a scientific universe, but that is not where it is happening. The text offers a rather homogeneous reading; it proceeds by addition. The reader makes a little supplementary progress. When this is not the case, another style intervenes with violence. The moment when the parataxis is interrupted, the text explodes. It marks the text. At that moment, the kind of slow, circular flight around the egg is interrupted. There is an exemplary sentence in the system of parataxis: "In time, the egg became an egg of the chicken." It constitutes a whole. Pause.

"It is not."

Annulment. The chicken is seen everyday so that it appears like a modern animal. But Clarice refers us to a pretemporal time that is that of genesis and of originary exchange. She works on double origin. It is true that it is the egg that finds the chicken.

To See the Egg: The Passion according to the Chicken

One of the ruses of the text is that of reality. One cannot distinguish before and after. As we find ourselves in the dilemma of seeing—and the text does not cheat in that respect—we are told immediately that one cannot see without being in the past. The text begins by positing the egg in eternity. Then we roll back into time. We are told what is in the first chapters in *The Passion according to G.H.* on seeing and more than seeing: I look at the egg, but do not have time to see it. The egg does not exist. From the moment one admits the impossibility of the present. One knows that all one sees, like the light coming from the star, is a thing seen. The paradox of writing is the following: how does one write in order to inscribe nontime? The challenge is going to produce this broken, slightly mad form. Clarice says that she looks at the egg in a single glance, and at the same time she does not see it. It is this necessary correction that is being made from one sentence to another and which gives us a bizarre feeling. The egg is permanently in eclipse. When it is being announced that one sees it, it is also being announced that one does not. Depending on the point of view, one has the feeling of a necessary contradiction, of an eclipse. It is the *fort-da* of the subject of the egg. The egg is presented and withdrawn, like all the subjects of the text. It refers to the question of the present.

This question is going to be relayed by another: what is the relationship between two subjects that are so strongly linked? The egg and the chicken are extreme subjects since there is no structure that links as tightly as that of the egg and the chicken. Yet this couple could be replaced by any other couple. It is so tight that it is on the verge of being erased. That is why the chicken does not know that the egg exists. This refers to a recommendation by Clarice. One should not know that the egg exists. If you look at people too closely, you no longer see them; the more you approach them, the less you see them. It can go all the way to the kiss, and then one does not see anything anymore; one is already at the first stage of incorporation. How does one embrace the egg without swallowing it? That is what the text does. It gets closer to the egg and the egg suddenly disappears; then it pulls away and the egg reappears. This is what can be called the movement of grace. If one looks at a thing too closely, it disappears; if one is too far, it also disappears until the moment when it reappears. There is a constant passage to the infinite, through proximity or distance. The infinite of proximity and the infinite of distance rejoin and are interchangeable.

The text begins with a morning. In order to signify that there is no time, we find ourselves, in the last sentence, at dawn. At the end we attain the beginning. One has made the full tour and starts up again. It is a *clin d'oeuf*, a wink of the egg. The very condition of love is being treated here. Love makes one live, but it is accompanied by the cruelty of reality. Love is "not having." One can love only on condition of not having what one loves. Clarice constantly speaks out against clichés, against received ideas. She is constantly on the side of spending.

The egg can and cannot be seen. Clarice deals with reflection and narcissism. She works on "denarcissizing," and the labor is simplified with a chicken. She does not need to make the trajectory of delegitimizing. She can go further because she already speaks from afar. She can say: "The chicken loves the egg. She does not know that the egg exists. If she knew that she has the chicken in herself, would she run away?"

Here is the question of love. The chicken loves the egg because it knows that it does not exist: "As for what came first, it was the egg that discovered the chicken. The chicken was not even summoned. The chicken is chosen spontaneously."

This is an aporia. It refers to who began, the egg or the chicken. It also refers to the question of light. And Clarice answers: it is the egg who found the chicken. It has to do with a certain choice and puts her in an active passivity. It is absolute maternity or eternal maternity. The chicken is an unspoken yes, a pure yes with feathers. It is at that moment that the egg finds her. One could almost say that the condition of the egg is the invisibility of the chicken. But it is also the inexistence of the egg, the fact that it cannot be perceived. The egg does not exist for the chicken because she lets it be. Clarice pushes this paradox to the point of saying that any kind of consciousness of the other entails an altering of the other. She says it only about the relationship of mother and child. But love between any two human beings is not situated outside possession either. Love begins with something in the order of appropriation. Love lasts while the other has not been appropriated. The problem is that the moment of appropriation is quite extended, and while the other is still outside, still to be appropriated, the figure is lovable. But the labor of love consists in leaving the other outside. It begins between two beings other than mother and child, with this kind of relationship that is perhaps easier to deal with than what takes place so violently between the protagonists in *The Apple in the Dark*. There is a struggle for or against appropriation simply because among those beings a contract like that which supposedly exists between mother and child does not exist: to let the other be is the ideal contract of detachment, which, in reality, hardly ever happens.

The difference between the two types of relations takes place at the level of detachment. Between mother and child there is detachment. The chicken has to lay her eggs. A relationship between two strangers begins with a movement of attachment, after which one has to look for detachment.

If one raises the questions of the moments of fracture in the text, one can see the first one where, suddenly, the question explodes: "And the chicken?"

It is all the more noticeable as, until now, in the juxtaposition of sentences, there were only categorical insertions until the chicken enters, called by the *a*'s. The chicken comes after the egg, although at the beginning, the two were mentioned together. Another breakage occurs when, suddenly, we hear: " 'Etc. etc. etc.' "

This breaks the rhythm of juxtaposition. It is a sentence in itself. It is mimetic. At many levels, it is a cackling sentence. At the same time, Clarice inscribes her own cackle. She cackles: and the rest, the rest, the rest. To say "etc." is a kind of paradoxical redundance. One does not cease to annul the things that remain. The remains are sufficient to themselves: "Suddenly I look at the egg in the kitchen."

Suddenly something happens at the level of the sign. At the same time, we can signal this paragraph, which is important in the story of substitutions and of relays in the text, by tracing a line between the paragraph that says:

"In itself, the chicken does not recognize the egg, but outside of herself, she does not recognize it either,"
and
"Suddenly I look at the egg in the kitchen and I see in it only food."

The same story begins again. Except in the place of the chicken there is I, and the circumstances are different. The consequences of not recognizing if it is a question of the chicken or the I are necessarily different. If the chicken does not recognize the egg, it remains suspended. If I do not recognize the egg, I eat it. There is an exchange between the chicken and Clarice that modifies the story. The chicken is not simple any more; it is accompanied by predicates, definitions, relative clauses. It remains suspended. The passage is magnificent at the level of mimeticism. The chicken refuses and at the same time we are refused by the text until it is set forth.

"The one who did not know that 'I' is only one of the words people form with their lips when answering the telephone, a mere attempt to find some more apt expression. The one who thought that 'I' means to possess a 'selfness.' The chickens who are likely to harm the egg are those who show themselves to be a relentless 'I'."

The chicken is not the denominator of this paragraph. It is an inventory of chickens. All the harmful chickens are those who have an 'I.' They are not simple chickens but "chickens who."

"In the kitchen I take one more egg . . . ": a moment of addition and withdrawal, a moment of violent apprehension ensues. As soon as one breaks the egg, the egg is no longer. It is a banal and metaphoric scene. If I take the other, I take from him shell and form. From that moment on, he has never existed. For him to exist: "It is absolutely necessary that I should be kept occupied and distracted."

I do not take it, so that he can be: "I am essentially one of those who renege. I belong to the freemasonry of those who have seen the egg once and then deny it as a means of ensuring its protection."

This is one of the keys of the text. It is the position of the ideal chicken that has to ignore the egg in order to save it. It is reminiscent of a moment in Heinrich von Kleist's *Die Verlobung in Santo Domingo* (Betrothal in Santo Domingo), where Gustavus is saved in the same mode a first, then a second, time by two successive fiancées who declare that they do not recognize him. What looks like reneging is the only way of saving him. This joins the dilemma about knowing and not knowing in *The Apple in the Dark*. Vitória trembles at the idea of being understood. If she were really understood, she would be lost for herself. Does that mean that one should not be understood? It depends on who understands. One can be understood without dying on condition that there remains enough incomprehension.

In Clarice's text a struggle occurs in favor of the chicken, but she says that the chicken is the tragedy. It is the chicken who incessantly disappears in this succession without succession. As soon as she starts to work on the chicken, she has to say: "I began speaking about the chicken, and for some considerable time I have said nothing about the chicken. I am still speaking about the egg."

Between the egg and the chicken an endless battle of love takes place. On the first page, there is the struggle between the words *ovo* (egg) and *ver* (to see). As in *The Passion according to G.H.*, one cannot see. The first sentence offers something of a deceit: "In the morning I see the egg on the kitchen table."

If I see the egg, I am God. The first sentence is impossible. It is oriented in the direction of the universal, of the universe. That is why I said that only God can see the egg. To see always means to distinguish something. If I do not "speak" the egg, I cannot see it, unless a story had started before, but then it would not be in the present. It is the only deceptive sentence, a bit arbitrary: "I see the egg" makes sense only at the end of the second paragraph when she says: "Like the world, the egg is obvious."

With this equivalence, the world as egg is the invisible evidence. We do not see the world. In Maurice Blanchot's *The Madness of the Day*, the mad person who is not mad says: "I see this day and outside it there is nothing."[3]

He who sees the world is either mad or God, but we do not see it. That is where the white space makes sense: "Egg, you are perfect. You are white." It is limited in its perfection. It can be said that the perfect, white egg is not even white. In our view, eggs are not perfectly white: they are fertilized or eaten. We do not know of any eggs with other destinies. An ideal egg is being described here. But it could give birth to something else, perhaps to the Chinese nation, or everything that can be reduced to one. There could be political allusions here, like *a*'s and *o*'s of Mao Tse-tung, since the text was written around the time of his ascendancy.

"To you I dedicate the beginning of time." The egg engenders the totality of stories and even before the stories: "Only machines see the egg."

This is a challenging expression. No human beings can see the egg, since those who see cannot see the egg. Then who can see it? Those who do not look at the egg because as soon as one looks, one no longer sees. In Kleist's *On the Marionette Theater*, we could see that only the absolute automaton or God or the bear without a conscience is gifted with grace. It is indifference. Perhaps a crane put the egg on the shoulder. As in *The Passion according to G.H.*, to look and to see touch infinitely, that is to say, seeing that one has a chance to see without knowing, the way one has a chance of loving while not loving. As soon as there is a conscience, something is interrupted. There is a subject and it is too much. This is perhaps why the egg puts itself on the shoulder where one does not see it. Clarice did not take the egg. It first alights on her shoulder. "The egg is a suspended thing. It never settles."

The sentence contradicts what she just said about the egg resting on her shoulder. Meaning surges from the conjunctions of the utterances. It can be heard only in an ongoing movement. No sentence exists without the other. No egg without a chicken. No sentence without another. No meaning without another. There was no time for contradiction to be posited. Mobility and sublation come about: "When it comes to rest, it is not the egg that has come to rest. It is something that remains beneath the egg."

It raises a philosophical question: If one thing is put on another, which one is above and which one is below? What is the order? If one puts the egg on a pillow, the pillow is deformed. The table is not deformed. What is more important, the egg or the pillow? What is active, passive? The egg on the pillow is the signifier and the signified. They cannot be separated. Where the table is deformed by the impact of the egg and becomes an inclined plane, "It transforms the table into a slanting plane." It did not place itself. Something put itself underneath the egg, and the intermediary is removed. The human intermediary, without whom the egg would not be placed, is also removed. True, the egg is always "a suspended thing."

That is where one sees that the egg is not an egg. It is a more than egg. There is a slippage until the egg becomes the day, the child, and, of course, the chicken.

The Good Law

I accompany the egg to another text, "Felicidade clandestina" (Secret happiness), which I did not want to introduce right away. If I do not give it right away, it is out of love. Not to give something right away is perhaps one of the definitions of love. The text works on the theme of "not giving right away." It is literally the core of what preoccupies me and what could be called the Ethics of the Garden of Secret Happiness.

Kafka said somewhere in his *Conversations* that we live in a period that is so possessed by demons that soon we will no longer be able to do anything good and just, except under the seal of secrecy, as if it were a question of illegality. I would like to surround this message with chicken feathers. Illegality could be secrecy, something clandestine. The passage could be translated by being spliced with "The Egg and the Chicken," as in the Kafkaesque passage about the agents. The passage, bearing Clarice's mark though the transposition, is Kafkaesque. Upon first reading, it is rather mysterious and unreadable. The page is truly clandestine. Its theme is quasi-illegal, follows another law, calls for another reading, has a quasi-illegal theme. If we arrive at this passage from our own notion of illegality, from the side of what Kierkegaard calls the general (i.e., classical) moral law, the passage remains closed. We must essay another path of another seeming illegality, of another legality, in order to arrive at this page. The law is ubiquitous. But it should not be forgotten that the vital message of Clarice and Kafka is that there are *two* laws. For Kierkegaard, what is called in general the "good law" is not good in the absolute. The other law, the rare and absolutely good law, is perhaps bad for the general. It is never a question of being an outlaw — for that does not mean anything — no more than of being an extraterrestrial. The question is raised by Clarice and by Kafka in different ways. Kafka is on the side of despair, of defeat. Kafka's vision, based on the reality of dissolution, of madness, and of bureaucratic alienation in Austria, is that a bad law will win in such a way that there will be only one law, the paternal, repressive, punitive law, since everything for him is happening in the sense of punishment, of castration. There is no felicity, no life, unless one burrows holes. For Clarice, there is felicity. It is situated in an immense, infinite space in which Kafka did not arrive. For Clarice, the good law exists. The without-law is not good. At the beginning of *The Passion according to G.H.*, Clarice insists on the necessity of cutting the meat into pieces, of regulating something, of assigning a limit to what is without limit. This new limit will not be repressive but aesthetic. It engenders form:

"A form gives contours to chaos, gives a construct to amorphous substance . . . the vision of an infinite flesh is a madman's vision, but if I cut that flesh into pieces and spread those pieces over days and famines . . . then it will no longer be perdition and madness: it will be humanized life again."[4]

In Clarice, we have a magnificent logic, that of a feminine libidinal economy, of an overabundance, directed toward a question rarely pondered, but always a feminine question about the unexpected drama of pleasure as excess. This joins what I said about happiness felt as threat. One can feel happiness as pleasurable submersion, or as excessively fragile, not because it is too small, but because it is too immense. One can have a vision or an imaginary structure that, as was the case of Freud in his open letter to Romain Rolland entitled "A Disturbance of Memory on the Acropolis," is closer to unhappiness than to happiness. Deep down, we often prefer being unhappy to being happy. Unhappiness puts us in a rather comfortable state. Happiness is work. It is never in the order of the "just barely enough," or of satisfaction. It is always of the order of "too much," which is at the same time "just right." It is somewhere between jubilation and satisfaction. So what do we do? I am not on the side of Kafka. When an interminable piece of meat is on a plate, one has good reason to be terrorized. Clarice says it well with her carnal metaphor: when one has too much to eat, what does one do? One begins to vomit or one is never hungry anymore or one works on the interminable meat. One has to do something unknown, give it form and be aware of the paradox, restructure one's relationship to poverty, to wealth. This can only be done with an invention of limits: "A form gives contours to chaos."

One has to put reins on a wild horse. The art of limiting oneself by a minimal law is quite difficult and delicate. That is where I join the idea of clandestinity, of secrecy, of going around the world starting from the other side. The question is: how does one keep happiness when there is not enough and when there is too much? There is a bible of this economy in *The Passion according to G.H.*:

> Oh, everything in me is aching to leave what was the world for me. Leaving is so harsh and aggressive an attitude that a person who opens her mouth to talk of leaving should be arrested and held incommunicado—I prefer to consider myself temporarily out of my own control rather than have the courage to think that all that is true (153).

Love as not having may be considered paradoxical, unexpected, since we would tend to believe that love is having.

In *The Passion according to G.H.*, each sentence is the continuation of the previous one. Beginnings are always in view and the reader has the desire to see where the logic comes from. But in "The Egg and the Chicken," because of the system of parataxis, juxtapositions form an affirmative system. Something of the meaning—and that is why it is a clandestine, secretive text—is really concealed from sentence to sentence. It is characteristic of this text, gives it its special form. One could even say that the text is performative because it is the story of the egg and the chicken: no egg without a chicken, no sentence without another sentence. A sentence depends on its other, not only on the sentence that accompanies the text, but on the hidden sentence. While working on the text, one can complete a number of sentences, render them more precise, add something that was there in transparence, in a kind of necessary and invisible way. For example, around the survival of the chicken, some sentences do not have meaning by themselves:

"And the chicken? The egg is the chicken's great sacrifice."

Or:

"The egg is the cross that the chicken carries through life. The egg is the chicken's unattainable dream. The chicken loves the egg. She does not know that the egg exists."

All these sentences are completely separated. The logic is not expressed; all articulations have been removed. It is a light, airy text, which requires a lot of work from the reader.

"Were she to know that she has an egg inside her, would she be saved? Were she to know that she has the egg inside her, would she lose her condition as a chicken?"

The chicken is defined as not knowing herself. If she knew, she would lose her state of chickenness. We are not on the side of sacrilege, but on the side of prohibition. She has recourse to white spaces. But a white space, once it is enunciated, is no longer all that white. That is why Clarice announces the theme of whiteness. Then, she prepares the work on whiteness through naming as white space. We could put this text side by side with Blanchot's *The Madness of the Day* where the unknown narrator says, "I see the day." That is impossible. One cannot see the light. If I see the day, I am in the space of a law called madness by doctors, lawyers, literary critics, and average readers.

Clarice attempts to speak, to say something in such a way that it would be confused with the thing. She reduces the gap between what is to be said and what is said, between the living and the saying of the living. The problematic condition of language is that while I speak of the egg, I forget the egg. I was speaking of the egg, and during that time there was "not egg." There was a "word of egg," a word "on egg," but no egg. What Clarice says is more complex: "Egg seen, egg lost."

There are people whom she will call agents, who are capable of avoiding this impossibility of speaking. To be able to say that the egg is white is simple and marvelous. Clarice chose to speak of the simplest and most living form: a word is always complicated, it has legs, feet, arms — she took the egg for object of meditation. She could have taken a pebble, a grain of sand, but she took the egg as a living geometric form. It is here to substitute, to disguise, and make pass what would be of the order of white speech, *le blanc-dire*, the perfect white space, a perfect speaking that would not betray but coincide. This evocation-creation is the dream of all poetry: that the forest be and it is! And on the side of poetry this is possible. Clarice hides under her text on the side where the impossible is possible. First, she herself does that of which she claims one dies. She puts herself among the destroyers of humankind. By saying that the egg is white, she destroys classical humankind, which obeys not only moral but also physical laws. "Egg for the moment will always be revolutionary."

Clarice works on the instant. The egg is a kind of materialized instant rendered visible. If we take the instant-egg, which is hardly to be perceived, it will always be revolutionary. "Revolutionary" is a humorous way of saying that it is ahead of our times. The egg will have made one more turn in relation to the period in which its story takes place. In the race between the look and the thing, a gap is opened because of the diachrony of language. Clarice says that the person who would call white what is white is a dangerous person both for herself and for others. "It cannot be called white."

It must not be called white in general terms, but absolutely. It must not be because: "The persons who call the egg white die for life."

They cannot remain in this world. This reminds the reader of the story of Abraham in Kierkegaard's *Fear and Trembling*. Abraham takes a leap from the general space into the absolute. He then believes the incredible in a general way. At the same time, he cannot say so, even to his wife, or else he falls back into the general sphere that judges attitudes like Abraham's. His difficulty is that of saying: I told God that I am going to sacrifice my son. I draw no conclusion. I expect nothing. I am in the instant of absolute obedience to God, without any calculation. I must believe that I am going to kill my son and at the same time I must believe absolutely that my son does not die. But I must not believe that my son will not die because then, I would betray God. His is an infinite double bind. He can only say yes. Abraham utters a silent yes. Any additional word would be like a blemish on the white egg. He saw the white, he spoke white. He becomes dangerous for humanity because he obeys an exemplary moral law. Therefore Abraham must be declared mad. He must be excluded, killed.

The general law in the sense of Kierkegaard allows society to survive. It says: If you want to continue living, begin by not speaking white, the absolute, but cover it with feathers, disguise it as a chicken. If you are a poet and are capable of speaking the truth, cover it with lies if you want to remain in this world where legality reigns. This passage works on illegality, on the limit. The right things can only be spoken in illegality. The people who are dying for life are the illegal people. Clarice is illegal. This entails the general opposition between disguise and nudity. Here, one sees the political quality of the situation. In *The Child and the Emperor*, only the child sees the emperor and finally says that he is naked. Clarice is the child. She says that one cannot speak without making the institution tremble. What is poignant is that it is an illegal, dangerous power of the poetic word. Philosophy does not have the advantage of the poet. Philosophy is legal. It carries on a discourse of justification, demonstration, knowing that it aims at illegality.

The story is taken up again at the other end of the text with the agents:

"Many advantages are given to all the agents so that the egg may take form. It is not a question of being jealous, because even some of the conditions, worse than those imposed on the others, are simply the ideal conditions for the egg."

There are cases of agents who commit suicide:

"They find the few instructions they have been given are insufficient, and feel a lack of support. There was the case of the agent who publicly revealed his identity because he could no longer tolerate not being understood, just as he could no longer tolerate not being respected by others; he died after being run over as he was leaving a restaurant."

That is the series of failed agents who wanted to see white but could not bear it. Or they realize that saying it is dangerous, for them as well as for society. They are examples of people who went mad, like the German romantics, Hölderlin, Kleist; or those who became wise but died, like Clarice and Kafka; or those who have seen the "incommunicable" and had to choose between staying in secrecy and clandestinity alone, or becoming keepers of the law, but without truth; or those who did not have Abraham's strength and committed suicide.

Clarice's egg is philosophical. It is an Orphic egg. It is the absolute egg but relativized, qualified. The chicken is not simply chicken; she is chicken even if she is unaware of it.

"From this exact moment on, never an egg did exist."

Eggs are breakable. It is a story of the disappearance of form. The time of the "has never existed" is a strange one. It erases the surface of time as if on the surface one had passed the hand, the way the foot went over the surface of the egg. Something has been totally erased. There is no negation of the egg through the breaking of its shell. It is on the other side. Clarice says that she must be careful not to break the egg: "I look at the egg in the kitchen with superficial attention in order not to break it. I take the greatest care not to understand it."

Here is the dilemma of the invisible egg, which is different from the edible egg, but the question is always: what to do in order not to break the egg. The remaining egg is visible and invisible, nonvisible because it is an egg in the instant but it can be seen by some. Not to break it is the condition of being able not to understand it, to let it be egg, to let it be free in space. When one takes an egg and breaks it, it is no longer an egg. The same happens when one says, "Egg seen, egg lost."

The egg must remain virgin, absolutely intact in order to be an egg. Even a broken egg is no longer an egg. Something is added to leave its surface intact. A superficial attention, which is also the most delicate, is needed. The egg remains only as superficial. The depth of the egg is something else. As soon as the egg has been touched violently, as soon as the shell has been broken by a look, it no longer exists. It disappears. That is why "it is absolutely indispensable that I be a person who is occupied and distracted."

Occupied to awake over the egg and at the same time distracted, the value of which is important in Clarice: when one is not distracted, one starts appropriating and it is all over. One has to be attentively superficial and distracted.

"I am indispensably one of those who renege." Here, problematically, Clarice shifts from the feminine to the masculine plural, to masonry. The text performs the reneging, which is going to be enunciated later when she says, "An egg has never existed."

It is a protection, but also a tomb. The egg has disappeared, has really been broken, and broken in such a way that it never did exist. It has been completely erased: "I am a part of the masonry of those who having seen an egg once renege it as a form of protection."

Even if I have seen the white egg, I will never say so, otherwise I would be in the position of Abelone in Rilke's *Notebooks of Malte Laurids Brigge*. The egg has to continue to exist in the silence that protects it. Masonry is explained through the agents: "We are of those who abstain from destroying and in that consume."

The tragedy of the agents is that of not speaking, and when they do choose to speak, they choose to be hit by a car. Through recognition one can neither tell the truth nor dissimulate. We are left with a passage that brings about a shift from the feminine to the masculine. Clarice speaks of herself in the feminine. As soon as she enters in the masonry, she switches to the masculine. This is a tragedy she does not describe because she accepts it. She finds her place, but the world of agents, initiated people, poets, is in the masculine. The question is not asked. The question of the mother is present; the tragedy of the chicken, admirable at the level of writing, is there. But the fact that she goes as a feminine individual into the masculine group is not something she analyzes like everything else. She theorizes everything, the look, madness, freedom, but not the question of femininity. She simply says, "And the chicken?"

But she does not say: "And the woman?" Is this a historical problem? At the time Clarice was writing, the question of woman was not asked. Does she repress it? In love, for her, there is equality of the sexes, almost an identity. One could say that a man capable of saving the chicken has feminine qualities. It seems to be a historical phenomenon. The passage goes by quickly and we find Clarice back in the kitchen. She is given back to the reader with her children. But for two entire pages, she had disappeared.

In *The Passion*, Clarice had worked as woman. In *The Apple in the Dark*, there is a classical narration, and in appearance she identifies herself in an astonishing way to a male protagonist. It is imaginary. What is even more passionate and terrible is the position she takes when she writes one of her last texts, *The Hour of the Star*, where she decides to tell the story of a woman. At that time she is absolutely compelled for mysterious and unknown reasons to use a male narrator-author. And that goes far. In order to speak of the little girl who is the heroine in *The Hour of the Star*, she needs a beard, though she shaves it. It is not only because the brotherhood of agents is massively masculine, but also because of a simple obedience to reality and its grammar. But it is also for reason of a certain rapport with the body and with woman that she cannot sustain as woman. She disguises herself at certain moments to speak the truth—not to protect the truth, but to protect herself from truth. It is touching and passionately interesting. There is a wound due to a historical period, almost a malediction on the body of Clarice, which is perhaps related to her precociousness, to the fact that she is a revolutionary egg. When she writes *Coração selvagem*, she is too much ahead of her time and to find someone else, she has to go beyond the limit of the sexes and go from the neuter to the masculine: "This is what they want to happen to me."

That is the story of the agents. The "they" are the world. It is the law, the general. *They* are those who do not want the truth to be spoken. It is another way of saying "one." It is the social or the general. They are the instances regulating conventions of lies, for example. She does not implicate herself in the agents who commit suicide. But she is one of those agents, threatened by these cases of agents. It is the juxtapositon of grammatical genres that raises the question. Otherwise, the agents of the story have all been almost exclusively men. It is a culturally undeniable fact. In a world where such a majority of men prevails, one finds the masculine plural. In these two pages, the agents begin to protect the eggs while until then, there was a direct rapport between egg and chicken that could have deceived us a little. This leads us back to:

"the chicken who did not want to sacrifice her life."

1982–83

Notes

1. Clarice Lispector, "O ovo e a galinha," in *A Legião Estrangeira* (Rio de Janeiro: Editôra de Autor, 1964). Translated by Giovanni Pontiero as "The Egg and the Chicken," in *Foreign Legion* (New York and London: Carcanet Press, 1986), 45–57. All quotations are from this translation.

2. "Escrevendo," in *Para não esquecer* (Rio de Janeiro: Editora Atica, 1979), 100. All translations mine.

3. Maurice Blanchot, *La folie du jour* (Paris: Fata Morgana, 1973). Translated by Lydia Davis as *The Madness of the Day* (Barrytown: Staten Hill Press, 1981), 6.

4. Clarice Lispector, *A paixão segundo G.H.* (Rio de Janeiro: Editôra do Autor, 1964). Translated by Ronald W. Sousa as *The Passion according to G.H.* (Minneapolis: University of Minnesota Press, 1988), 6.

Chapter 5
"Felicidade clandestina":
The Promise of Having What
One Will Have

In order to make a sketch of the landscape in which we are roaming about, I surround myself with elements from other countrysides. I will take a little text by Freud entitled "A Disturbance of Memory on the Acropolis: An Open Letter to Romain Rolland on the Occasion of his Seventieth Birthday."[1] We may wonder what the disturbance was all about. Freud narrates a series of memories that he examines with something that analytically goes very far, since it invokes a father-son relationship. It is upon the latter that psychoanalysis is founded, as *The Interpretation of Dreams*, Freud's first book (which begins with a magnificent introduction written under the sign of the father-son rivalry), shows. We can also find this at the other end of his life in "A Disturbance of Memory," except with this singular aspect of there being no disturbance, apart from memory itself. Memory regurgitates something the way Loch Ness regurgitates its monster. It is a masculine fairy tale, a novel in miniature, an extraordinary short story, a voyage into the unconscious triggered by a real and imaginary voyage. My lesson for this reading is: "Too good to be true." Freud in his beautiful Goethean German includes foreign expressions. Here in this text, addressed as an open letter to Romain Rolland, appears an expression in English. Freud also sends him, to give him pleasure, a few expressions in French: *déjà vu, fausse reconnaissance*, expressions borrowed from the analytical field. "Too good to be true" is in English. The expression exists in German. But Freud can only get at it in another language. The use of English leads him to meditate between the good and the beautiful.

I am working on the "I can't get over it! It's amazing!" in relation to something that has happened. Whatever one's experience of the Acropolis might be, Freud's is totally inscribed in the masculine. With his remark "too good to be true," I shall aim at a reading of "Felicidade clandestina" (Secret happiness).[2] Everything is in the title. I open a parenthesis that I would like to see fade away. It is clandestine, that is to say, secret. "Felicidade clandestina," if one lets the title float, can be a felicity hidden from the other. But the secret's very own is to be hidden from itself. The secret is secret for its carrier too. The true secret, one that is kept, is also one that is lost. It is without exteriority. It does not exist. When Clarice refers to "The Egg and the Chicken," the egg does not exist insofar as what could exist of the egg would exist only if one could have access to the inside of the egg, for example, by breaking it. It is only at the moment when the egg is broken that it begins to be an egg. But a broken egg is no longer an egg. I trace a path backward toward a problem of the value of silence. Silence is in a necessary relationship with the protection of the beautiful.

We work on a certain silence as equivalent of clandestinity but also as a different equivalent. That is why it is interesting to listen to "Felicidade clandestina." Perhaps there can be an equivalent or a secret that would be marked by libidinal differences. How one keeps a secret — a treasure, a paradise — may depend on one's libidinal economy.

For quite some time, I have been musing, using myself, amusing myself with — and I encourage you to listen to me with more than one ear — the problematic, almost tragic dimension of how to have, how to see (*comment avoir, à voir*) what one has. As soon as one has something, it becomes almost something of the order of not having. I work on erosion (*usure*). I use myself up on erosion. I am trying to wear down erosion (*user l'usure*). Erosion could be called habit. But that is not what it is. Do I aim at something that cannot be used? It could all be gathered under the theme of abuse. One can work on the abuse of the ear. Perhaps the ear drank it (*a bu*)? Is it possible to drink life and to keep it? In "Felicidade clandestina," it is a question of abuse.

All this could also be worked through on the mode of a movement of grace, of this perfect kind of balancing we have in Kleist's *On the Marionette Theater*. In order to have what one has, to keep a little bit of having, one has to make having move a little. One has to agitate it, disquiet it and, maybe, when Freud speaks in "A Disturbance of Memory," that is what he is talking about: we have to disquiet our memory a little bit, so that it gives us something, so that we can have what we have.

Read in flight, in survey, "Felicidade clandestina" reveals itself on first sight. Later on, other elements reveal themselves in addition. The movement in space of the text is seen right away, and so are its temporality and a whole semantic system. It is a double text. At first, one could say that it reads like another marvelous version of "Sunday, before falling asleep." But to come back to Freud's text once more, one could also say that there are similar elements in his and Clarice's texts. The story of school, for example, when a rapport holds between what one learns from books and from life. For Freud, it is as if what is printed in books were true. This raises the question of Freud's rapport with reality. Freud completely separates books from reality. Clarice does not separate them. In "Felicidade clandestina" the book is not referred back to the symbolic, as in Freud; bookish knowledge is not disincarnated. It is in direct rapport with orality. In Freud, the two areas are completely separate. To join what one learns at school with what one sees, for example, is impossible for him. In addition, for Freud there is a prohibition that comes from the relation with the father: So what I read in books does also exist in reality? How does one go from one to the other? The question of a passage is not even raised in "Felicidade clandestina."

Finally, what Freud keeps on saying is that he does not arrive at the Acropolis. He is there, but he does not arrive there. It is a confession of impotence. He analyzes it himself as something that is not happening to him. What does not happen to him is his own pleasure in himself, of where he is. He compares this extraordinary event to being back at the Acropolis, of being in the presence of something incredible that is and is not an apparition and that has its equivalent in the Loch Ness monster. The monster exists; there is pleasure, and we talk of the monster as a substitute of whatever we want. It is a penis story from one end to the other. It is so obvious, it is almost too simple. The details become quite succulent. In order to approach something, Freud has to take his immense detours of desire. When he wanted to go to Rome, it took him forty days; it took him forty-eight years to get to the Acropolis. One could say that it was absolutely accidental. He did everything not to get there. He decided to go to Corfu and not to Athens. All these immense detours, this formidable expenditure to get to a pleasure that will not take place, describe a masculine economy. Freud did get something from it, he drew a text from it. What came out was a little text.

Now, in "Felicidade clandestina," the mother of the little fat girl gives something to Clarice—not so that she will have, but so that she is led to desire. To desire, in general, is to be on the side of lack. Admirably, it is on the side of "more." She knows how to go on having in the middle of having, how not to have a closed, but an open, trembling kind of having. Because it still takes place in childhood, she shows the mechanism of nonpossession in possession. This allows her to keep something that is lost but can be, is, found again at every instant. And all this happens in the space of the promise of having what one will have. Clarice is exactly the opposite of Freud. "Felicidade clandestina" is the story of two little girls, a fat one and a thin one, Clarice. The fat girl promises to give the thin girl a book but keeps her waiting indefinitely, until the end, when the mother gives her the book. From the moment the little fat girl tells the little thin one: come, I will lend you this book—an admirable, biblical sentence—from that moment on, Clarice already has. She has the secret of desire, whereas, in general, desire is accompanied by a negative. She has what she desires. For her, desire has a positive power. The attempt of the little fat girl to castrate her may be interminable because she cannot be castrated. She can wait eternally without having the feeling of not having but always having the feeling that she will have. In this struggle between removal, retention, and the tremendous abundance of which the little girl Clarice disposes, she is always victorious. She will have, and this "she will have" in the future is a present. She conjugates her present in the future; she is mistress of a certain temporality. Time is what scans the text. Incessantly, the question of how much time is raised. It does not matter. The present is eternity.

This text is about a most refined practice of happiness. Clarice as the thin child gathers everything. She is already a grown person: "She is everything a person big or small could have the audacity to desire."

Freud, by contrast, invokes Napoleon! He does it on several occasions. Every time there is a question of libido, Napoleon appears. But he says to himself: if one can compare something small to something very big, Freud to Napoleon, then I find myself in the same situation as Napoleon with his crown. If it were "Felicidade clandestina," at the end of the crowning, we would have a crowning with the Twelfth Night cake.

In Clarice Lispector, a marvelous element of guessing oneself, of preceding oneself, always takes place. She says: everything I did not yet know, is under the appearance of a negation or of an anticipation, but it is already there. In fact, she was capable of discovering, while preceding herself, that she already had because she would have it, even if she never had it. The rhythm of this kind of possession without dispossession is extraordinary. Happiness being never but secret, in a certain way she is happy before being happy. She has before having. It is in this trembling movement, with this genius she has of having always known that to love (she says at length in "The Egg and the Chicken") is not to have in order to have. That is where the secret of a "feminine" pleasure is inscribed.

If, with Freud, one is under the sign of the father, one is never without a father in Clarice. He is present in an inaugural way in her text. But if Freud's text is made of father and brother, Clarice's text—and this is rare—is taken in a feminine space. Her admirable text can be a delight in our times where we know what we know of feminism. It is a text where all the tendencies, if we may say so, of the women's movement are gathered, including the little fat girl. Clarice is no saint. She writes in absolute nakedness of the relation to the other, without shame or lack of shame. She is going to tell us about the sadism of the little fat girl, but for sadism, sadism and a half. She writes of women as they are. Clarice is direct: "She was fat, short, covered with freckles, and with excessively frizzy, somewhat reddish hair."

To go from "Felicidade clandestina," which could be the name of a woman, of Clarice Lispector, to the little fat girl, shows the gap between what is desirable and what is less so.

A lot can be said about the presentation of the characters. All the differential terms in this text could be noted: two readings, two bodies, two temporalities, two types of pleasure and non-pleasure. There is a *fort-da* on both sides. The diabolic side of the little fat girl consists in making her spool of the thin one. She makes her come and go. She winds her around her spool. The little thin one can be at the place of the diabolically manipulated object, if she did not work herself her *fort-da*. She disengages herself from the rhythm that is imposed on her in the temporality of the other, while keeping the initiative at the level of the body. Before the ecstasy, a full development of the body in space begins at the moment when the antagonism is posited violently: "She told me to stop by her house the following day and that she would lend me [the book]."

Here begins the transformation into pure hope for pleasure: "I was not living, I was swimming slowly in a sweet sea whose waves carried me back and forth."

She is transformed into waiting. She is waiting to be born. Unspeakable pleasure exists. She already thwarts the thread of the spool and lets herself be submerged by something on the side of the mother that makes her completely happy. She appears passive. What she begins to know, but will find out only later, is what will become one of the themes in Clarice's maturity: happiness in hoping, happiness before happiness. That is the first movement of the body. The second one will come afterward.

"The following day I went to her house, literally running." What she does in her gait is played out through running, walking, leaping, a whole scale of drives connected to a fall that never takes place. Before the story turns to the open disadvantage of the little fat girl, it has already turned as, unbeknownst to herself, she has given to the little thin one what she never intended to give, and what, in fact, she even suppressed, by not giving the famous postcard with the landscape of Recife. Instead of this flat reproduction, the little fat girl gave the thin one the space of a city animated and populated. Through the promise of the book, she gave her the universe. She has given her all the streets that she did not give her with the postcard, and the little thin girl takes possession of the universe with all of her body. She also gave her time. For the little fat girl, time is hell. For the thin girl, it is the time of pleasure.

There is the stop before the door. The little thin girl never enters. It is a question of entering, of the closed book and the open book, or the going out of the house of the book. For movement, something else has to be noted. The story Clarice Lispector tells could be called a childhood memory. But it is much more than that. The memory is poured into a kind of narrative mode whose principal feature is scansion, suspension, articulation over time. The narrative is extremely faithful, and then, a moment arrives when it questions itself. It appears as a narrative at the moment when the story can no longer take place:

"How can one tell what followed?"

In this sentence, there is an impossible story, that which cannot be told. From that moment on, we are on the side of the "too good to be true" that is situated beyond words. There we join what had been said about "The Egg and The Chicken," Kafka and the story of Abraham in Kierkegaard: Something happened beyond what can be told. One crosses over to the impossible narrative:

"I think I didn't say anything."

We were waiting for the promise, for retention, for something that was not happening and that, at last, has happened in a certain mode. Now that the miracle has taken place, one of Clarice's sentences preserves the miracle, as a kind of positive negative:

"No, I didn't leave skipping as usual,"

and in the next paragraph:

" I didn't begin to read."

From the moment she has the book, another type of spacing is put into movement. This other kind of spacing preserves something living. It is not a way of holding on, in a masculine mode, whose most extreme example is Edgar Allan Poe (who kept his women buried). It is not on the side of burial but on the side of delicacy, of putting into proximity, of establishing a more refined and more delicate distance. There, one finds all the imperceptible physical, imaginary, and mental movements. The creation of the other space is not that of streets. It is as if now she created an immense but minute space that is going to open to an interminable pleasure of the book that, upon arriving at home, she begins by not beginning.

That is Clarice's way of starting her story. If one arrives at this stage at the end of a story, reading is to be questioned, redefined. What is reading? That is our question. Here she says, in other words, to read is to make love by taking care of the other. There is a marvelous little detail: "A few hours after I opened it, I closed it again. I went walking in the house, and I delayed even further by going to eat bread and butter."

The delay while eating bread and butter is in fact something of the extreme precision of her relation to alimentation. It is a question of eating from one end to the other of the story. She eats bread and butter, a ritual meal, a celebration but also a sign that she separates the different types of eating, of consuming. She distinguishes real from sublime food. She is not going to swallow the book that makes her hungry. She does not take the wrong object. It is a lesson of reading. To know how to read is to take infinite time to read; it is not to take the book for a little geometric object, but for an immense itinerary. It is knowing how to scan, to pace, how to proceed very slowly. To know how to read a book is a way of life. One reads while eating bread and butter, while walking, while opening and closing with the book the whole space of a lifetime. At the beginning, in the play of desire, something enormous takes place that will be discovered in the text. It is the very nature of the object of desire. Not the nature of the book but the situation in the world of property. Her book comes from the father. It is not hers. Something of the gift is in suspense and refers to a very absent father. The trajectory consists in going to the place of the promise, on a path toward paradise, which is the opposite of what we learn in school where we are taught that we lose and leave paradise. What she does is to go toward paradise. This paradise is inhabited by the devil. But hell opens onto paradise. It is an active paradise because nothing can make the little thin girl lose it for reasons that are written in the text. The story of who inscribes or who writes touches upon what was in "The Egg and the Chicken." There is an intense contradiction between what is said all the time: speaking about the egg, I forgot it, but from such speaking there emanates a silence that sustains life. Rimbaud's silence, for example, will keep what is most beautiful. Silence is interrupted in Rimbaud's poem "Bruxelles":

Let us keep silent.[3]

Period. Then another stanza that does not keep silence ends on silence. How does one keep silence without losing silence? One is constantly before the aporia of writing and silence, before the fact that to keep is to lose. One has to agitate it constantly in order to make something tremble, bring it back to life, so that it does not end up as loss. Finally, writing betrays something, says something that cannot be said or should not be said, as in "The Egg and The Chicken." Without this betrayal nothing of this "thing" would exist or appear. It is a necessary, happy, painful betrayal that Rimbaud would express thus: "It is too beautiful, it is too beautiful. But it is necessary," with all the ambiguity of this type of syntax. Perhaps what is necessary is the contrary of the "too beautiful." Perhaps the necessary is synonymous with the "too beautiful." The too much is necessary.

"Felicidade clandestina," works on time. Clarice's preoccupation is similar to mine: how can one, after possession, still be before possession? At the level of the body, this was inscribed by the comings and goings, by the movements of the little girl who was going to the house of the little fat girl.

When she says: "The following day I went to her house literally running," one can see, by transparence, the story of the law, with all the architecture of the place with doors, windows, with the possibility of going in, of not going in. This calls for a double reading: "She didn't ask me to come in," could seem repressive. Underneath the prohibition of the little fat girl who diabolically marks her blows, a factual prohibition occurs. The "do not come in" already belongs to an economy of keeping, of holding, but of the good keeping, in the sense of protection of the place, not of the avaricious conservation. The little thin girl arrives running. She leaves open mouthed, first slowly, then she accelerates: "This time, I didn't even fall."

The theme of the fall in this text is related to the paradise ahead. She falls out of hell without falling. It is upon leaving paradise that one is supposed to fall.

Here, to the contrary, paradise is outside, in the streets. She starts again. Hope, the promise of the book, take on biblical overtones: "The promise of the book was guiding me. The next day would come, the following days would later be my entire life . . . ." She works in the present, but the days that follow are now. Future is present, present exists insofar as it is full of future, but a future now:

"The love for the world was waiting for me, I went skipping through the streets as always and I did not fall a single time."

She exits from hell, "but it didn't simply stay at that." She goes back to hell, back to paradise. This is indicated very lightly by "diabolical."

"The following day I was there, at the door of her house with a smile and a pounding heart."

Opposition is evident at the level of the body. Her heart is working incessantly while the other one stays calm:

"In order to hear the calm answer"

which joins the theme of fixation,

"that the book was not yet in her power"

as a matter of speaking:

"and that I should come back the following day."

Adds Clarice: "And thus it continued. How long? I do not know."

The little fat girl's incessant work is undermined by the thin girl. In this combat between the two, one is tortured by the other. It seems that the evil in the little fat girl could, from spending itself, exhaust itself:

"I had already started to guess that she had chosen me so I would suffer, sometimes I guess. But, even while guessing, sometimes, I accept: as if whoever wants to make me suffer infernally needs me to suffer."

This goes beyond the story with the little girl. Something redeeming is on the side of Clarice. The sadism of the little fat one is undone. Clarice escapes it completely, since she accepts suffering also as having its reason for being and its efficacy.

Movement continues until the end. But the narrative stops. Something else continues — not of the order of narrative — that has almost the end of a fairy tale. It stops when life continues, when something more than the story has taken over. The narrative functions only as repetition of something that can be told and that has an end. Once the narration is over, either nothing remains or one has to link with the continuous, the eternally infinite living.

Now we go on the other side. The place is not the house of the little fat one but that of the thin one. At that moment displacements of all kinds take place. Time has changed its nature: now a time of having, no longer of hope is instaured. And in place of hope, there is going to be creation of the secrecy of having, of having that is going to be in a relation with the world so that a kind of discontinuity in continuity will ensue, linking the book with all kinds of vital activities that project its infinity. The time for reading is a time of living, which largely exceeds the book as volume, as the closed book. It is the open-closed-open book, the palpitation of the book. This kind of deferred movement is inscribed very lightly in the last microscene:

"Sometimes, I sat in the hammock, swinging with the open book on my lap . . ."

At the moment where one could expect a final immobility — and the book has to be open — movement radiates erotically through this kind of marvelous balancing of the hammock, which comes in place of what I would call the trembling, when she says: " . . . without touching it, in purest ecstasy." She sits without touching it, but the book touches her. Her hands, her movement of prehension are suspended. But there is proximity, a slight brushing, and a caress. The book is on her knees. She does not take it. It is given to her.

This story could be a double of "Sunday, before falling asleep." There, we have a loss of clandestinity. But something goes toward its accomplishment, toward a summit, toward the "top of the world." Here there is a summit that recurs, *cima* (summit). Its exact function can be found in the sentence:

"It was a big book . . . "

and

" . . . completely above [*acima de*] my means."

The book remains, a bit above, a bit beyond. It is beyond her financial means, her vital means; therefore it can never be exhausted.

The "too good to be true" is an exclamation of reception that can mark anguish before something that happens unexpectedly. Now I wanted to work on the unexpected, the unhoped for (*inespéré*), on how surprising that can be. Clarice was transformed into hope. There is hope, but in the process, which constantly takes her before the house where nothing happens, hope ends up becoming pure hope. The feat of strength of the little thin girl is that with time, with the repetition of her tests, what she counted on disappeared to the point of becoming an object indefinitely hoped for. In place of a precise hope, there is going to be an interminable patience. It is pure hope that the little fat girl gave to the little thin girl, without having done it on purpose. At the limit, one could say that — as with Kafka's man from the country, although on another mode — she would wait all her life and she would be capable of it.

The "too good to be true" was brought about in "Felicidade clandestina" through the mother who marks the unexpected arrival. It is not as clear in this story as it is in "The Egg and the Chicken." The *inespéré*, the unexpected, can happen only on condition of not being expected. That is why I spoke of pure hope, of an open hope that would give its chance to what could happen. This hope is like an open window. It is expressed better in "The Egg and the Chicken," since the egg can arrive only when she stops waiting for it, when she has forgotten that it can happen. I can almost interchange what is unexpected with what is undesired, which does not mean undesirable. The "too good" is not the realization of a desire. It is only in the aftereffect that it leads one to discover something that could have been desired, but everything takes place beyond a locus of desire. It is not the realization of a desire that is shown in "Felicidade clandestina." When desire has the generosity of the little thin girl, it is already satisfaction; it is already realized. It is a desire that gives her the world, the movement, what she will or will not have. In this type of economy, one already has what one desires. And also—but this is not what happens in "Felicidade clandestina,"—one has what the other wants, desires, to give us. I say this away from an economy of lack.

It is "too good but necessary." This disquieting note is perhaps in relation with the uncertainty about the origin of the gift. In Freud's story, when he says, It is too good for me because I am but the father's son, this is not necessarily what Rimbaud says:

It is too good . . . but necessary.

It comes in place of an impossibility of rendering grace, which is inscribed in "it is necessary." It is an immense gift. To whom can one give, render, grace? Whom can one thank? It is one of the questions Clarice often raises; it is a question Rimbaud raises. What troubles the person exclaiming this is that the gift comes from no one. It is not Abraham who will tell God that it is too good; that would be an insult. It is atheological, a matter of to whom to render, whom to thank, and if the gift is from no one, it becomes magic. One may have the feeling that the gift disappears the way it appeared. All of Clarice's text is a way of saying "thank you" to nobody, or to life; it is a way of recognizing a gift so that it does not disappear or become erased. She thanks the thing itself.

What now needs to be articulated are feminine secret happiness and masculine secret happiness, that is to say, Clarice's "Felicidade clandestina" and Freud's, "A Disturbance of Memory on the Acropolis." I am going to concentrate on the analyses of certain economies. I will redefine some possible approaches of reading, since my project deals with problems of reading.

I am going to be more specific: we have to pause once more on "Felicidade clandestina" which is for us a spring, or an egg. The object of love or desire—since that is what matters in this text—is a book, and not just any book. What I like, and one cannot not see this essential detail, is that it is a big book. One could talk of the question of size, of the big book. But I want to go back to our different economies of pleasure once more. Besides, in "Felicidade clandestina," there is also a story of an economy. It is the elaboration of an economy that spans, from the first age to the adult age, the variation of an economy that could be defined, for example, as a feminine economy. Clarice elaborates the changes of this economy, not only in relation to different economies—masculine and feminine—but inside the very economy said to be feminine. She traces the unfolding, the span of the possibilities of this economy and in particular its imaginary treasure that allows it to be displaced. She elaborates on the possibility of this economy to be moved onto several planes at once and to go—especially through waiting—from something immediate to something mediate, to, I am going to say, not the genital stage but the sublime stage. In order to turn around a sublime economy, I have to make the distinction between a masculine and a feminine sublime economy. In *Economimesis* (a continuation of *Parergon*), in a reading of Kant's aesthetics, Jacques Derrida makes an analysis of the masculine sublime economy. The latter does not offer itself as such. It considers itself as a total reading, as an analysis of the sublime in equal terms, without difference. I see in it a difference I situate in the movement of sublimation. The movement is double, made of attraction and repulsion. It would join what I said earlier: How can one have what one has? How does one shake up having? One could speak of a quivering, of an agitation, which makes it such that in a gesture of having there is nonhaving. But as I say, this movement, in fact, leads to all sorts of differences. It tips the balance, depending on the analyses, on the point of insertion, on what produces movement, to the side of a libidinal masculinity or femininity. In the feeling of the sublime that can be read in Kant's sublimely beautiful passage remarked by Derrida, in this kind of trajectory, this kind of genealogy of masculine pleasure, a state of mind can be seen. The sublime, as a category emerging from the eighteenth century, has completely overtaken literature and the arts in general. There are paintings of the sublime, writing of the sublime. The sublime was figured in literary and plastic representations by natural elements, by high mountains, gorges. It is analyzed as attracting and repulsing. The mind is both attracted by its object and repulsed. The insistence is even on repulsion. There is a cut, an interruption of pleasure that is completely readable in the texts by Kant taken up by Derrida. Derrida marks the identity of the analogy between the corporeal schema and ejaculation: inhibition and effusion, or discharge. The form that is being articulated is that of a masculine pleasure. It is determined by a resistance to castration. This leads to a "negative pleasure." It engenders all the reflections on negative pleasure to the point of being built over masochism. It is a masculine position. This negative pleasure can be drawn inside of something that is precisely not cut, which would be inscribed in a continuous mode of feminine pleasure, where there are negative moments that never have the time to be negative, that are carried on in incessant resurgence. Here we find that the metaphor we have in "Felicidade clandestina" is one of swinging. It is the same as in Kleist's *Marionette Theater*, where there is a moment in the curve that this movement describes, a zero moment where one passes, but without stopping. There is passage through zero or the infinite, but without cuts, without any stopping.

What is admirable in "Felicidade clandestina" is its composition of two great periods that correspond to two great moments of the story: the first moment occurs when she does not have the book, whence the whole question of having pleasure is in not yet. The second time is when she has the book. At that moment,

she does not simply have it, she *still* has it. To have something still, by means of
having it, is very strong. To come back to my variation on having, Clarice does
not answer theoretically but practically. It is truly a lesson in having what one
has, in a most mobile kind of having. It goes back — and I go around the world
and come back to the Acropolis — to the story of Freud's trouble of memory. In
"Felicidade clandestina," because it is a violent text and not one of simple pleasure, something is insinuated that one must recognize in passing. It is also a text
of struggle, of hatred. Between the two little girls there is this tacit drama with all
the commentary brought to it by Clarice. One of the most striking passages is the
little paragraph in the middle of the page on acceptance of suffering. For reasons
she explicates afterward, the little girl accepts being tormented. This instant in
the text, an aside that opens onto another dilemma, is crucial. Something very
important is situated here: the price of pleasure. To have pleasure and to suffer
always go together. It is also the question of the Acropolis, the question of the
price of pleasure that articulates the two texts. Who pays whom? The definition
of the debt is invoked in both texts, but the answers are very different. But one
always pays a price.

Now in Freud's Acropolis such a place is highly analytic. There the unconscious is going to unfold. We go there only thinking that we are awake, as Kafka
would say, but really profoundly asleep. One sleepwalks in these places and begins to act in one's own story, in one's own text. When we read Freud's letter to
Romain Rolland, much can be said about the "genre" of the text. But I would
rather work on its excess, and not on the problem of genre. Had I been more
disinterested, I would have made something of its atmosphere. It is a melancholy
text, on the side of mourning, a text signed in advance by a man "who has
known better days." These better days are not better days; they are days that
never were, that never took place. The true story of Freud, of his passion, of his
love, goes through this little text. What one sees is something awful, of the order
of not being able to get there, of the order of not being able to arrive, of the event
that did not arrive, or even of the event as not arriving. This is brought about by
Freud's narcissism, which can be read elsewhere. He gives, allows himself this
narcissism when it is too late. When Napoleon was retired to his island, he was
able to say: I was Napoleon. As Napoleon, he did not dare to say it. From the
moment when Freud says in the opening of his letter, I am an old impoverished
man, we can ask how do we understand that? Because we read the letter after it
has become cold. But in reading this letter at the time, Romain Rolland must have
thought strange things. How can the great Freud say this? It sounds incredibly
bitter. It is from complete loss that he can assert a gigantic will to pleasure that
had been decapitated on the Acropolis through the imaginary appearance of his
father. The presence of the brother summarizes the general relation of Freud to
his little brothers, his disciples. There has always been an incorporated brother.
All along the text, one feels an uneasiness because of it. There is an atmosphere

of bourgeois comedy. The two brothers do not talk to each other, but they communicate in permanence through telepathy. The episode of the Acropolis is the moment when Freud invented the interpretation of dreams. He had a phantasm of celebration with the history of the plate that would be affixed in a Viennese street and that would read: Here Freud interpreted his first dream. It is the moment of absolute triumph, and at the same time a triumph he cannot completely enjoy. It is related to the questions: Whom does one have to pay for one's pleasure? Who lays down the law of pleasure? Freud's text of the Acropolis constantly says that to have pleasure is prohibited. Now others, like Balzac, tell a story with great pleasure about nonpleasure. Freud does not have pleasure in telling his story, which is sad from one end to the other. Quite different from "Felicidade clandestina," the waiting is not joyous but morose. At one point, there is this lovely sentence by Napoleon to his brother during the coronation:

"What would *Monsieur notre Père* have said to this, if he could have been here to-day?" (247).

And:

"I might that day on the Acropolis have said to my brother . . . " (247.)

But I did not. All this refers incessantly to, Do you remember our youth? One sees that since he did not pay, his ticket included, he does not have pleasure. He lacks a giving instance, in this case a father, who would have given him what he has. Had the father been there, things would have happened to him and he would have been the beneficiary. But all is locked in silence. It is a great struggle against the father. Freud's interpretation is: I exceeded the father, so I feel guilty. It is an Oedipal story but also more than that. We never do anything that is not, in fact, dedicated to the person who pushed us to go that far. And even further than the father. This is not true. It is from an erased "from there" that he went. By erasing the origin he also erases the arrival. Freud says that for several years, it has come back to him continually. One can say that a man who evaluates his life in such a terrifying manner is seeing its summit. At forty-eight, he sees himself in the middle of life. He is not in a forest like Dante, who must go through something marvelous that is the mother. He is at the summit, in the place of the father, and furthermore, he negates it. It is not dialectical, and nothing advances. In Freud, everything fixes itself; there is an arrest. If reality is "strange," one could ask if there *is* a reality and if so, where it is situated. We could explicate the atmosphere of the text through Freud's own situation. It is a tragic moment, the moment of Hitler's accession to power, when Freud does not know what is going to become of himself. He is incredibly sick. But the mechanism says that there is no recognition of debt, and to take up again the story of destination, from the moment when Freud cannot name the origin, he cannot arrive at the other end either. Pleasure does not fall from the sky. It comes from somewhere. Recognition is not necessarily legitimation. It is something that can be completely positive, of the order of transmission. One can transmit only what one received. To whom does one have to pay the right to have pleasure? Here, it would have been to the father, but the father was absent, covered by silence.

If we come back to the side of "Felicidade clandestina," there was already a response. Clarice's position is extremely forceful. What is striking is not only that she recognizes a debt and accepts paying on the side of women, but that, in addition, her position is exceptional. It can be seen already in *Coração selvagem*: Clarice's position is one of innocence. Someone like Freud says constantly: I felt guilty, hence explanation by the superego and work on the "too good." I did not deserve it. I am not worthy of it. Freud cannot accept it, even in humility. He reacts by saying: "It is too good to be true." It is a way of rejecting onto reality his own problem of narcissistic evaluation. If he could have said to himself: Yes, I am Napoleon, he could have had pleasure. But the mechanism of narcissistic defense is created. Maybe inside me something is lived as Napoleon. But I do not dare to say it publicly. That would be pride. On the side of Clarice, one can imagine something that is situated right away beyond pride and joins extreme humility. "Felicidade clandestina" is a text of infinite pride. It is a passage to the infinite, but one falls back on the side of humility. I read from the short paragraph I quoted a while ago, about the way we are given to read the narcissistic opposition between the two little girls. Clarice Lispector is not embarrassed. She is not ashamed of her self-portrait. She is not on the side of modesty. She simply has *le beau rôle*. We can recall the passage from *Coraçao selvagem* where she places herself in innocence when she steals a book. She is surprised by her horrified aunt, who says to her: What did you do? And Clarice answers: Yes, I took the book. And she adds that if she considered that it was bad, she would be on the side of evil, of guilt. But she followed her desire. She does not forgive herself; she situates herself in the legitimate right, in innocence. Her right is not legitimated by a social tribunal.

Freud and Clarice are at opposites. In Freud's text, the mother comes back as a kind of Loch Ness monster, a dead, omnipotent, penal mother. Psychoanalysis is filled with penal mothers. She comes back again at the end, as the sea, this time much more peaceful. Freud has to vanquish the mother. It is almost the opposite of Clarice's position. The theme of "I can't get over it! It's amazing!" can have a positive or a negative value. True, Freud *n'en revient pas*, in the double sense of not coming back from it and not being able to get over it, for the good reason that he never arrived there in the first place. Clarice does not come back because she goes in order not to come back again. She keeps the astonishment as a flame and not as something negated, repressed, or kept silent, underground.

In "Felicidade clandestina," something is exchanged that is an equivalent of life itself. The something happens to be a book, and in the space of this text, the field from which the inscription of the book emerges, goes with food, with nourishment. At the same time, the story of the becoming of the book starts with a desired book that, at the end, as in a fairy tale, leaves its place and joins the lover.

But we are still at the stage of the piece of candy. The adversary economies of the two girls had been rendered in a detail in the first paragraph:

"As if this weren't enough, (the little fat girl) filled the two pockets of her blouse, above the chest, with candy."

If we worked as closely as possible to the body, we would see that, as when one is little and one does not have breasts one puts handkerchiefs in their place, the little fat girl fills the space with candy. What does this mean at the level of absorption and consumption? What is this little fat girl going to do? Is she going to eat herself? Her own breasts? If we follow the trajectory of the body, much can be said about the bodily localization of this text. We leave from the bosom. The differentiation is not made at the sexual level, of who has and who does not have; rather, it is going to reverse itself into what a certain type of having that "does not know how to have what it has," means. The little fat one has books that she perverts because she does not read them.

"I continued to implore her to lend me books that she was not reading."

As locus of inscription of desire in the text, the breast comes back incessantly as with the motif of the beating heart, and in the scene during which the book is given to the little girl:

"How can one tell what followed? I was dazed, and that is how I received the book in my hand. I kept the book with both hands, pressing it against my chest."

All is happening in this space, inside, outside, a supplement of chest, between the heart, the breast, and with the book that is subject to transformation. She compresses the book as if it were an outside heart, or a child. There is going to be a slight displacement until she has the book like a lover on her knees.

I will take up again the question of book-nourishment. The book is in a relation of exchange, of substitution with good nourishment. And here we have a classical problem, something that we feel when we read passionately, and that has to do with poetic nourishment. What distinguishes poetic nourishment from the other is that it is sublime, that in a certain way it ought to be inexhaustible. It cannot be that. Something is playing on inexhaustible, hence on pleasure. The quality of pleasure that arrives from the object "book" is the mystery of reading. First of all, not everybody takes pleasure in reading. The drama of the little fat girl is that she does not take pleasure in reading. Something of a certain type of pleasure is not accessible to her. Maybe it has to do with the fact that she does not have access to pure pleasure, to free pleasure, to what one would call aesthetic pleasure, which can be communicated but not exchanged or commercialized. That is the the essence of art. It is its freedom in relation to use value or exchange value. One could go very far in the analysis of the relations of power between the two little girls. They do not have the same desire; they do not dispute an object, but one keeps back what the other one wants. One is outside of exchange, the other is in an economy of "more." There is a kind of negative pleasure of the little fat girl because she has pleasure as long as she still has in her possession the object of desire of the other. There is some sadism, and also the fact that it is her own sad pleasure that is displaced. Instead of the pleasure of reading, she takes pleasure in deceiving the other. She is a little fat girl, overfed and underfed. The text is unpleasant and ferocious, cruelly realistic: "the calm ferocity of her sadism."

There is evident sadism, but there is something else that is not evident but very active in the text: the tall thin girl with her inexhaustive capacity of letting herself be tortured, breaks the economy of sadism. It can be imagined that, in fact, the little fat girl does not succeed in making the other suffer. This can be interminable. One wonders what would have happened if the mother had not arrived. In the hard-wearing, everlasting thin girl, an inexhaustible force of resistance to castration is located where there would be only martyrdom for those caught in the space of castration:

"I did not even notice the humiliations to which she subjected me."

It is only in the after effect of adulthood that it is called humiliation. In childhood, there was nothing.

I come back to the paragraph:

"How can one tell what followed?"

It is a turning point, the main break in the text. Just before, we had:

"That is all a big or a small person can have the audacity of wanting."

She has had everything. She has everything. More than everything. Because the mother has more than given:

"You can keep the book as long as you want."

There is a complete adequation with her desire, only so long as her desire will last. "Keep it" is the absolute realization. The story is over. Once over, what is there to be told? She has everything. Now, the second story begins, from an enormous interruption. We do not know if what followed was told or not. It raises the question about the impossibility of narration, the impossibility of telling something that belongs to what is nonnarratable, nonrecitable. By definition, the narration picks up, repeats what can be repeated. Here, something happens of the order of the nonrepeatable. It is a unique event. It is no more repeatable than the story of Abraham. It is totally noncommunicable because it happens only once. How to tell also raises the question of narration, of who does the telling. The fading, transformation, and evaporation of the narrating subject are put forth in this sentence. Who would tell? Where is she, she who would tell? She says it:

"I was dazed."

She is in another transitory state. There is no more subject, no more words. There is no more time. At the same time, I know nothing. There is a passage to another economy that does away with *não*, with no. In Portuguese, there are two consecutive negations:

"Não, não saí . . . [No, I didn't leave . . .]."

How is this sentence written? To whom does she address herself? We go through a negation that is not negative. Something begins to take a distance from the first economy, which can lead to a positive economy of sublimation only by repulsing, by pushing aside, by sending back to the past, to her first economy. Everything she once did she no longer does:

"No, I didn't leave skipping as usual."

" . . . I didn't begin to read."

"I pretended I didn't have it."

This could be compared to a dialectical movement through elimination of the first term, or to a moment of birth. She does it to extricate herself from one economy in order to go over to another. It is the moment of passage that marks this paragraph:

"I was dazed, and that's how I received the book in my hand."

She receives it in a state of astonishment, of absence:

"I think I didn't say anything."

"I did not say anything" would be affirmative, but she is absent; she is not even a witness of what is happening: "I think."

"I took the book."

That, yes, that is the thing that remains. The rhythm has changed. We are in another world. After the agitated comings and goings around the book, another movement, quantitatively and rhythmically different, begins:

"I left *very* slowly."

Then, there is this moment:

"I know I held the big book with both hands, compressing it against my chest."

And the whole world disappeared. Only the child remains, forming a body with what is no longer a simple book. One does not know very well what this is going to be. Little by little, it is being sketched for us. But for the time being, it is pure object of love, since the first thing the girl proceeds to do is not to read it.

Something marvelous comes at the end of the text in relation to clandestinity. She never lies:

"I created the falsest difficulties for that secret thing that was happiness."

To create difficulties, in spite of everything, is a gesture of creation. One could believe that it is a type of behavior that could be classified as masochism, but not at all. We notice that it is taken in the space of maintenance. What is put in place is a whole maneuver to protect the book. And then, we notice "false difficulties." The first part of this story presents the real difficulties. Once the real difficulties have disappeared, they have to be replaced by false difficulties, which play the same part. One could think that it is too classical, a kind of deferred negative, a not wanting to have pleasure. But not at all. It is an extraordinarily forceful leap from a passive waiting to an active waiting. The little girl goes on waiting for what she already has. To narrate the active waiting is much more difficult than to narrate a passive waiting. It is easier to narrate the search than the actual finding. This is also related to the fact that the position of narration is always a position of distance, at the limit of exclusion. When the gap is infinitesimal, when there is a movement toward cohesion, there is no more space for narration. What can come in place of what made up the movement of narration, the empty space between subject and object, would be something completely different. It would be what Clarice describes here, as another type of consumption. It could be another form of echo of reality. It could be musical. She has the book on her knees. A bodily relation is immediately established. This also tells us that the book has always been more than book. It is the essence of the true book to be more than book.

"And thus, it continued. How long? I don't know. She knew that it was an indefinite time until the venom had flowed entirely along her fat body. I had already started to guess that she had chosen me so that I would suffer, sometimes I guess. But, even while guessing, sometimes I accept: as if whoever wants to make me suffer has an infernal need for my suffering.''

This is unheard of. If she is like that, we have to believe that she belongs to the order of sanctity. It is a story of selection. At the beginning, there is an indistinct ''us,'' and little by little, two protagonists are detached from it. The little fat girl chose the thin one because she is the one who has the greatest capacity for having pleasure, while she herself has the least. That makes her suffer. The little fat one knows the value of pleasure. Being someone who knows, who feels the riches from which she is barred, she belongs to the race of the damned; she is in hell. That is what is being guessed on the other side. The tall thin girl guesses this need of the other, which consists in exhausting hell, in going so far in sadism and nastiness that she would have a chance to exhaust what is figured under the name of venom. One has to say that at that moment, little Clarice has an incredible capacity for compassion. She is no fool. But she does not attribute it to anything but hell, the hellish need of the other. So she does not defend herself. She says:

"Even while guessing, sometimes I accept.''

Her hypothesis is that she can offer it to herself. That is what the little fat girl also thinks: she can pay the other because she can pay it to herself. She has the secret of inexhaustible pleasure and of inexhaustible suffering, since it amounts to the same thing. She has a greater strength than the fat girl. The same source is at times on the side of suffering, at times on the side of pleasure. The extraordinary thing in this paragraph is that suffering does not wear her down. She is going to suffer immensely, but in relation to the immense feeling of pleasure of which she is capable. Any suffering is but the traversal of something that is, in fact, the suffering of the other, until she comes back to her own pleasure. This is why she is going to pay "to herself.'' While doing this, she accepts paying for the other because she has won in advance. She is never in hell. She may be afraid of hell, but she is in the difficulty of those who are endowed with paradise. She lives an immense force that nothing cuts, interrupts. She is in the world of happiness, in the world of pleasure. She never leaves it, and suffering for her comes from the other. It will never be a destructive suffering. I would even say that this is why she is so cruel. Hers is a neat cruelty because she has no resentment for the other. In this kind of laying bare (*dépouillement*) to which she accedes, she accepts. She does not answer, but she accepts. And when I say that she has no resentment, it is because she is absent from a desire that wants to give back to the other. The little fat girl wants her destroyed, tormented, but the thin girl has no desire for it. That is the worst of cruelties. It is a kind of bare, superhuman cruelty.

The way she asks the other to lend her a book, she lends herself to the other. She is the book herself. She is herself what lends itself to the terrible and negative pleasure of the other. Something other than a book could be at stake. The one who desires makes herself rich from her desire, and has pity on the one who does not desire. Because it is a book, it goes further than if it were a rabbit. It raises the problem of reading as consumption. It is because of the question of knowing how to take pleasure in what one has without putting an end to it. How to continue, how to maintain, how to entertain the inexhaustibility of something that could be exhausted if one were not situated in an economy with a total opening.

I spoke of cruelty. As we can read in Kierkegaard, there are two worlds, that of the absolute and that of the general. Abraham, seen by his wife, is a being of monstrous cruelty. That is what the little girl carries, what she accepts being. What makes it so strong is that she never apologizes. She remains in the place of innocence, in the cruelty of innocence, in all the cruelty of her riches, except that she is willing to pay for it. That is why the text is dazzling. It dares to say what a well-ordered charity would not say, for example: "The little fat girl." Clarice writes outside of precaution. She is totally shameless.

Freud, in his text, disembarks in Athens without having made the trip. Clarice, to get to the book, makes a very long voyage. The longer it is, the happier she is. The trip is part of the general pleasure. But once she has arrived on her Acropolis, she is going to begin reading the Acropolis itself as a mode of voyage. And there is going to be a whole interior voyage.

When somebody brought me *Agua viva*, it gave me such joy that I did not read it. It took me at least a year to do so. And all of a sudden, the book was divided into a thousand books. Each sentence seemed to me to be another book. That is how I consoled myself with the fact that it was enclosed in a single volume. When I was little, I had experienced pleasure when the third volume of *The Three Musketeers* was missing from the Municipal Library. When we are little, we imagine that once a book has been read, it has been read. Later on, we realize that we are never done reading a book. We can read in all tranquillity, read again interminably even the smallest of volumes, like *Agua viva*. The text opens up. It is a book full of books. That is what a book and reading are all about. Commercially, a book full of books disgruntles readers and editors, who ask for a book consisting of one and only one book. And if it is a book consisting of one page or one word, that is even better for them!

1982–83

Notes

1. Sigmund Freud, "A Disturbance of Memory on the Acropolis," in *Standard Edition*, ed. and trans. James Strachey, vol. 22 (London: Hogarth Press), 239–48.

2. Clarice Lispector, "Felicidade clandestina," in *Felicidade Clandestina* (Rio de Janeiro: Editora Nova Fronteira, 1981), 7–10. All translations mine with the help of Claudia Guimaraes.

3. "Et puis, C'est trop beau! trop! Gardons notre silence [And then, It is too beautiful! too much! Let us keep silent]," Arthur Rimbaud, in "Bruxelles," *Oeuvres*, ed. Suzanne Bernard (Paris: Garnier, 1960), 167. Translation mine.

Chapter 6
The Hour of the Star:
How Does One Desire Wealth or Poverty?

Clarice Lispector's last text, *The Hour of the Star*, is similar to, yet very different from, her other texts.[1] In its density, it is the opposite of *The Apple in the Dark*. It is also a book on love. But whereas *The Apple in the Dark* is a rich, almost abstruse book (though it may be about stripping away and beginning again) that examines the slightest movements of passion, *The Hour of the Star* is its opposite. Once more, we can take up the Kleistian metaphor and say that it is a passage through zero, to the infinite, a passage to the stars. *The Hour of the Star* is not the most nourishing text; it is a text of poverty, and, as such, it is absolutely grandiose. It is a text on poverty that is not poor. Not by chance, it approaches a little protagonist called Macabea. She is a little working girl, tubercular, illiterate. She is absolutely miserable, socially, culturally, but not at the level of the heart. It is a text of great pity. One should really have paid for the right to write such a text; to speak from such riches on the topic of such thinness, or such modesty, one should really have paid. The text raises the general question of how to narrate. How can one know, how can one tell the infinitely small? It does not mean either that in something small, there cannot be something big.

Clarice's lesson is to tell us to go and find the interplay of life and death in the quotidian, the insignificant, the ordinary, in what she calls "the nerve" in *Agua viva*, the tiniest detail—a street corner, a grocery store. In a certain way, *The Hour of the Star* is an epic, but at the same time it is a beggar's story. It is absolutely faithful to the infinite riches of Macabea. Our problem, when we want to write, speak, evoke the other, is how not to do it from ourselves. Imagine that I want to evoke an African tribe. If I do it from what I am, I will see in difference,

143

nevertheless, that which is not. Because, inevitably, I would be, if I did not pay strict attention, in a register of lack, of subtractions or absences. In a relationship to the other, there is everything that is not of the same, of the same that is not, and of the other that he or she is. Generally, one notices all the same that he or she is not. It is much easier. It is harder to see the other he or she is. That is where the real work begins. In *The Hour of the Star*, Clarice gathers up what Macabea is, which is not much. She is just a little bundle, but for Macabea that is everything. Clarice describes it. She unpacks the bundle while giving this person, simply through minute attention, without any kind of faking, an absolutely poetic dimension.

One could work on all the modes of narration in a classical manner. It could be of interest to take *The Hour of the Star* as the North Star on the modes of perception of what magical qualities there might be in every living thing. That is what Clarice constantly does in *Agua viva*. But I want to take another direction. I want to work on the color gray, on dust and on mud, on matter that can be transformed into gold, and on the unusable. There I think of Jean Genet's texts, which have the same qualities as Clarice Lispector's. In a certain sense, he is as unreadable or invisible by means of being subtle. His texts, for example, "L'atelier d'Alberto Giacometti," can be read both ways. The textual surface gives very little to see, although it is very rich. It has an enormous philosophical content but as usual, it slips into textual play. Reading distractedly, one can hear almost nothing. Genet writes with the same lightness of touch as Clarice. His lightness is also that of a true heaviness, of what could be called a gravidity. I often use Kafka or Kierkegaard to read Clarice. But I can also take other texts, like Genet's. I am, of course, not going to work on male homosexuality of which Genet gives a sublimating interpretation. There is a kind of originary phantasm in everything Genet writes. For him, everything that exists in a living way, open onto death, is caused, suscitated, by what he calls a wound. The wound is a rather complex representation of what would be the pain (*douleur*) of femininity. It is completely imaginary. From there, he constructs monuments — and that makes him different from Clarice Lispector, who does not move from the wound. But little by little, this difference is erased. If one takes a distance, one begins to see the world emerge in an analogous fashion. Genet or Lispector cherishes a world that for us, for them, is tenderly and violently other. In *A Bela e a Fera* (Beauty and the Beast), for example, there was the sudden apparition of the one-legged beggar. In Clarice, the chain of the other, the violently other, contains a terrifying beggar as well as a brigand, and the psychotic child as well as the cockroach. It is a universe quite removed from the human sphere. This problematic world can also be found in Genet with differences, for example, in the choice of those who represent otherness. In Genet the others are often the Arabs. I allude to the blind Arab who has his white cane to protect himself from the violence of the white man. Genet's comments are infinitely rich, almost sacred. This is a detail. But it also works as an ensemble. The Arab is almost blind. Genet works on the side of insufficient sight, on the white eyes without a look. Giacometti, who is supposed to have especially good eyesight, is marked by broken glasses. Throughout the text, Genet puts on and takes off Giocometti's very carefully broken glasses. I am going to read the two texts, Genet's and Lispector's, side by side. It will allow me to work on something that could be called the technique of the novel.

The Hour of the Star is absolutely unequaled in terms of signification, audacity, and invention. She who appears as the main protagonist is a woman who is so little, so miserable, so thin that she would not be useful for anything if she had not been picked up by the look of the author of *The Hour of the Star*. But this is wrong because she was not sublated. Maybe it was she who invented the author. What carries me off, into my reading, is precisely the question of the author.

The title explodes with titles. It is starred. The title is composed of fifteen titles and none of these titles is the title.

THE HOUR
OF THE STAR

The Blame is Mine

or

The Hour of the Star

or

Let Her Fend for Herself

or

The Right to Scream

Clarice Lispector

.As for the Future.

or

Singing the Blues

or

She Doesn't Know How to Scream

or

A Sense of Loss

or

Whistling in the Dark Wind

or

I Can Do Nothing

or

A Record of Preceding Events

or

A Tearful Tale of Cordel

or

A Discreet Exit by the Back Door

[translation modified]

Typographically, one sees a very striking, slightly pyramidal form. There is something that could be read like the inscription on a monument. The series of titles would mime a chain. Each title could function as a key to the text. At the same time there is a series of very striking effects. The most noticeable is Clarice Lispector's signature, which can be read like the undoing of a hierarchy. One title is like another, in a critique of value. I want to work on what is not useful, that is, on the valorization of nothing, on devalorization. Giacometti told Genet to valorize whatever has no value.

I want to remark something else on this page: Clarice Lispector's signature comes right after "The Right to Scream." The right to scream, and . . . it is Clarice's signature. In a certain way, Clarice is the scream of the text. In the typography of this astonishing page, in place of "or," we have Clarice's signature. Under the signature, the printed signs continue. It is like a piece written in the tradition of Cordel, a kind of oral literature, with a special rhythm, that we find throughout the text consisting of a system of inversions and almost a kind of metrics. It reminds us of ancient ballads, of the origins of theater as well as of nursery rhymes. Clarice recreates a genre, a kind of literary space that disappeared long ago.

In the system of equivalences established by Genet, "or" would be Clarice's common name. "Or" is going to be the name, the mark of a possibility of exchange (I am taking up Genet's words) between equivalents. It is this *or*, both as gold and conjunction in French, that makes a person identical to all that is "more precious than the rest of the world."

Genet continues to say that the identical is precious. The same experience recurs in his texts. In the text on Giacometti, Genet writes about having a painful revelation while encountering a nasty, ugly old man in the train:

> Any man was "worth" exactly—please excuse me, but it is on "exactly" that I want to insist—any other. "Anyone," I said to myself, "can be loved beyond his ugliness, his stupidity, his meanness."
>
> It was a glance, insistent or quick, that had crossed mine and that made me become aware of it. And the fact that a man could be loved beyond his ugliness or his meanness precisely allowed the latter to be likeable. Let us not be mistaken: it was not a question of a generosity coming from me, but a recognition. Giacometti's look had seen this for a long time, and he restitutes it to us. I say what I feel: the proximity expressed in his figures seems to me to be his precious point where the human being would be brought back to what is most irreducible in him: his solitude exactly equivalent to any other.[2]

This experience in Genet is a kind of recurring, primal scene. Different versions invite comparison. In "What Remained of a Rembrandt Torn into Small, Very Regular Little Squares and Rammed Down the Shithole," we read:

> When, one day, in a train compartment, looking at the traveller opposite me, I had the revelation that any man is *worth* any other, I was not suspecting—or rather yes, I felt it obscurely, for suddenly a blanket of sadness came over me, and more or less bearable, but noticeable, it no longer left me—that this knowledge would bring about such a methodical disintegration. Behind what was visible of this man, or further–further and at the same time miraculously and desolately close—in this man—body and face without grace, ugly, according to some even ignoble details, . . . through the look that crossed mine, I discovered, receiving it like a shock, a kind of universal identity to all men.[3]

The question of universal identity of all people has to be taken as far as possible, in Genet as well as in Clarice. Here we can distinguish between categories of communication and people capable of communicating. People like Clarice or Genet are people who exposed themselves to the other. They let themselves be impregnated, penetrated, invaded by the other, Genet in an almost exemplary fashion, by the repugnant other. They accept the most painful, the most denarcissizing, alteration. Next to this, we can see something entirely different in the way someone like Rilke, for example, chose his partners of alteration. In contrast to Clarice and Genet, he kept to himself. When he let himself be penetrated, it was by trees, by works of art, by flowers, angels. He is very selective. However, I would like to borrow a little sentence from his *Testament*. In this text, Rilke gathered the leaves of a kind of journal, defensively, furiously, against the threats of love. One does not know whose testament it is. Somebody is threatened by death. The poet is threatened by man, by love. Since he does not want to die, he chooses to kill love. Rilke's thematics are cruel, absolutely. And Rilke knows that there is someone in him whom he kills, that there are two, and that one has to die who is always the same. It is terrifying and beautiful. Rilke says of Rimbaud that he wanted to shake up language with all the strength of his heart so that it would become, if only for an instant, divinely unusable—and then leave without looking back, and become a merchant.

The paroxysm of Rimbaud's enterprise is reminiscent of Kleist's movement toward the infinite. At the infinite, the image disappears and comes back, upside down, as its opposite. That is what Rimbaud does when he becomes a merchant. The choice of vocation is admirable. To be a merchant is so unpoetic that, perhaps, Rimbaud continues to be poetic. Of importance for us is the theme of whatever is good for nothing.

I take off again from *The Hour of the Star* and from the signature that comes in the place of "or." As if the "or" were the general equivalence of Clarice Lispector? She is the "or" of her text, of her protagonist. The first page reads:

The Author's Dedication

(in truth Clarice Lispector)

This is not an artifice. The reader cannot not be alarmed by the "in truth." Are there two Clarices? There is a doubling, a superimposing. The book has to be read upside down, over and under.

"I dedicate this narrative to dear old Schumann and his beloved Clara who are now, alas, nothing but dust and ashes. I dedicate it to the deep crimson of my blood as someone in his prime."

A metamorphosis precedes the writing of the text. Clarice will write as a man. All women writers have done it, but with her, it is voluntary, both as a game and as serious business. It is carried to extreme maturity here. The inaugural "or" of exchange is drawn in the direction of the masculine. She tells us that this text can only have been written by a man. The man she is does not fall into the category of virility. He is so masculine that he becomes very feminine. He is the most refined man of masculine sex. The masculine appears right away in the text, at the level of blood. It is an inner masculinity that takes its source in blood. The text had to be written by a man in order to approach the most and the least woman of all women, who belongs to the category of the "almost." She is so light, made of so little matter, that she is hardly a woman. She is hardly capable of gathering affective sentences, and at the same time, she is, of course, hypersensitive. Perhaps the author is below sexual difference in order to make the sketch of this "hardly-a-woman." This is a hypothesis. There are many others.

I return to "The L'atelier d'Alberto Giacometti," where I read an admirable sentence by Genet:

> After leaving the atelier, when I am in the street, nothing that surrounds me is true. Can I say it? In this atelier, a man is slowly dying, he consumes himself and is being metamorphosed under our very eyes into goddesses.[4]

For Genet, the mystery of creation is the transformation into one's creatures. With Clarice, there is metamorphosis, although not "under our very eyes." Clarice is being transformed into a man who is being transformed into "hardly-a-woman."

First, there is the signature that Clarice slipped into the text. This is, of course, close to Derrida's concern with the signature and the nature of appearance that a signature represents. This goes with another important motif: naming. Names, pronouns, pseudonyms. "I" explodes into "me," following the theory of general equivalences of which Genet speaks and which he practices in hist texts. I have read few texts that have given me a stomachache: *The Hour of the Star* is one of them. Hunger produces effects of mutation in the universe, and in the relation to the other. When one is hungry, one is close to devouring. In most texts, there is somebody, a protagonist, who struggles. This is not the case in *The Hour of the Star*, where the "protagonist" is so infinitely small that she is not even noticeable.

The reader is struck by the strange, nontraditional dedication. There is no patronage. There is only endless skidding. One wonders if there is something of an exchange. In a certain sense, there is alteration and substitution of "myself" for "this thing." The book is already thing; it is no longer a book.

I return to the dedication, a head severed from the textual body. There is a double dedication, one big and bold, the other between parentheses. I underscore this hesitation, which is like a sexual hesitation, between the suspension of dedication and the author. We have to remember what kind of clever effects Genet draws from the word "suspension." Our textual reminiscence brings us back to Mallarmé's texts, reread by Derrida, to the suspension as *lustre*, as luster and chandelier, where the oscillation happens less from one border to the other, than as a crossing through space. Such a "thing" can also be a body that—animated by a movement of space—goes through different zones of marking. Truth and Clarice in suspension give the movement to the text. Clarice Lispector is suspended because the author is well settled in higher case. Clarice Lispector's name inaugurates the series of proper names that are in the middle of the text. Usually, the proper name is proper. But here the first one is suspended and the others are immediately transformed—I do not want to say transfigured—into bones. Those who are properly named are subjected to death. The passage through death, toward something else, is indicated right away. We are all Schumann and Clara, who are now nothing but bones.

In the dedication (7–8), we are on the side of someone who has lost his poverty. The movement of the story is going to be the attempt of the author, "in truth Clarice Lispector," to find by way of meditating on a poor being, a little bit of lost poverty.

"I dedicate it to the tempest of Beethoven. To the vibrations of Bach's neutral colors."

With "tempest," "vibration," what had been given to her through music, is something that shakes her up, that brings about a destructuring of her person, to the point of softening her bones. She quotes all those who gave her a good death, including Stravinsky:

"who terrifies me and who makes me soar in flames."

And Richard Strauss:

"To Death and Transfiguration, in which Richard Strauss predicts my fate."

That would be a key of the text but especially this:

"Most of all, I dedicate it to the day's vigil and to day itself."

Clarice gathers everything. She owes something to a great many people. One has to remember the insistence on the present in Clarice. In *Agua viva*, there was a passage where music provoked effects of metamorphoses, of bursting.

Coming back to the question: what is dedicated? By whom? To whom? I begin with the story of equivalences in "L'atelier." There is a passage where there is a conversation between Mozart and Frederick II. There is a hesitation in Genet:

"Frederick II (I think, listening to, I think: *The Magic Flute*), to Mozart: So many notes, so many notes!—Sir, there is not one too many."[5]

For Genet, this is a fable. For Frederick II, there might be only one note containing all notes. Maybe we have in the text notes that could be equivalent, but at the same time, every note is necessary. Maybe Macabea, the protagonist, is a kind of note that, according to the king, could be done away with. At the same time, she is not *de trop*. From this dedication, music is going to be transfigured. Through death, it is reduced to a note, a scream, a protest. But this reduction is not of the order of restriction. A single note can go up in an inverse direction from poverty. With some notes, it is technicolor—the way we had *Ovomaltine* in "Sunday, before falling asleep":

"It is a story in technicolor to add a touch of luxury, for heaven knows, I need that too."

It is *A Thousand and One Nights*; it is Ali Baba's cave for Macabea. It suffices that the note, the music-scream, or the word, reach the period and make "I" explode into "me." The *I* is untenable, suspended. It cannot be defined:

"To all those prophets of our age who have revealed me to myself and made me explode into: me."

At the end, there is a proximity between meditating and living. Writing is outside. When someone is meditating, there is nothing and nobody:

"What can one do except meditate in order to plunge into that total void which can only be attained through meditation."

That is what she calls life, brute living. It is without limits, without end:

"Meditation can be an end in itself."

What troubles her is writing. Clarice surges, saying "I," and that is already writing. In *Agua viva*, she wrote a paragraph in which she was trying to explain who was writing. Who is writing? How does one tear oneself away from the self in order to go out and write? In *The Passion according to G.H.*, writing had to cut the flesh of the living into little pieces. Here, we have a similar situation, but life is made of a substance of meditation. The text deals with the relationship between living and writing. The latter nevertheless always interrupts something of the flow of life. Writing is triggered by a kind of vibration, a kind of bodily music, but, even though it traverses the body, it begins in the head. Another, more violent kind of writing goes further, deeper, as a musical writing, signed, bearing a proper name, but detached from the author, in the direction of death.

I come back to the last sentence of the dedication:

"Amen for all of us."

The last sentence is linked to a yes, to acceptance. It is something situated between the gift, the story of dedication, what is given back, and something that is related to a strange prayer ending with these words. It is important to see that one moves on to a communal "we." Who is "all of us"? It is a human community, of course. But since it is a book we are reading, we are called into the book with much more intensity. We are blessed, author included. This *I* that is suspended from time to time is an *I* that leads, but especially someone who receives the impulse to write from the other and who receives the other in the text itself. When we read in the last paragraph of the dedication, "This story unfolds in a state of emergency and public calamity," this story also happens to the author. No text gets rid of the author as much as this one. Genet is similar, but he theorizes. What he theorizes is the furtive movement of the author, his hiding, his disguise into something else. In Clarice, there is a much greater abandonment in an effort to let herself suffer what she describes when she says:

"I explode into: me."

And:

"It is an unfinished book because it offers no answer. An answer I hope some-one somewhere in the world may be able to provide. You perhaps?"

This book cannot be ended without the intervention of the other. Perhaps it is we?

The text itself begins with a yes:

"Everything in the world began with a yes."

One can put it side by side with the opening of Genet's text:

> Every man will have perhaps felt this kind of sorrow, if not the terror, to
> see how the world and its history seem taken in an ineluctable
> movement, which is amplifying more and more, and which seems to
> have to modify, for ever coarser ends, only the visible manifestations of
> the world. This visible world is what it is, and our action on it will not
> be able to make it absolutely different.[6]

Genet is close to Clarice, but the differences between the two styles are also noticeable. Genet never writes a sentence without disguising himself. In Genet, every sentence interminably puts on its own costume. Whereas Clarice goes toward nakedness. The point of departure is the same: everything. We tend to take ourselves for the whole universe, which is silly and narcissistic. But here, the address and the place are not *I*. It is: "Amen for all of us," which links with the problematic of the equivalence of the whole world.

What does it mean when one desires wealth or poverty? What does one desire? What wealth? What poverty? They are interchangeable, be they material or spiritual. It is the same, since we translate affectively, the material into something spiritual, and vice versa. Genet writes that absolute paradise for him was the children's home. There he encountered absolute happiness because even a piece of candy was paradise. It is well known that a rich child needs more and more and can no longer be saved. The question is not that of poverty and wealth that can be exchanged. The question is, can one take a vow of poverty? In the little fragments of Clarice collected by Olga Borelli, published in *Sketch for a Possible Portrait of Clarice Lispector*, we read:

"Sensuality is to have a lot of money."

"I like humble people. Many prefer a humble life."

"Humility comes easily to those who have everything. It is hard to maintain oneself poor in the soul when one has nothing. When one has nothing and one obtains peace, humility is a substantive. In the wealth of life, humility is a brilliant and beautiful adjective."

"Blessed be those who abandon everything in favor of at least a facsimile of peace. The humility of those who have everything is to abandon everything. It is necessary to have everything in order to abandon everything."

"I want to preserve my humility. And I want that for being humble, I do not have the vanity of being humble."

What she says is cruel and true. Those who have can never have nothing. True peace can be obtained from having nothing. By means of having, one can strip away, but there always remains something. Those who have had, always will have left that memory and a trace of narcissism, be it ever so slight, of the effort made to impoverish themselves. There are always remains of having, even if one no longer has. That is Clarice's dilemma in *The Hour of the Star*. Clarice is going to work, as she says, on a girl who has never had anything. She has this "having nothing" that the author, through the added maneuver of sexual difference, will never have. Clarice states in the first pages of the text that one can never purify oneself from one's social origins. Although the author tries to approach the girl who has never had anything, she is someone who belongs to the world of social classes, to the bourgoisie, even if she says that she does not belong to any class. Outside of any social class, the girl cannot be classified.

One of my points of departure was to work on poverty from the point of view of poverty or of wealth. Our point of view is that of wealth, with a few exceptions. The most ambitious project can be to work on what, to most readers will be forever inaccessible: real, primitive poverty.

To work on someone who possesses "nonhaving" to such a point, Clarice tries to dispossess herself from everything, sexual signs included. The author is going to use a certain number of techniques, gestures, artful procedures. She is going to invent an art that will allow the author to make the portrait of someone who never had the slightest rapport with the world of art.

Let us come back to the question of form, of style and technique. *The Hour of the Star* is the opposite of the classical novel in which an author shows and makes believe that he is not on stage. When we read *The Hour of the Star*, the music and the narrative have already started, at the same time that the story itself has not yet quite begun. However, the musicians, the drummers, are already fully engaged in activity. The arrival of the main character on stage is a bit deferred. The protagonist is both absent and present. This expectation is part of the spectacle. From the beginning, there is a narrator as in more traditional narrative forms. The effect is to undo the old distinction between inside and outside. It is not just a simple artistic device. It is for Clarice the only way to be as close as possible to Macabea. Genet constantly speaks of going down into the street. One could say by analogy that Clarice goes down into the text, little by little. The process engenders something very complex, which is the birth of the author. The author is in the text as well as in his own protagonists.

In "Le secret de Rembrandt," Genet gives us the name of the secret in the first words of the text: "A strong kindness."[7] The association is rather strange. Genet is going to talk about Rembrandt's trajectory from pompous display to decrepitude. It brings the reader in contact with a value of ugliness that joins Clarice's. Genet's ugliness is slightly different from Clarice's, which is already sublimated. In Genet unbearable ugliness goes far. He notes how in paintings before 1642, Rembrandt makes sumptuous biblical portraits with rich decors. His paintings are of conventional wealth, but the sensuality of clothing, of fabric is never present in his faces, which always look old. Genet notes a transformation. Rembrandt takes off the riches and goes toward decrepitude:

> They are the two portraits of Mrs. Trip (National Gallery), these two heads of an old woman, which decompose, which rot under our eyes, which are painted with the greatest love.[8]

In the French passage, one takes off from the masculine; then the genders are blurred and decompose through a gesture of leaving behind sumptuous wealth. "Painted," in Genet's sentence, refers to portraits, but for us it seems to refer to the heads. Says Genet:

> Later on I will have to explain why I use this word when the painter's method becomes so cruel. Here, decrepitude is no longer considered and restituted like something picturesque, but like something as likeable as anything.[9]

Genet's space is the same as Lispector's. There is equivalence. Madame Trip in decomposition is as important as Saskia, the Oriental queen. Genet's aesthetic morality signifies the dignity of those who seem to be deprived of it. Decrepitude is beautiful. Genet's definition of beauty becomes visible: beautiful is whatever is without simulacra, without veil. That *is* purely beautiful. Genet continues:

> It has been written: Rembrandt, in contrast to Hals, for example, did not know well how to capture the resemblance between his models; in other words, to see the difference between one man and another. If he did not see it, maybe it did not exist? Or is it a *trompe-l'oeil*? His portraits, in fact, rarely give us a personality trait of the model: the man who is there, a priori, neither crass nor coward, neither tall nor small, neither good nor bad: he is capable, at every instant, to be all that. But there never appears a caricatural trait brought about by prejudgment.[10]

Hence, Rembrandt does not seize, in a strong, judicial sense, the resemblance among his models. He does not know how to see the difference between one man and the other. This seems paradoxical, since what he is going to produce is the common of mankind, not something outside universal resemblance.

> As for painting, this miller's son who at twenty-three knew how to paint, and admirably at that, at thirty-seven will no longer know how to. It is now that he is going to learn everything with an almost gauche hesitation, without ever risking into virtuosity.[11]

Do you see Clarice's world through this? First stage: he knows. Second stage: he will no longer know. This is everything we can also read in Clarice, the whole question of not understanding, from which the question of incomprehension can take off. From the moment he no longer knows how to paint, Rembrandt can learn how to paint. When he knows how to paint, he makes paintings in good, theatrical likeness. Then, he becomes hesitant. Genet tells us that we have to burn knowledge, theatricality, sumptuosity, in order to learn how to know nothing. Here we begin to work on decrepitude. In *Agua viva*, Clarice says:

"I like the ugliness of a love from equal to equal."

In Genet's territory, *laid*, ugly, slips into values of *lait* (milk), *lais* (a medieval lay). In Clarice, we can work on values from equal to equal. She is saying that we all are also ugly. It is this value of equality in ugliness that I want to study in *The Hour of the Star*. This equal to equal is not one of confusion. There is difference, a difference that does not differ, not that of the wound, but one with a possibility of risk, of danger. We are going to begin with confusion. I take the word etymologically. I can take it as a possible fusion, from *fondre*, to fuse, to melt. It is the terrifying experience that Genet lived in "Ce qui est resté d'un Rembrandt" and which was similar to the one retold in "L'atelier." After having described the filth in the third-class train compartment and the ugliness of the other man, he writes:

I flowed from my body and through my eyes, into that of the traveller, *at the same time that the traveller flowed into mine.*[12]

This is really what one calls a confusion: to flow (*s'écouler*), to melt (*fondre*) with the whole semantic field of the word, the way one says a bird of prey swoops down (*fond sur vous*), to be suddenly the other and nevertheless oneself. Confusion is one of my themes, the other being commiseration. I borrowed the latter from Clarice:

"It is the minimum I can do with my life: to accept with commiseration the sacrifice of night."

Commiseration means "to be miserable with." One does not say: compoverty, comwealth. Let us remember Clarice's landscape from *Agua viva*:

"I like burnt and dry landscapes with twisted trees and mountains made of rock with a pale and suspended light. That is where I find secret beauty. I know that you do not like art either. I was born hard, heroic and solitary."

This kind of countryside is everywhere in *The Hour of the Star*. It can be read metaphorically, allegorically. In Genet, in "L'atelier d'Alberto Giacometti," we had landscapes of streets and ateliers that meant much more than a simple frame.

When I speak of poverty, I am also speaking of questions of libidinal economies in an absolutely glaring way. It is even more visible and more obviously readable than when I speak of love, which also takes up a question of economy. I can work on Genet's theme of equivalence: every man is worth another man. ("Tout homme en vaut un autre.") In Genet, *vaut*, to be worth, also stands for *veau*, calf, an idiot. In terms of economy, to say 'tout veau en vaut un autre,' every calf (*veau*) is worth (*vaut*) another, makes it no longer marketable. That is what it is about. Nonmarketability, the withdrawal of the exchange value, of the use value is operated through a look that produces equivalences. In my general reflection on economy, I can situate myself at the paradoxical limits, overturning and overturned (*renversantes et renversées*), of all markets, of all that is of the order of economy. We are situated, as Derrida said, in excess, or beyond the market (*pardessus le marché*), hence on the inside of this meditation on "nothing," on ugliness, on the milk-fed calf (*veau de lait*). We deal with economies said to be human — to take back the Freudian economic model — with libidinal economies, our own personal economies of affective and psychic investment, our ways of winning and losing, of possessing, of stripping away, of desiring, which all have more or less specific traits. When I speak of libidinal economy, I speak of the way in which we manage our own existence, accept poverty, misery. I speak of the way in which we transform into poverty, misery, or wealth, the way in which we acquire goods. I speak of all the movements of our different ways of having or of acquiring. When I qualify this libidinal economy by masculine or feminine, I do it with ten thousand precautions, because the words I use are deceptive. They are easy to use; they are facile, current words. We should do without them, but we still use them. A feminine economy does not refer to women, but perhaps to a trait that comes back to women more often, that of the possibility of accepting what is socially intolerable, for example, general equivalence. We do not accept it; nobody accepts it, in fact. One has to do an extraordinary kind of labor — except in a case of congenital sanctity — to tolerate love of ugliness from equal to equal. We are quite selective, through high or low. But the texts I have chosen here deal with a capacity not to have. It is most difficult and hard to tolerate.

"One cannot prove the existence of what is the most real, but the essential thing is to believe."

This sentence in the "Author's Dedication" can be detached from its context. It could gather the totality of Abraham's story in Kierkegaard's volume. It refers to something that we can know, intuit, experience. At the same time, it is an index of what is happening in the text: an absence of proof. There is a long reflection on not giving proof. The worst, or the best, part is that the text itself cannot give proof of Macabea's existence. The text is about "almost," to speak in Clarice's terminology. Macabea is the nonexistent "almost." She exists less than the least existing girl in Brazil. That is what Clarice keeps telling us. The "author" has to transform himself incessantly, to turn around his protagonist, in order to slip into this kind of mobility of true existence. The whole text, not only at the level of themes but also at that of style, is going to stay very far from what could be its narrative convention, in order to be integrated in a kind of proof, of legitimate identity. As soon as one opens the book, one is suspended, beginning with the dedication and the multiplicity of titles. The title, which usually fixes the identity, naming a proper name, can barely hold on to a text where it is precisely a question of "barely" a person.

The tearful moments of the text have to be noted:
"To weep and believe."
To cry and to shed tears are not the same thing. There are differences, as between poverty and misery. "To weep one's heart out" is derogatory, whereas, in "to weep and believe," to "believe" functions as limit. It is an absolute believing. But believing bursts into crying. It is suspended; it functions as an opening. To believe while crying has to do with mourning, lamenting. To believe and to weep are almost synonymous. Weeping is a revealing moment in the reading of the text. It turns around the difference between a scream and tears.
"For one has a right to scream."
We deal with legitimation.
"So I am screaming."
But to scream is not to cry.
"A simple scream that begs no charity."
We have already seen in Clarice an attitude that is without pity. For a moment, the spector of the alms intervenes, with the possibility of asking and the possibility of the beggar. A whole dilemma of an economy is opened where the position of the author is: I scream without asking. While in the passage of the dedication one waits for someone in the world to provide an answer, here one does not. What comes next?
"I know that there are girls who sell their bodies, their only real possession, in exchange for a good dinner rather than the usual mortadella sandwich."
Those girls do not just scream, they ask for alms. We enter into an economy of vindication. All this is situated in Northeastern Brazil, where misery is such that it is hard for us to imagine. If we said earlier, a calf is worth another calf, we must say here: a girl is worth, equals, a mortadella sandwich. But Macabea is less than a person. So she is less than a sandwich? We wonder who is writing. Here it is "another":
"It strikes me that I don't need her either and that what I am writing could be written by another. Another writer, of course, but it would have to be a man for a woman would weep her heart out."
The tears are not absolute. A naive reading would fall back into stereotypes. But we should not forget that it is a woman writing about a woman. "A woman writer is going to weep" is not true, since she herself does not do it; she only

writes it. Clarice uses a stratagem, not constantly, like Genet, but just for once. It is a necessary ploy that is not directed toward disguise.

"And—and not to forget that if the atom's structure is invisible, it is nonetheless real."

The "not to forget" is troubling. Unless the paragraph really separates the remark on trouble from the next remark. The division of the "and" is fascinating. It cuts something that is not usually cut. The cut is extremely violent. In oral discourse, one can possibly hesitate, but not in writing. It alerts the reader to a text made of leaps and bounds. All links in the paragraphs are interrupted. The linkage of genres is also interrupted, capricious, and proceeds by leaps and bounds. A cut in the imaginary always refers to a masculine structure. I am struck because in *Agua viva*, one could not cut. There were paragraphs but in order to analyze them, one had to go back to the preceding paragraph. Even if one had the illusion of an arrest, the thread of reflection was not absolutely cut. *Agua viva* can only be read in one trait. To read it by paragraphs is to do it violence. We had to operate the cuts ourselves. But in *The Hour of the Star*, that is not so at all. There are constant cuts. One gender cuts another; one scene cuts another. The scene in which the text is being written and where the author performs a kind of pseudopresent, from time to time stops abruptly, cut, as if Macabea came in and left again. There is really a doubling (and much more) of two universes that are not conjugated, but follow each other, intersect, and—as Genet would say—at times fuse. The points of fusion, of confusion, between the author and Macabea have to be followed closely.

The first time Macabea sees herself is when she looks into the mirror and discovers that she has a mustache. The passage is exemplary of the technique of the text:
"I see the girl from the North-east looking in the mirror and—the ruffle of a drum—in the mirror there appears my own face, weary and unshaven"(22).
There is a double scene. The *I* of the text sees her seeing herself. The *I* is positioned at the outer limit of an inside. The technique is close to Joyce's. In *Ulysses*, an episode in a hallucinating chapter on Circe has Joyce stage a moment when the main protagonists, Bloom and Stephen, walk around in Dublin and go to the brothel. The brothel is by definition the locus of exchange, of annulment of differences. In this brothel, everyone plays at being everyone else. At a certain moments, Bloom looks at himself in the mirror and sometimes sees himself other. Stephen, sometimes, is Stoom, because there is a mixture of Stephen and Bloom. Or he sees himself as Shakespeare, who sticks out his tongue. He sees himself as other. This is similar to the very brief moment where the author appears in Lispector's text. I want to work on this scene of interruption of one by the other. The cut is rendered typographically and produces interruptions that are

surprising in Clarice but that function as such, with the help of some extraordinary procedures: ruffle of drums, thunderclaps, toothaches, an event and—off we leap into another world. But to leap into another world is also to question genres. We constantly go from one genre to the other.

The physical volume of this tiny text, *The Hour of the Star*, is exactly like Clarice's beard. It either produces an illusion, an illusion that does not deceive, or, very quickly, through the illusion, like the image in the mirror, one notices what remains for us from the book, that is to say, something gigantic. The *tour de force* of the book is that it is small. One could have said that to bring alive someone like Macabea, who is but a grain of dust, an atom, so much work is needed that one could expect an enormous book. Instead, not only did Clarice succeed in bringing something tiny into life at the price of a colossal amount of work, but she also succeeded in giving it the form of something small.

One is constantly thrown into a paradox. The pain of that paradox consists in making the portrait of the invisible, in rendering visible what has never been seen, to render it visible indirectly. We have a vision that Clarice is in the habit of calling *oblique*. We can see obliquely whatever is not seen. Says the author that when he sees the northeastern girl looking at herself in a mirror, if he looks straight into the mirror, he sees his tired and bearded face. In order to reveal what is not seen, Clarice has recourse to all kinds of ploys, of techniques, of sidestepping. She lets herself be seen. She has to make space for someone as tiny as the northeastern girl. Clarice has to efface herself. But a total effacement would bring about that of the northeastern girl as well. Defying conventions of literary description, Clarice is drawing attention to the very locus of disappearance. And our attention is drawn to the locus of disappearance by signs that one could find amusing, striking: mustaches, a beard, a whole paraphernalia of masculinity that goes beyond ordinary masculinity. It is a way of drawing attention to the locus of Clarice's disappearance, which is at the same time her locus of manifestation. We will not forget. Clarice produces something we cannot forget. It is the disguise into the masculine that calls attention to what is being disguised. One sees only the disguise. Obliquely, one remembers the parenthesis:

"(In truth Clarice Lispector)"

The text is full of parentheses. Those are the places in the text where Clarice goes the furthest. One can only make signs of what Clarice Lispector is, because they are so obviously false that they give off signs on the side of truth. The more it is feigned, the coarser it is. It tells us: Watch out! This is where the invisible truth lies. We feel the truth at work all the time. In a way, through the number of often comical choices this text inflicts on us, it reminds us constantly of the invisible truth of Clarice, which is to be a woman. I say this; she does not. Truth can be made palpable, obliquely discernible, by people with special training. It may also completely disappear. A great many people can be deceived.

It is not the same problem in Genet's "L'atelier d'Alberto Giacometti." As Giacometti's art is an art of reduction, of effacement, of miniature, one has to make oneself smaller, more minute than the minute in order to create difference. That is what Genet does. But it is at the level of the painting, not of the creator. Because the creator is here, he does not run the risk of effacement.

The text of *The Hour of the Star* does not begin. All along, Clarice, while almost theorizing it, speaks of nonbeginning. She says so from the first page, throughout incessant unfoldings. The dedication precedes the titles. The titles themselves are an ensemble of folds that do away with the title since there are only titles. The first page of the story tells us something that could reassure us:

"Everything in the world began with a yes."

In the following sentence:

"One molecule said yes to another molecule and life was born."

One is already in the indefinite, in nonbeginning. This is developed for those who have not yet understood in the following sentence:

"But before prehistory, there was the prehistory of prehistory and there was the never and there was the yes."

The first sentence is a ploy. The book ends with yes. But, in fact, it is the first sentence. A yes that would already be a kind of answer and an affirmation. She also says:

"There was the never."

And right afterward, there is:

"It was ever so."

If one begins with never, where is the place of always? That is why she says:

"Let no one be mistaken. I only achieve simplicity with enormous effort."

The first paragraph and the whole text are infinitely complicated. Where do we arrive at simplicity? At the other end, with "yes." Everyone is mistaken, but there are traces of truth somewhere.

Clarice puts the beginning into the past. The beginning would precede everything. But that is untenable. The first paragraph is untenable. All we know is that "the universe never began." At the same time, Clarice tells us from the beginning of the paragraph that it has begun. In a certain way, she tells us the equivalence, the exchange between "having begun" and not "having begun." It tells us that we are entering into a world of stratagems. The supreme trickery consists in warning us while saying:

"Let no one be mistaken."

This leads us to be mistaken more than once. Of course, she also says things that do not deceive. But she develops a critique of the illusion of truth. There is a sentence that sums it all up for me. The kind of serious play is announced thus:

"I should explain that this story will emerge from a gradual vision—for the past two and a half years, I have slowly started discovering the whys and the wherefores.''

Present, past and future merge in this text inscribed in the present. I leap ahead and back in order to recall one of the titles:

"*.As for the Future.*"

It comes immediately after Clarice Lispector's signature and makes the whole question of titles explode, since it is situated in the list of titles as a title that it is not, or else, it is the title. And below, is there an order or not? Seemingly, there is an order, so that below the name there is the title between two periods. A little further on, in the text, she picks up this title:

"A story that is patently open and explicit yet holds certain secrets — starting with one of the books' titles, preceded and followed by a period, '.As For The Future' ''(13).

To begin with a period implies that there is neither beginning nor end. Between two final periods, one has perhaps a calling and a future that would be the "result of a gradual vision." The curtain is not situated in its habitual place. The curtain is going to go up, or it is going to be brought into the book at a certain moment. And then it appears or disappears in a mode other than what we have in our theater. It is future, present; it was here, it will be here. Clarice says:

"Just as I am writing at the same time as I am being read."

These moments, these white spaces, have to be indicated. *The Hour of the Star* is not one of Clarice's traditional texts. All her moral motifs, her whole ethics, her philosophy can be found in it, but not the form. The book has an absolutely new form. It is almost too easy to read but, as usual, it is full of ploys. These ploys also indicate where the truth lies.

"It is the vision of the immanence of."

The sentences are suspended. In Genet, we had:

" . . . rich of."

This is the best expression of wealth since it is no longer defined. In Clarice one finds the theme of immanence, or of emergence. Here it is the epitome of provocation because with "immanence of," something is going to happen; it is going to be an apocalypse, the end of somebody. Of what, of whom? Will we ever know? Is it a vision of something? No, it simply is the vision of the invisible, which may be an idea, or the secret of life. It is not worth filling with a content, since what is important is the final period.

The Madness of the Day by Maurice Blanchot does not cease to inscribe what is being enunciated at the end of the text:

"A story? No. No stories, never again." [13]

The text inscribes something of the impossible story, the very story in question. We constantly work on texts that subvert the notion of story. A story is a very precise and frightening mode of enclosure of the living thing in a verbal form, in a membrane, which gives the subject of enunciation a special place. If one tells the story of something, one is no longer there. It is of the order of the *après coup*, the aftereffect. One can be cold; one can cut off one's hand; one is in the space of fiction without being implicated at the level of the body. It is the contrary of what Clarice does, that is to say, to write the now. She accomplishes a form of writing that does not tell, that does not come back to something. To the contrary, she produces a kind of event that is being progressively transformed. This is very rare.

One has to be careful with the question of story. In our times, it has been completely displaced. We are left with the novel, the great narrative that is completely codified, and the story with a question mark that exits nowadays and that we find in Blanchot as well as in Clarice. In Clarice there is a great variety of possible stories. In *The Foreign Legion*, she tells memories that have taken place and are forgotten. There is an extremely subtle play of temporality. This kind of a "story question mark" supports the textual grounding that serves to bring back events that cannot be told. That is what happens in Blanchot. In Clarice's story, the most important cannot be told—for example, what pertains to birth. I do not refer to Clarice as an example of nonstory, except for *Agua viva*. There is something of the order of demonstration in Clarice, but there are possibilities of nonstory in her writing. There are nonstories that are not without meaning. The problem is that there is a lexical tradition of literary analysis that makes it so that the story can be told. And then there is the "story question mark," which is absolutely nonnarratable. The *récit* tells a story. But Blanchot did everything to write in such a way that things are happening that at no point can be told. The partners of narration in *The Madness of the Day* are the police and doctors, or the readers, who say: So, are you going to tell us what happened, yes or no? The guy answers: I already said it, but nobody heard it because it is said in such a way as to remain protean. Instead of the report, he makes the trial of a narratable story.

Next to this, there is the art of Clarice Lispector. She tells something that in any case cannot be captured in the frame of a story and that is reality. When, in *The Foreign Legion*, she tells what happens in Ofélia's eyes, it is not what one finds in Balzac. Clarice tells what is happening *now*. The story tells what has already happenend. Clarice writes about what is happening in slow motion. The classical story is accelerated, gives a survey, comes back to events. Nobody in the world can write and live at the same time; there is always a discrepancy. But one can write as closely as possible to the living. One has to learn to live in slow motion, to let things happen. It requires a psychological and ethical position that is very hard to adopt and which is that of supreme patience. The *récit* precedes and one should never precede.

One has to reread *The Passion according to G.H.*, or Kierkegaard's *Fear and Trembling,* in which a single thought is being developed in three hundred pages. What can happen, by chance, is the moment of encounter between oneself, a space capable of thought and something else. It produces a vibration. If one has been receptive, that is where one can begin to work, at the very point of impact. And it opens up an inexhaustible font, an interminable labyrinth. If we want to understand why something has touched us, it will take us to the end of the world, and there we cannot go faster than real thought. Afterward, there are certain practices of thought, like writing. To write, one sits down. One is in a position of general slowing down of activity. One reads faster than one writes. We have to listen to the lesson of the poets. I will never be a poet, I am too impatient. I will never write what Rilke has written and which presupposes an extreme slowing down. If one asked Blanchot how long it took him to write his little text, he would probably say a whole lifetime. It is a difficult text, written at the point of reversal of contradiction; and, of course, language only wants to say one thing at once. Language wants to go straight. To force it to produce ambiguous statements requires extraordinary strength and labor. It is precise, minute work that requires a lot of time.

1983–84

Notes

1. Clarice Lispector, *A hora da estrela* (Rio de Janeiro: Livraria José Olimpio Editora, 1977). Translated by Giovanni Pontiero as *The Hour of the Star* (New York: Carcanet Press, 1986). All quotations are from this translation. Modifications have been indicated.

2. Jean Genet, "L'atelier d'Alberto Giacometti," in *Oeuvres complètes*, vol. 5 (Paris: Gallimard, 1979), 51. Translations mine.

3. Jean Genet, "Ce qui est resté d'un Rembrandt déchiré en petits carrés réguliers et foutu aux chiottes," in *Oeuvres complètes*, vol. 4 (Paris: Gallimard, 1968), 21–22. Translations mine.

4. Jean Genet, "L'atelier d'Alberto Giacometti," 72.

5. Ibid., 53.

6. Ibid., 41.

7. Jean Genet, "Le secret de Rembrandt," in *Oeuvres complètes*, vol. 5, 31.

8. Ibid., 32.

9. Ibid., 32.

10. Ibid., 33.

11. Ibid., 35.

12. Jean Genet, "Ce qui est resté d'un Rembrandt," 22–23.

13. Maurice Blanchot, *La folie du jour* (Paris: Fata Morgana, 1973). Translated by Lydia Davis as *The Madness of the Day* (Barrytown: Station Hill Press, 1981), 18.

Index

Index

Compiled by Robin Jackson

Aesthetics: of Kant, 25-27; postmodern, xv.
See also Pleasure
A hora de estrela. See The Hour of the Star
*A paixão segundo G.H. See The Passion
according to G.H.*
A Bela e a Fera. See Beauty and the Beast
Agua viva. See The Stream of Life
Angst, viii
Antony and Cleopatra (Shakespeare), xiv
Apple in the Dark, The, x, xiii, xv, 60-97,
112, 114, 143; and narration, 121

Balzac, Honoré de, 135, 162
Bataille, Georges, xii, xviii, 20
Beast in the Jungle, The (James), 96
Beaujour, Michel, xi
Beauty and the Beast, 89, 92, 144
Beyle, Henri [pseudo. Stendahl], xv
Birth, 39-41, 44, 62, 63
Blanchot, Maurice, x, 103, 114, 118, 161,
162, 163
Bosch, Hieronymus, 103
Brazil, xv, xviii; oral literature, 146

Celan, Paul, x
Child and the Emperor, The, 119

Close to the Savage Heart, x, 6, 13, 15, 50,
78, 89, 98, 122, 136; and *Agua viva*,
29-31, 35, 40-41, 44-47

de Beauvoir, Simone, viii
Derrida, Jacques, x, xi; and aesthetic
judgment, 25-27, 47, 49, 99, 156;
Economimesis, 133; *Glas*, x; and
masculine sublime economy, 133;
Parergon, 25-27, 133; and signature, 149
Descartes, René, xii
Dionysus, 34
"Domingo antes de dormir," *See* "Sunday,
before falling asleep"
Dostoyevsky, Fyodor, 67

Economimesis (Derrida), 133
Economy, libidinal, 76-78, 124, 155-56
L'éducation sentimentale (Flaubert), 53

Faulkner, William, 81
Femininity, and writing, vii-viii, xii, 76-78
Finnegans Wake (Joyce), 98
Flaubert, Gustave, 53-54; *L'éducation
sentimentale*, 53
Foreign Legion, The, xiii, 162
Foucault, Michel, xi, xvi

167

Francis, Saint, 34-36
Freud, Sigmund, xi, xii, xvi, 156; and animals, 12, 65, 82; "A Disturbance of Memory on the Acropolis," 116, 123-26, 132-36, 141; Interpretation of Dreams, 123, 135

Genet, Jean, x, xii, xiv, 90; and reading Lispector, 144-61
Genre, 134; and Cordel, 146. See also Narration
Glas (Derrida), x

Hegel, Georg Wilhelm Friedrich, viii, xi, 49, 104
Heidegger, Martin, viii-xv passim; and Clarice's "things," 28-29, 38, 42
Hölderlin, Friedrich, 32, 120
Hour of the Star, The, xiv, 121-22, 143-63

Interpretation of Dreams, The (Freud), 123, 135
James, Henry, 96
La jeune née (Cixous). See Newly Born Woman, The
Jensen, Wilhelm, 82
Jerusalem Delivered (Tasso), 66
Joyce, James, viii, x, 35, 78, 98, 158; Finnegans Wake, 98; and Lispector's technique, 4, 158; and montage, 15, 44; Portrait of the Artist, 4, 6; Ulysses, 158

Kafka, Franz, x, 62, 83, 120, 131, 134, 144; and the law, 11, 102, 115-16; Letters to Milena, 66-68; and narrative, 98; "Vor dem Gesetz," 11
Kant, Immanuel, 25-27, 133
Kierkegaard, Søren, 116, 119, 141, 144, 156, 162
King Lear (Shakespeare), 3, 4
Kleist, Heinrich von, x, xv, 61, 114, 120, 143, 148; and Heidegger, 28; On the Marionette Theater, 7, 55, 61, 115, 124, 133; Der zerbrochene Krug, 28
Kristeva, Julia, xi

La Fontaine, Jean de, 100
Lacan, Jacques, xiii, 98, 109; and the mirror, 47, 50; and pleasure, 15-16

Language: and naming, 32-33; and negativity, xi; poetry, 119, 163; relation to the body, 12-13; and sexual difference, xiii; and symbolic castration, xiv
Legião estrangeira. See Foreign Legion, The
Letters to Milena (Kafka), 66, 67-68
Lévi-Strauss, Claude, xviii
Limonade, viii
Lispector, Clarice: and allegory, 155; and music, 150-51; mysticism of, 43-44; and naming, ix, 32-33, 149-50; and oral literature, 146; and psychoanalysis, 136; and sexual difference, xiii, 77, 80-83, 148-50, 155-56; syntax of, 22, 70-74, 102-3. See also Metaphor, Narration, Subject, The Apple in the Dark, Beauty and the Beast, Close to the Savage Heart, The Hour of the Star, The Newly Born Woman, The Passion according to G.H., The Stream of Life, "Sunday, before falling asleep"

Madness of the Day, The (Blanchot), 103, 114, 118, 161
Mallarmé, Stéphane, ix, 149
Marx, Karl, xi
Mauss, Marcel, xviii
Metaphor, 17-20; of birth, 39-41, 44; of mirror, 46-52 passim

Narration, 17, 52-54, 98-99, 139-40; in The Apple in the Dark, 121; in The Hour of the Star, 143, 153; and the law, 14-15; and story, 72-74, 127-28, 161-62; and syntax, 21, 27-28
Newly Born Woman, The (Cixous), xiv
Nibelungen (Wagner), 28
Nietzsche, Friedrich, xi, xiv-xv
Notebooks of Malte Laurids Brigge, The (Rilke), 102, 121

Parergon (Derrida), 25-27, 133
Passion according to G.H., The, x, 76, 77, 82, 109-14, 151, 162; and The Apple in the Dark, 62, 63, 66, 67, 78; intimacy in, 41, 79; and the law, 115, 116; relation between subject and object in, 23, 25; sex of protagonist in, 121
Perto do coração selvagem. See Close to the Savage Heart

Pleasure, xii, 18-20, 27, 126-27; aesthetic, 137-42; feminine, 15-16; genealogy of masculine, 133-36
Poe, Edgar Allan, 101, 128
Portrait of the Artist (Joyce), 3, 4

Reading, 3-4, 99-105, 136-42
Rilke, Rainer Maria, 32, 38, 70, 102, 121, 147, 163
Rimbaud, Arthur, xiv, 54, 69, 75, 129, 132, 147
Romanticism, xiv-xv, 120

Sartre, Jean-Paul, viii
Schiller, Friedrich, xv
Schlegel, Friedrich, xv
Shakespeare, William, xiv, 3; *Antony and Cleopatra*, xiv; *King Lear*, 3, 4
Sketch for a Possible Portrait of Clarice Lispector (Borelli), 152
Stendhal. *See* Henri Beyle
Stream of Life, The, vii-viii, xii, 11-59, 84, 98, 99, 110, 141, 144, 150, 155, 158
Subject, viii, 29-30; and birth, xviii, 15, 44; and object, xviii, 22-25, 33-34, 74-75; and writing, xi, xii
Sublime, 133, 137
"Sunday, before falling asleep," x, xvii, 3-10, 124, 131, 150

Tasso, Torquato, 66
Testament (Rilke), 147
Text: and genre, 134; and the law, 14; meaning of, 99-101. *See also* Narration, Reading, Writing
Three Musketeers, The (Dumas), 141
Thomas, Saint, 35
Tsvetayeva, Marina, x

Ueber das Marionettentheater. See Kleist
Ulysses (Joyce), 158

Valéry, Paul, 47, 49
Verlobung in Santo Domingo, Die (Kleist), 114
"Vor dem Gesetz" (Kafka), 11

Wittgenstein, Ludwig, 35
Writing, 104-11; and ambiguity, 163; and birth, xi, xvii, 15, 39-41, 44; and femininity, vii-viii, xii, 3, 60, 76-78; and grammar, 70-74; and the law, 11-14; and music, 150-51, 153; and the subject, xi, xii, 70, 74; and technology, xv; *See also* Lispector, Metaphor, Narration, Reading

zerbrochene Krug, Des (Kleist), 28

Theory and History of Literature

Volume 43. Michael Nerlich *The Ideology of Adventure, Volume 2*
Volume 42. Michael Nerlich *The Ideology of Adventure, Volume 1*
Volume 41. Denis Hollier *The College of Sociology*
Volume 40. Peter Sloterdijk *Critique of Cynical Reason*
Volume 39. Géza von Molnár *Romantic Vision, Ethical Context: Novalis and Artistic Autonomy*
Volume 38. Algirdas Julien Greimas *On Meaning: Selected Writings in Semiotic Theory*
Volume 37. Nicolas Abraham and Maria Torok *The Wolf Man's Magic Word: A Cryptonymy*
Volume 36. Alice Yaeger Kaplan *Reproductions of Banality: Fascism, Literature, and French Intellectual Life*
Volume 35. Denis Hollier *The Politics of Prose*
Volume 34. Geoffrey Hartman *The Unremarkable Wordsworth*
Volume 33. Paul de Man *The Resistance to Theory*
Volume 32. Djelal Kadir *Questing Fictions: Latin America's Family Romance*
Volume 31. Samuel Weber *Institution and Interpretation*
Volume 30. Gilles Deleuze and Félix Guattari *Kafka: Toward a Minor Literature*
Volume 29. Peter Szondi *Theory of the Modern Drama*
Volume 28. Edited by Jonathan Arac *Postmodernism and Politics*
Volume 27. Stephen Melville *Philosophy Beside Itself: On Deconstruction and Modernism*
Volume 26. Andrzej Warminski *Readings in Interpretation: Hölderlin, Hegel, Heidegger*
Volume 25. José Antonio Maravall *Culture of the Baroque: Analysis of a Historical Structure*
Volume 24. Hélène Cixous and Catherine Clément *The Newly Born Woman*
Volume 23. Klaus Theweleit *Male Fantasies, 2. Male Bodies: Psychoanalyzing the White Terror*
Volume 22. Klaus Theweleit *Male Fantasies, 1. Women, Floods, Bodies, History*
Volume 21. Malek Alloula *The Colonial Harem*
Volume 20. Jean-François Lyotard and Jean-Loup Thébaud *Just Gaming*
Volume 19. Jay Caplan *Framed Narratives: Diderot's Genealogy of the Beholder*
Volume 18. Thomas G. Pavel *The Poetics of Plot: The Case of English Renaissance Drama*
Volume 17. Michel de Certeau *Heterologies*
Volume 16. Jacques Attali *Noise*

Volume 15. Peter Szondi *On Textual Understanding and Other Essays*
Volume 14. Georges Bataille *Visions of Excess: Selected Writings, 1927-1939*
Volume 13. Tzvetan Todorov *Mikhail Bakhtin: The Dialogical Principle*
Volume 12. Ross Chambers *Story and Situation: Narrative Seduction and the Power of Fiction*
Volume 11. Edited by John Fekete *The Structural Allegory: Reconstructive Encounters with the New French Thought*
Volume 10. Jean-François Lyotard *The Postmodern Condition: A Report on Knowledge*
Volume 9. Erich Auerbach *Scenes from the Drama of European Literature*
Volume 8. Mikhail Bakhtin *Problems of Dostoevsky's Poetics*
Volume 7. Paul de Man *Blindness and Insight: Essays in the Rhetoric of Contemporary Criticism* 2nd ed., rev.
Volume 6. Edited by Jonathan Arac, Wlad Godzich, and Wallace Martin *The Yale Critics: Deconstruction in America*
Volume 5. Vladimir Propp *Theory and History of Folklore*
Volume 4. Peter Bürger *Theory of the Avant-Garde*
Volume 3. Hans Robert Jauss *Aesthetic Experience and Literary Hermeneutics*
Volume 2. Hans Robert Jauss *Toward an Aesthetic of Reception*
Volume 1. Tzvetan Todorov *Introduction to Poetics*

Hélène Cixous, born in Algeria in 1937, is head of the Center of Research in Feminine Studies at the University of Paris VIII. Since the publication of *La jeune née* in France in 1975, Cixous has become one of the major writers and theoreticians to come out of the French feminist intellectual movement. She received the Prix Medicis in 1969 for her first novel, *Dedans*. Her latest novel, *Manne* (about the Mandelas and Mandelstams), appeared in 1988 (Ed. des Femmes). Many of her books have been translated into Dutch, Danish, Japanese, Brazilian, German, and English, including *The Newly Born Woman* (Minnesota, 1986). She has written several plays; her two latest, one about Cambodia, the other — *The Indiad* (on the partition of India) — were performed by the Théâtre du Soleil.

Verena Andermatt Conley is professor of French and women's studies at Miami University in Ohio. She attended the University of Geneva and received her Ph.D. in 1973 from the University of Wisconsin. Conley is author of *Hélène Cixous: Writing the Feminine* and contributes to *Diacritics, New Literary History, Enclitic,* and *Esprit créateur*.